Land Causes,
Accomack County, Virginia,
1727–1826

LAND CAUSES
ACCOMACK COUNTY, VIRGINIA
1727–1826

Stratton Nottingham

CLEARFIELD

Originally published 1930
Retyped, re-indexed, and reprinted by
Genealogical Publishing Co., Inc.
Baltimore, Maryland
1999

Reprinted for Clearfield Company by
Genealogical Publishing Company
Baltimore, Maryland
2020

ISBN 9780806359045

PREFACE

The records included in this volume are invaluable to anyone interested in Eastern Shore genealogy, and, the compiler believes, will prove to be a valuable addition to Virginia genealogy in general. The Land Causes or chancery suits for dower, division of lands, ejectment proceedings &c., give in full the declaration of the plaintiff, the answer of the defendants, the verdict of the jury, depositions, in many instances giving the date of birth, death and marriage of the parties; land is traced from the original patent to about 1825, showing the various owners and their descendants and next of kin through many generations. The records include those of the District Court as well as those of the County Court. In suits for division or ejectment when any of the interested parties have left the county or State, their then place of residence is given.

The abstracts in most cases are the special verdicts of juries, which sum up and give in concrete form the declarations and answers - Depositions of unusual interest, or which show anything not set out in the verdict, are also fully abstracted.

The compiler wishes to acknowledge his appreciation to Mr. John D. Grant, Jr., Clerk, and his Deputies, for the many courtesies extended him while making these abstracts.

Ejectment proceedings between Peter Peaceable, plaintiff vs. Thomas Trouble-some, defendant, for lands in Accomack County, which Dennis Blake devised to the plaintiff, &c. Rebecca Wilson appeared in open Court and entered herself defendant instead of said Thomas Troublesome, &c. Jury impaneled and returned the following verdict:

That the said William Blake, late of Accomack County, dec., was possessed in his life time, in fee simple, in the lands in question, which by his deed duly executed 2 Apr. 1688, conveyed to his son, William Blake for his natural life, with remainder to his heirs, the remainder to John Blake, another son of William Blake, the elder, and the heirs of his body, and the reversion of the fee simple to the heirs of the said William Blake, the elder, at common law.

That William Blake, the younger, entered into the lands and was thereof possessed during his life, and died without lawful issue.

That after the death of the said William Blake, the younger, the aforesaid John Blake entered into the lands and was thereof possessed during his life.

That the said John Blake is intermarried with a certain Sarah Ratcliff, by whom he had issue the defendant.

That the defendant is the only surviving issue of the said John Blake.

That the said John Blake departed this life before the commencement of this action, and that Dennis Blake, the lessor of the plaintiff, is heir at common law to William Blake, the elder.

That John Blake, the defendant's father, was married to the defendant's mother, whose maiden name was Sarah Ratcliff, the 5th day of November, 1692, and that the defendant was born of the body of the said Sarah in the life time of the said John Blake.

That the said John Blake and Sarah lived together as man and wife until the death of the said Sarah, and that before the commencement of this suit both the said John and Sarah departed this life. 3 July 1827 - p. 2

Elizabeth Welburne, by Daniel Marshall and Sarah, his wife, her nearest friend and guardian.
vs. - Partition Suit.
Ann Welburne, daughters and heirs of Samuel Wolburne [sic], dec.

That the said Elizabeth and Ann Welburne together hold an undivided interest in one orchard, one garden, dwelling house, barn, kitchen and 500 acres of land, and also 100 acres of land, and also 100 acres of Marsh land in the Parish of Accomack. Daniel Welburne guardian of Ann. 14 Feb. 1729/30 - p. 6

Hancock Nickless
vs. - Partition Suit.
John Rowles

That the said Hancock and the said John Rowles, by virtue of a deed of conveyance from Daniel Rowles, brother of the said John Rowles, to the said

Hancock of the said Daniel's part of the land given by the last will and testament of John Rowles, late of the County Aforesaid, dec., to his sons the aforesaid John and Daniel Rowles, containing 350 acres at Andua, in the County aforesaid, &c. 20 July 1730 - p 8

John Jackson
vs. - Partition Suit
Thomas Parramore & Joanna Custis, his wife.

That the said John and the aforesaid Thomas and Joanna, in right of the said Joanna, together and undivided hold two orchards, 1 garden, four dwelling houses, two kitchens, one barn, 1013 acres of land and 200 acres of Marsh, upon Matompkin Creek, in the Parish of Accomack, late the inheritance of William Custis, dec., whereon unto him the said John and to his heirs it belongs to have one orchard, one dwelling house, 200 acres of land and Marsh, and to the said Thomas & Joanna, in right of the said Joanna, the residue of the premises according to the last will and testament of the said William Custis, the said 200 acres, being devised by the said William Custis, dec., to his wife, Bridget, and conveyed to the aforesaid John by William Arbuckle and the said Bridget, then his wife - 27 Nov. 1732 - p. 11 (Joanna Custis Hope, wife of Thomas Parramore, dau. of William Hope and Gr. Dau. of Capt. George Hope; also gr. dau. of Capt. William Custis.)

Peter Bowdoin & Susanna, his wife, & Hannah Preeson,
vs. - Partition suit.
James Gibson and Sarah, his wife.

That the said Peter Bowdoin and Susanna, his wife, in right of said Susannah, Hannah Preeson and James Gibson and Sarah, his wife, in right of said Sarah, together and undivided hold 1000 acres of land and appurtenances, at a place called Assowoman, in the County aforesaid, under the last will and testament of Thomas Preeson, late of Northampton, Gent., dec., father of the said Sarah, Susannah and Hannah. 18 Sept. 1731 - p. 16

William Willett
vs. - Ejectment Proceedings.
Francis Ayres & Scarburgh Drummond.

Jury Impaneled and returned the following special verdict:

That Richard Hill, formerly of the County of Accomack, Gent., dec., was possessed in fee of the land in the declaration mentioned; we also find the last will and testament of the said Hill bearing date 24 May, 1687; we also find a deed from Francis Ayres, late of the said County, father of the defendant Francis Ayres, to William Willett, grandfather of the plaintiff, bearing date the 7th day of January, 1696, which was duly acknowledged the same day in the County aforesaid; we also find a deed from the said Richard Hill to the said William Willett, bearing date the 18th May, 1678, which was acknowledged in the Court aforesaid the 16th May, 1861; we also find the plat of survey made for the said Francis Ayres by

Edmund Scarburgh, late surveyor of the said County the ___ day of December, 1698; we also find that the aforesaid William Willett by his last will and testament left to the plaintiff the land on which the trespass aforesaid is supposed to be committed; we further find that the mill built upon the acre of land by William Willett, dec., and mentioned in the deed from the said Richard Hill to the said William Willett, grandfather of the plaintiff, and George Middleton hath gone to decay &c. We further find that the defendants are heirs at law to the said Richard Hill; we further find that the defendants felled two trees on the 200 acres of land in the aforesaid will of Richard Hill mentioned &c. 7 May, 1733 - p. 18

Henry Custis
vs. - Partition Suit.
Robinson Custis.
That the said Henry and Robinson together and undivided hold a certain tract of land in the County of Accomack on Matompkin, containing 1303 acres, left by the last will and testament of Henry Custis, late of Accomack County, decd., to the said Robinson - Henry Scarburgh, Jr. appointed guardian of Henry Custis; John Kendall appointed guardian to Robinson Custis. 26 June, 1735 - p. 23

George Hope, an infant by John Jackson, his guardian,
vs - Ejectment proceedings.
Richard Justice.
Jury impaneled and returned the following special verdict.
That we find a patent bearing date 12 February, 1671/2 hereto annexed; that we further find a deed from Daniel Jenifer and Ann, his wife, to George Hope, father of Thomas Hope, who was father of George Hope the plaintiff, bearing date 7 Sept. 1686, and that the lands in the said deed are parcel of the lands in the patent above mentioned, and also that the lands in question are parcel of the lands in the said deed mentioned.
That by virtue of the said deed the said George Hope, the grantee, therein mentioned, was possessed of the lands and died so thereof possessed.
We further find the last will and testament of the said George Hope, dec., bearing date the 12 January, 1721/2;
We further find that George Hope, plaintiff, is eldest son of Thomas Hope aforesaid who was son of George Hope, dec., aforesaid.
We find a lease from Thomas Hope to Ralph Justice bearing date 14 July, 1727, of the lands in question, and we find that Ralph Justice by his last will devised the farm in the said lease mentioned to his son Richard, the defendant. 3 Apr. 1735 - Suite instituted 2 July 1734 - p. 24

3

George Hope, an infant, by John Jackson, his guardian,
vs - Partition Suit
Robert Justice & Comfort his wife, in right of said wife (Comfort daughter of
Capt. George Hope and widow of Mark Ewell)
    That the said George Hope and Robert Justice & Comfort, his wife, in right
of said Comfort, together and undivided hold three messuages, 3 orchards, &c.,
and 700 acres of land and 200 acres of marsh in the Parish of Accomack, near
Keckotank, whereof to the said Robert Justice, in right of the said Comfort, it
pertaineth to have 30 acres of land, and to the said George Hope the residue of the
property. That the said George Hope and Comfort Justice hold the said land by
virtue of the last will and testament of George Hope, the grandfather of the said
George Hope. 6 Jan. 1735/6 - p. 26

Edmund Allen and Ann, his wife, formerly the wife of Thomas Custis, dec.
vs - Suit for dower.
Thomas Custis, minor, son and heir at law of John Custis, dec., Gent., who was
the son & heir at law of the said Thomas Custis, dec.
    Petition for 1/3 part of 1750 acres of land and appurtenances lying at a place
called Deep Creek, which was by the last will of the said Thomas Custis, dec., her
former husband, given to his son, John Custis, Gent., dec., and by the last will and
testament of the said John Custis given to his son, the said Thomas Custis, as the
dower of the said Ann of the endowment of the aforesaid Thomas Custis, dec., her
former husband - Peter Bowdoin gdn. of Thomas Custis, minor. 4 July 1738 - p.
40.

William Beavans, Jr.
vs. - Partition Suit.
John Riggs and Jemima, his wife, late Jemima Melichop, late of Accomack
County, spinster.
    That the said William Beavans and John Riggs and Jemima, his wife, in right
of the said Jemima, hold an undivided one messuage and 216 acres with the
appurtenances in Pungoteague Neck on Assowoman Creek. 23 Feb. 1741 - p. 53.

William Thrustout
vs. - Ejectment Proceedings.
George Drummond, by Ann Drummond, his guardian appointed to defend this
suit;
    Jury impaneled and returned the following verdict.
    That a patent was granted to Elizabeth, Sarah and Margaret Dye for 690 acres
in the County of Accomack, alias Northampton, bearing date 31 March, 1671/2,
which includes the land in dispute;
    That William Freeman and Elizabeth, his wife, Richard Williams and Sarah,
his wife (the said Elizabeth and Sarah surviving heirs and partners of 690 acres of
land granted them and their sister Margaret), by deed dated 17 January, 1677,

conveyed to the said John Cole, his heirs and assigns, the said 690 acres at Matompkin, in said County;

That John Cole, the lessor, is the grandson and heir at law to John Cole who bought the above mentioned land.

That the said John Cole, the plaintiff's lessor, was born 1706 on the 2 day of August.

That John Cole, the father of the lessor of the plaintiff by his deed poll dated 16 December, 1685, in consideration that he was indebted to Col. John West, to secure the same made over to the said West all his estate, real and personal, that is to say all his personal estate and both the seats of land he purchased of Mr. Richard Bailey and the other of William Freeman; and whereas the said John Cole had built a house upon his own cost and charges for the County of Accomack's use to keep Court in, and had given the said house to the County gratis during his life, and also had given the County a prison & liberty for the use of the said bounds of the said prison being late laid out, the same privilege to remain and continue for the county's use aforesaid so long as the county thought fit to use them;

That when the said West was satisfied he was to surrender up to the said John Cole the aforesaid estate, and that the bounds of the prison then laid out contained about 50 acres, and that the Justices about 11 years ago bought 10 acres of land from Thomas Wise for the Court to use for a Court House and prison, and hath been out of possession of the remaining 40 acres about 40 years;

That the 10 acres was laid out by the county surveyor 30 June 1729;

That John Cole, Grandfather of the lessor of the plaintiff, and Mary his wife, by deed dated 12 Sept. 1693 conveyed to Jarvis Baggaly that dividint of land he purchased of William Freeman, late of Accomack County, situate at Motompkin, containing by estimation 345 acres;

That in consideration of the said John Cole having given the aforesaid Court House and Prison to the County, &c., made this agreement with the said Boggerly; that Mary, the wife of the said Cole, was to have the privilege during her life to make use of the old orchard and making liquor, &c., and should the said John Cole survive the said Mary he to have the same privilege.

That an escheat patent was granted for the premises in question to Charles Baley and John Sparrow, dated 23 March, 1715;

That the said Charles was survived by the said Sparrow;

That the said John Sparrow by deed dated 6 May, 1728, conveyed to Thomas Wise a parcel of land containing 450 acres, which land was taken up by the said Bayly and Sparrow;

That Thomas Wise by deed dated 26 Feb. 1729, conveyed the said land to Richard Drummond, which land lies in Accomack County where the Court House now stands, being the land which the said Thomas Wise bought of John Sparrow;

That Richard Drummond by his last will and testament devised the premises in question to the said George Drummond;

That the defendant and those he claims under have been in possession of the premises from the year 1693 until the institution of this suit. 28 Dec. 1742 - p. 60

5

Elizabeth Hutchinson, late Elizabeth Bayley [sic], and late the wife of Richard Baley, deceased.
vs. - Suite for Dower.
Richard Baley, eldest son & heir of Richard Baley, dec.
Answer of Richard Baley by Mitchell Scarburgh, his attorney.

That the aforesaid Elizabeth ought not to have dower of the land because that after the death of the aforesaid Richard Baley, in times past her husband, &c., and before the day of issuing forth of the original writ of the said Elizabeth, to-wit: on the 1st day of March, 1730, one Richard Baley, grandson of Richard Baley the elder, and sole heir of the said Richard Baley, assigned to the said Elizabeth 300 acres on the North side of Craddock Creek, which said land the said Elizabeth received as her dower of her late husband. Elizabeth Baley states that her husband in his lifetime, to-wit: 18 April, 1725, was seized of the land in the plea mentioned, and assigned to the said Elizabeth her dower, and being so seized on the 19 April in the year aforesaid by his last will and testament devised the said land (by the name of 250 acres of land in Accomack County, &c.) to his grandson, Henry Baley, son of Richard Baley and Rosanna then deceased, and to the heirs male of his body, and for want of heirs to his grandson Southy Baley and his male heirs, and having so made his will died of the premises aforesaid seized; after his death, to-wit: on the 4th day of June, 1728, the said devisee Henry Baley entered into the premises and was thereof seized in fee tail male, and afterwards died so thereof seized without issue, by means whereof the said land according to the devise & gift descended to the said Southy Baley, who after the death of the said Henry, to wit: on the 1st day of March, 1728, in the county aforesaid, by Henry Baley, his guardian, entered on the premises in the possession of the said Elizabeth, and the lands and profits thereof the said guardian for the use of the said Southy Baley did receive, and ever since hath received, &c. 28 Dec. 1742 - p. 66

Richard Faldo, Lessee of John Drummond, son of Robert Drummond,
vs. - Ejectment Proceedings.
Southy Littleton -

That John Drummond, grandfather of the plaintiff's lessor, was seized of the land in question in fee on the day of the date of his will, 10 October 171- and in his said will bequeathed to his two sons, James and Robert land lying at the seaside containing 550 acres to be equally divided between them, James to have that part lying in Arcadia Branch, and should either die without issue his part to pass to the survivor; to his son Richard Drummond, son Hill Drummond, granddaughter Patience Allen, daughter Margaret Bagwell, daughter Mary Chance, grandson John Drummond, son of Hill Drummond. "Whereas my son John has alienated and confirmed to my son Robert a parcel of land containing 100 acres, should my said son John or his heirs, or any other person or persons, claiming right, title or interest under him, disturb my said son Robert in the quiet enjoyment of the said land, then my said son John, or his heirs or assigns shall forfeit & loose all and every part of my estate." Five sons, Richard, Hill, James,

6

Drake & Robert executors. Grandson James Allen, grandson Scarburgh and Richard, his brother.

In that the said John died so thereof seized, that the lands devised to the said Robert Drummond are the lands in question, and that the said Robert Drummond after the death of the said testator John, entered into the lands in question & was thereof seized & made a deed thereof to Samuel Thomas as follows: 7 Jan. 1717, between Robert Drummond, of Sussex County in the Territories of Pennsylvania, Bricklayer, to Samuel Thomas of the County of Accomack in Virginia, Bricklayer, sale of 275 acres in Accomack which land was devised to the said Robert Drummond by the last will and testament of his father, John Drummond, &c.

That Samuel Thomas by virtue of the said deed entered into the said lands and was thereof seized and died so thereof seized.

That after his death the defendant & Betty, the wife of the defendant, heir at law to the said Samuel Thomas, entered into the premises and was thereof seized and still are of the premises;

That the lessor of the plaintiff is the eldest son & heir of the devisee Robert Drummond,

That Samuel Thomas and those claiming under him have been in possession of the premises in question from the death of the said Robert Drummond;

That the plaintiff's lessor at the time of the death of the said Robert Drummond was an infant under the age of 21 years, and at this time is of the age of 27 years & no more. 1 Jan. 1743 - p. 75

Thomas Goodright, lessee of Fisher Bradford
vs. - Ejectment proceedings.
William Bradford.

July impaneled and returned the following verdict.

That a patent was granted to William Bradford, father of the lessor of the plaintiff for 3000 acres on the Seaside at Watchapreague, near Matchapungo, 2400 acres of which was formerly granted to Nathaniel Bradford in two patents, one of 1000 acres dated 26 March, 1662, and the other 1400 acres dated 6 Sept. 1664, and 600 acres, the residue, being found within the old bounds, dated 16 June, 1699;

That the said William Bradford made his last will and testament, dated 14 July, 1735, and devised to his three sons, Nathaniel, William and Thomas Bradford 1 s. To his son Bailey Bradford 1s. To his son John Bradford cattle; to his son-in-law Jeodiah Bell & Sarah, his wife, land and marsh containing 10 acres; to his son Fisher Bradford the plantation where he (William) then lived, with 600 acres belonging to it, reversion to his son John and for want of heirs to grandson William B. Gascoigne. To his wife Bridget Bradford. To his son Fisher Bradford all his land not already given to all kind soever. To Comfort the daughter of Henry Armitrader when she arrives to the age of 16 years. To daughter Anne Bonnewell.

That Fisher Bradford, lessor of the plaintiff, is the said Fisher Bradford mentioned in the will;

7

That William Bradford, the defendant, is grandson and heir at law to William Bradford the elder, patentee of the land in question;

That William Bradford, patentee, made a deed of gift to his son Nathaniel Bradford, his heir at law, to whom the defendant is son & heir for 500 acres in Bradford's Neck, dated 2 March, 1710.

That William Bradford, the grandfather of the defendant and patentee, was present at a survey made by Mitchell Scarburgh, surveyor, December 30, 1724;

That the said William Bradford made a deed to his son Bayley Bradford for 400 acres of land in Bradford's Neck dated 28 July in the 13 year of the Reign of our Sovereign Lord the King, recorded 1 August, 1728;

That the defendant and those he claims title under have been in possession of the land in question about . . . (blank) . . years. 23 Feb. 1745 - p. 92

Arthur Emmerson, Clerk,
vs. - Suit for Partition.
John Brotherton Saunders.

That the said Arthur Emmerson, Clerk & John Brotherton Saunders hold together and undivided 500 acres of land and marsh, being at Guilford, otherwise called Muddy Creek, which was by the last will & testament of . . . (blank). . . Brotherton, dec., devised to Mary Brotherton, his daughter, who intermarried with Southy Rew, Gent., of the aforesaid County, & the son of Rachel Saunders, wife of the said Richard Saunders, of the county aforesaid, planter, who is the aforesaid John Brotherton Saunders, and which said Southy Rew and Mary, his wife, have conveyed their moiety of the said premises to the said Arthur Emmerson. Richard Saunders appointed guardian to John Brotherton Saunders to defend this suit. 24 Feb. 1746 - p. 101

Peter Plumtree,
vs. - Ejectment Proceedings.
John Cole.

Jury impaneled and returned the following verdict.

That a patent was granted to Ambrose White for 2130 acres in Northampton County at Matompkin (now Accomack - S.N.), the land in question being a part thereof, dated 25 March, 1672.

That there was a conveyance from the said Ambrose White and Comfort, his wife, to John Cole for 1200 acres of land, being part of the land granted in the said patent, dated 20 August, 1678;

That there was a conveyance from the said John Cole & Mary, his wife, for 1100 acres of land, being part, to John Michael, bearing date 25 June, 1684.

That the said John Michael by his last will and testament dated 12 Sept. 1684, devised a part of the land in question to his son Simon Michael, with reversion to his son John, and in case both died without issue to descend to their female issue.

That John Michael, son of the above said John, and Sarah, his wife, with the consent of his mother, now the wife of Capt. Richard Drummond, by deed dated

3 October, 1715, conveyed to his brother Simon Michael 200 acres of the said Matompkin land in exchange for that part;

That the said John Michael is heir at law to John Michael the testator.

That John, the testator, was dead before the date of the last mentioned deed.

That there was a conveyance of the lands in question from Simon Michael and Susanna, his wife, to Alexander West, bearing date 30 November 1715, 100 acres descended to the said Simon to his father, John Michael, Sr., described as "the Point of land belonging to the Matompkin plantation."

That the said Alexander West by his last will and testament dated 30 November 1727, devised the land in question to Mary, his wife, with reversion to her daughter Mary Hurtly, and for want of issue to his grandson, Alexander West;

That after the death of the said Alexander the said Mary intermarried with John Darby, the lessor, and that the said Mary is now living.

That John Cole, the defendant, is grandson to John Cole the grantee of Ambrose White.

That Robert Cole, son of the vendee & heir at law, was possessed of the lands in question about 15 years, and that the defendant is heir to the said Robert Cole, and that the said John Cole is of the age of 42 years. 22 July, 1747 - p. 104

Sarah Walker, widow of John Walker, dec.

vs. - Suit for Dower

Ann Walker, spinster, dau. & heir at law to John Walker, dec.

Petition for ⅓ part of a messuage and plantation containing 240 acres; ⅓ of one other messuage and plantation containing 766 ¼ acres; of one other messuage and plantation containing 100 acres; of one other messuage containing 25 acres of Marsh land and one water grist mill lying in the Parish of Accomack, which she claims as dower &c. 25 April 1749 - p. 121.

Harry Holdfast

vs - Ejectment Proceedings.

Thomas Custis.

That Thomas Custis was seized in fee of the lands in the declaration mentioned, and was also seized in tail of 1750 acres adjoining the said lands, and being so seized made his last will and testament dated 3 Oct. 1719, & bequeathed to his wife Ann Custis all the lands that he had with her, lying near Oak Hall, to his son John Custis the plantation whereon he then lived containing 1750 acres, being on Deep Creek. To his son Edmund Custis 1000 acres adjoining the land where he then dwelt, whereon Joseph Walker now dwells, "I give all my lands and interest in the lands on Jengoteague & Morry's Island which was given by the last will of the Hon. John Custis of Arlington to me & my wife Elizabeth Custis, to my son Edmund Custis;" To his son Thomas Whittington Custis 300 acres on Old Plantation Creek in Northampton County; should Edmund die before coming to full age & without issue, I give the land given him to my son Thomas, & should Thomas die before full age & without issue, then my son Edmund to have the land given him. To daughter Tabitha; to daughter Sarah; to daughter Elizabeth; son

John Custis (under age); To sister Tabitha Scarburgh Custis; wife Ann and friends Capt. John Bradhurst & Mr. Charles Sneed & Mr. Henry Custis Executors. Sons to receive their estates at 18 and daughters at 18 or marriage. I give the first child born after this date of my wife Ann Curtis 700 acres in the said county adjoining the lands of William Parker, near to Burton's Branch, which land descended to me from my Hon. grandmother, Mrs. Tabitha Hill.

That the 1000 acres therein mentioned is the lands devised to his son Edmund, and the 1750 acres of land therein mentioned is the land devised to his son John by the said will.

That the said Edmund Custis made his last will dated 27 March 1747, in these words: "I Edmund Custis of Northampton County" &c. To his son Edmund Custis the plantation where I now live; to wife Catherine; to daughter Ann Custis. I give 600 acres of land that I have in Deep Creek to my Ex'rs. to be sold, and after the payment of my debts the residue to be divided between my wife, son and daughter; son to have ½ and wife and daughter the other half between them. To kinsman Hancock Custis; Should my son Edmund die without issue I give my plantation where I now live to my daughter, Ann Custis, reversion to my kinsman Hancock Custis, son of my brother John. Wife Exec. & guardian of children till they come to lawful age or marry.

By which will the said Edmund devised 800 acres, part of the 1000 acres devised by his father, the testator Thomas, to be sold for the payment of debts;

That the lessor of the plaintiff purchased the same of the testator's executrix as by deed dated 23 June 1750, to-wit: This deed between John Wilkins of Northampton County, Gent., and Catherine, his wife, executrix of the last will and testament of Edmund Custis, late of the said County, Gent., her late husband, dec., to Littleton Eyre - Sale of 800 acres, being part of the aforesaid 1000 acres. The said Edmund Custis a short time before his death granted and sold unto Joshua James late of Accomack County, dec., 200 acres, part of the aforesaid 1000 acres.

That the said testator Thomas' dwelling plantation whereon there stood a negro quarter, extended into the said 1000 acres as far as the defendant now claims of the said 1000 acres.

That the aforesaid John Custis is eldest son & heir at law of the testator Thomas, and that the defendant is his eldest son and heir at law;

That the defendant Thomas agreed with the lessor of the plaintiff that the plaintiff and a certain John Wilkins, who intermarried with the widow & Exec. of the said Edmund Custis, on the 30 day of November, 1749, to run the division between the said 1750 acres and the 1000 acres of land agreeable to a deed from John Custis and Tabitha his wife to the aforesaid Thomas Custis, for the said 1750 acres, which deed is in these words - - -

John Custis, Sr., of the County of Northampton, Esq., & Tabitha, his wife, to "our well beloved nephew & grandson Edmund Custis, of the county of Accomack, Gent. & Tabitha, his now wife, our granddaughter, & their children after them" - Deed of Gift - All that tract of land where the said Edmund and Tabitha now live, situate at Deep Creek containing 1750 acres on the North East side of Deep Creek, & bounded on the Southern parts therewith, on the North

West by a point of marsh facing the bay; on the North Eastward by a part of a little creek called Drummonds Creek and a line of marked trees drawn from the said Drummond's Creek South; South East half a point, Easterly 342 poles unto a corner tree marked at the western corner of the land formerly belonging to William Gower, and from thence on the South Eastern side by a line of marked trees drawn S.W. by West 508 poles unto Deep Creek, including in the said 1750 acres all the marshes, necks and branches within the aforesaid bounds, being ½ of 3500 acres more or less granted by patent to the said Tabitha, now the wife of the said John Custis, Sr., & her sister, Matilda Scarburgh, now the wife of Col. John West, both the daughters of Col. Edmund Scarburgh, dec., patent dated 29 March, 1656, to the said Edmund & Tabitha for and during their natural lives, and after their decease to their son Thomas Custis and the heirs of his body, and in default of such heirs to the next heir or heirs of their bodies, and if all such as are before mentioned are extinct, then to the next heir or heirs of the said Tabitha, now the wife of the said Edmund, male or female, and in failure of them to our grandson Smart Whittington, son of William Whittington, Gent. & brother of the said Tabitha Custis, wife of the said Edmund Custis, during his natural life, and then to his heirs male, and for want of such heirs to our grandson John Custis, the son of John Custis, Jr., of the County of Northampton aforesaid, Gent., & his heirs, and for want of such issue to the heirs of the said John Custis, Sr.

That the defendant, together with the plaintiff's lessor, and the said Wilkins employed Edmund Scarburgh, Surveyor of the County of Accomack, to run the said line the next day, and for which the said defendant agreed and hath since paid the surveyor ⅔ of the fees, but on meeting the next day to complete the agreement the defendant told the plaintiff's lessor & the said Wilkins that the Surveyor might run the line, but that it would not be binding up on him.

That Edmund, son of the testator Thomas, at the time of making his last will was of lawful age, and left issue; that the testator Thomas' and son, Thomas Whittington Custis, to whom the remainder of the aforesaid 1000 acres was given in case of Edmund's death under age or without issue, was brother and died an infant. 28 Jan. 1752 - p. 129

John Taylor
vs. - Partition Suit.
Robert Carruthers & Tabitha, his wife.

That the said John Taylor and Robert Carruthers and Tabitha, his wife, together and undivided hold 200 acres of land in the Parish & County of Accomack, near Little Matomkin; that ½ the said land belongs to the plaintiff, and the said Robert Carruthers and Tabitha, his wife, in right of said wife, to have the other 100 acres. 25 Aug. 1751 - p. 128

William Drummond & Bradhurst, his wife
vs. - Partition Suit.
Sarah Scarburgh & Robert Coleburn, the younger.

Whereas the said William Drummond & Bradhurst, his wife, in right of said wife, and the said Sarah and the said Robert, together and undivided hold five messuages &. 975 acres of land at Great Matompkin, in the Parish & County of Accomack, & one messuage and 521 acres at Hogneck in the Parish of Accomack, and one messuage & 200 acres at or near Assawoman in the Parish aforesaid, of the inheritance which was Charles Scarburgh, brother of the said Bradhurst and Sarah and uncle of the said Robert by Elizabeth, mother of the said Robert and sister of the said Charles, whose heirs the said Bradhurst, Sarah and Robert are. Tabitha Bayley appointed guardian of Sarah Scarburgh and John Colburn guardian of Robert Colburn to defend this suit. 25 Aug. 1751 - p. 141

Thomas Tearless
vs. - Ejectment proceedings.
John Abbott, late of Accomack, planter.

That Robert Brinmer, alias Brimer, grandfather of the lessor of the plaintiff, was seized of 385 acres of land in Accomack County in fee, whereof the lands in question are part, and being so seized on the 2 May, 1710, did devise the same as follows: My dwelling house called & known by the name of Dunkirk & a tract of land containing 385 acres on the North side of Muddy Creek in Accomack County, I leave in the custody and management of my Executrix, Mary Brinmer, alias Brimer, until my sons herein mentioned arrive at the following ages, then I give & bequeath to my said sons as follows: To my son John Brinmer, alias Brinmer, a part or parcel of the said land of 129 acres when he arrives at 21 years of age. Unto my son Samuel Brinmer, alias Brimer, 126 acres, part of said tract when he arrives at 21 years of age, and unto my youngest son Brinmer, alias Brimer, 128 acres being the remainder of the said tract, together with the aforesaid dwelling house immediately after the decease of his mother, my aforesaid Exec. Should any of my sons die the survivor to inherit their part, and should all my sons die without lawful issue, I bequeath the same to my daughter Mary Brinmer, alias Brimer. Wife Mary executrix. Dated 23 Dec. 1709.

That Robert Brimer, the testator's youngest son after the death of his father & his full age of 21 years, died without issue, his brothers John & Samuel surviving him.

That Robert's part was equally divided between his two surviving brothers; that the premises in question are part of the lands devised by the testator Robert to his son John; and that the lessor of the plaintiff is eldest son of the said John, son of the testator.

That the said John Brimer, father of the plaintiff's lessor, died within three years of the bringing of this suit;

That after the death of the said Robert Brimer, the grandfather, by virtue of the devise in the aforesaid will mentioned unto John Brimer, the father of the lessor of the present plaintiff, Robert Brimer, the said John the father entered into and was thereof seized, and by his deed dated 29 July 1740, conveyed in fee unto Richard Abbott, father of John Abbott, the present defendant, 80 acres of land, being part of the land devised by the will of the said Robert Brimer, the grandfather, to John Brimer the father of the said Robert Brimer, lessor of the now plaintiff.

That Richard Abbott by virtue thereof entered and was thereof so seized, and afterwards died leaving then a son, John Abbott, the present defendant, his eldest son & heir at law, an infant and still an infant under the age of 21 years.

That after the death of the said Richard Abbott the said John Abbott, the defendant, entered into the said 80 acres of land & was thereof seized and still is seized thereof - 30 July, 1752 - p. 144

Richard Fenn
vs. - Ejectment Proceedings.
Simon Harman.

That a patent was granted to Edward Smith for 300 acres of land bearing date 3 Nov. 1660, and that another patent was granted to William Jordan for 400 acres in fee dated 20 Oct. 1661, and that one other patent was granted to Edward Smith for 300 acres of land dated 20 Oct. 1661, and one other patent was granted to Ambrose White for 450 acres in fee, dated 11 Nov. 1672.

That the right to the lands mentioned in all the said grants by several conveyances became legally vested in Arthur Robins, of Northampton County, grandfather of the lessor of the plaintiff, in fee, who entered into the same and was seized thereof, and that the lands in the declaration mentioned are comprised in some of these lands or patents;

That the said Arthur Robins being so seized made his last will and testament dated 24 Aug. 1692, and bequeathed to his son John Robins the plantation that Elias Garganus now lives upon, containing 450 acres, also 200 acres of land of the northern part of land contained in a patent granted to Edward Smith for 300 acres; to his son Arthur Robins all the rest of his land either in Virginia or England, and should either of my said sons die without issue the survivor to inherit the whole, he paying to his lawful sisters Elizabeth, Sabra, Esther, Scarburgh, Barbary, Margaret and Sarah the full sum of 5000£ of tobacco to be divided between them, and should both die without issue the land to return to their lawful sisters - Sons under 18. Lt. Col. John Robins, son Edward Robins, Capt. John Custis & brother-in-law John Wise overseers.

That after the death of the testator, Arthur Robins, eldest son and devisee and father of the lessor of the plaintiff, and John his other son & devisee, severally entered into the lands and were thereof seized;

That the devisee John afterwards died without issue in the lifetime of his brother, Arthur, after whose death Arthur Robins, the father of the lessor of the plaintiff, entered into the lands as aforesaid;

That Barbara, the wife of Arthur Robins the eldest, departed this life more than 10 years before the commencement of this suit.

13

That Arthur the devisee and father of the lessor, departed this life on the 1st day of March, 1746, and that the lessor of the plaintiff is the eldest son lawfully begotten of Arthur Robins, devisee of Arthur Robins the elder;

That Arthur Robins, the father of Arthur, the lessor of the plaintiff, after the death of the aforesaid John Robins & the entry & seizen as aforesaid of the said Arthur, the father of the said Arthur the plaintiff's lessor, to-wit: 4 April, 1722, conveyed to Simon Harmon 300 acres of land in fee, part of the land granted within some of the several patents above recited. &c. 27 March 1753 - p. 153

Edmund Allen & Anne, his wife
vs. - Suite for Dower.
John Custis &c.

Edmund Allen and Anne, his wife, who was the wife of Henry Custis -- demand against John Custis, son & heir of Robinson Custis, Tabitha Scarburgh Custis & Margaret Custis, ⅓ of the three messuages, plantations &c. & 1333 acres of land in the parish of Accomack as the dower of the said Anne of the endowment of the aforesaid Henry Custis, lately her husband, whereof she hath nothing &c. 27 May, 1775 - p. 167

Upshur, Teackle, & wife
vs. - Suite for Dower.
Henry Scarburgh

Upshur Teackle and Margaret his wife, late the wife of Henry Scarburgh &c. Charles West appointed guardian of Henry Scarburgh to defend this suit - 26 Jan. 1756 - p. 176

William Whealton & Scarburgh, his wife, in right of said wife,
vs. - Suit for dower.
James Watt.

Scarburgh Whealton, late the wife of Adam Watt, dec. &c. 25 Jan. 1756 - p. 179

David Martial, Jr., & Sophia, his wife,
vs - Suit for Partition.
John Dubberly & Annabella, his wife.

That the said David Martial & Sophia, his wife, in right of said wife, and John Dubberly and Annabella, his wife, in right of said wife, together and undivided hold one messuage and plantation containing 100 acres of cleared land, 200 acres of woodsland and 50 acres of Marsh. - 21 Feb. 1757 - p. 184

Anne Stockly, an infant under 21 years of age, by William Bevans, her guardian
vs - Partition Suit.
Isaac Smith.

That together and undivided the said Anne Stockly and Isaac Smith hold one plantation & dwelling house & 150 acres of land in the county of Accomack, near

Onancock Town, one moiety of which land and tenements belong to the said Anne & her heirs by virtue of a devise made to her by a certain Francis Stockly, late of Accomack, dec. and to the said Isaac & his heirs doth belong the other moiety of the said lands by virtue of a conveyance thereof to him made by a certain Phillip Witchard who purchased the same of a certain Denwood Turpin & Elizabeth, his wife, to which said Elizabeth Turpin the other moiety of the said premises was devised by the said Francis Stockly by his will aforesaid - 29 April 1760 - p. 197

Severn Guthrey
vs. - Partition Suit.
George Booth, Smith Snead, George Scott, John Scott, Jonathan Harding & Ann Snead.

Whereas a certain John West, Gent., late of Accomack, being seized as of fee in a tract of land near Deep Creek, containing by estimation 1200 acres, afterwards by is will dated Feb. 1702, devised the same to his four daughters, Catherine, Mary, Anne and Scarburgh, to be equally divided between them, and that they entered into the said lands after the death of the said John West and were thereof seized;

That on the --- day of --- A.D. ---- , the said Mary & her then husband, Robert Snead, conveyed the said Mary's ½ part of the premises unto the said John Snead & his heirs;

That on the --- day of --- A.D. --- the said John Snead conveyed the said ¼ part to a certain George Booth, which said Booth is since deceased and his said undivided ¼ part has descended to the first named George Booth;

That the said George Booth, the son, his deed dated --- conveyed to the said Severn Guthrey 150 acres of the premises and by another deed conveyed to a certain John Booth 50 acres of the said premises, which said land was conveyed by the said John Booth to the said Guthrey, so that the said Guthery now holds ⅓ part of one undivided ¼ part, the property originally of the said Mary, devisee and daughter of the said West, and the said George Booth of the other ⅓ part of the said ¼ part;

That the said Catherine, another of the said daughters, by her deed in writing devised to her son the said Smith Snead her undivided ¼ part;

That the said Anne, another of the daughters of the said John West, by her deed dated July 1746, conveyed to her son Scarburgh Sparrow her undivided ¼ part of the premises; That the said Scarburgh Sparrow conveyed the said ¼ part of the premises to the said Smith Snead, and that the said Smith Snead has since by his deed conveyed to the said George Scott & his heirs ⅔ of the last named undivided ¼ part of the premises, and that the said Scott conveyed to his two sons, the said John and George Scott, Jr., the one moiety of his ⅓ part of the said undivided ¼ part of the premises.

The other ¼ part of the premises originally the property of the said Scarburgh, another daughter of the said West, is descended unto the aforesaid Jonathan Harding, eldest son & heir at law to the said Scarburgh by a certain Jonathan Harding, lately her husband, now dec., and that the said Jonathan by his

15

deed conveyed unto the said Ann Snead one moiety of the said ¼ part of the premises. 24 Feb., 1760 - p. 203.

Covington Corbin, Daniel Martial, Jr., Peter Martial, Daniel Martial & Sophia, his wife, in right of said Sophie.
vs - Partition Suit.
William Martial Richardson.

 Covington Corbin, Daniel Marshall [sic], Peter Marshall, Daniel Marshall, Jr. & Sophia, his wife, in right of said wife, and the said William Martial Richardson together and undivided hold 75 acres of woodsland and 10 acres of cleared land in the County of Accomack;

 That 1/6 thereof doth belong to the said Covington Corbin and his heirs as purchasers under Annabella, one of the daughters and co-heirs of Charles Martial, dec., to whom 1/8 part of the premises did belong as devised under the will of John Martial, dec., and the other ¼ as purchasers under Mary Martial the elder, Mary Martial the younger & Comfort Martial, who were devisees under the will of the said John Martial, dec., and the said Mary the younger were also heir to Annabella Martial & John Martial the younger who were devisees of the said John Martial their father, now dec. One other 1/8 part of the premises doth belong to the said Peter Martial and his heirs as devisees under the will of said John Martial, dec., his father. One other 1/16 part thereof doth belong to Daniel Martial the younger & Sophia, his wife, and to the heirs of the said Sophia as the other daughter & co-heir of the said Charles Martial, dec., and the other 1/8 part thereof doth belong to the said William Martial Richardson and his heirs as devisees under the will of the said John Martial, dec. 27 May 1760 - p. 209

John Seekright, lessee of John & Littleton Harman
vs. - Ejectment Proceedings.
Hancock Belote & Richard West.

 Deposition of Esther Savage, of Northampton County, age 62 years - That she has often heard by tradition and believes that Nathaniel Littleton, late of this county, dec., was son & heir at law of Southy Littleton the elder, last of Accomack County, dec. That the said Southy had seven children as she hath likewise heard and believes, namely the said Nathaniel who died in the year 1702, leaving several children who all died without issue except the deponent; Esther, who married William Whittington of Somerset County in Maryland and died before the said Nathaniel leaving several children; Sarah who married first with Adam Michael and after the said Adam's death she intermarried with John Custis and died without issue in the year 1720; Elizabeth who married Richard Waters of the County of Somerset and died about the year 1753, leaving several small children; Gertrude married Henry Harmanson of Northampton County and died about the year 1737 leaving issue; Borman who died without issue, and Southy died about the year 1702 and left issue.

 That a quarter part of a tract of land at Gengoteague descended to her and her sister, Sarah Custis King, at the death of the above named Sarah Custis, and the said Sarah Custis King dying without issue the whole one-fourth thereof became vested in this deponent.

That this deponent purchased another ¼ part of the said tract of land of the said Elizabeth Waters when a widow, and that the said Gertrude, or her heirs, sold her part of the said land several years past, but to whom she knows now, and further saith not.

Jury impaneled and returned the following verdict:

That Southy Littleton in his lifetime and granted him in fee by patent dated 5 October, 1674, the land contained within the letters A.B.C.F. G.H.I.K. in the plan hereto annexed, and that the said Southy afterwards, to-wit, on the 16 day of September, 1679 by his last will devised 200 acres unto Richard Jones in fee, which 200 acres are contained within the figures and red lines 1,2,3,4, and also devised unto Henry White in fee 153 acres lying upon that branch illustrated by the name of Pocomoke Branch in the Plan, and adjoining that small branch marked by the figure 5: That he devised all the remainder of that patent unto his four daughters, to-wit: Esther, Sarah, Gertrude and Elizabeth, which will is in the following words, to-wit: (abstract) Dated 16 Sept. 1679 - To eldest son Nathaniel Littleton during his natural life a tract of land situate on Magatty Bay in Northampton County containing 4050 acres, reversion to his heirs male, and for want of male heirs to the heirs of common law. To daughter Esther Littleton a Neck of land at Jingoteague called the King's Neck. To youngest son Southy Littleton during his natural life plantation at Nandua in Accomack County, containing 2270 acres, reversion to his male heirs, and for want of male heirs to the heirs at common law of the testator. To John Rust 200 acres in Somerset County, Md., where he now lives, and which I laid out for him, and the rest of the land in that Neck to my daughter Gertrude Littleton. To Francis Williams 300 acres where he now lives in Somerset County, Md. provided he pays for it as by his bill and account in my book, which land is between the Neck of John Rust's land and King's Neck, the remainder of which Neck up to Capt. Robins' land I give to my daughter Elizabeth Littleton. All the rest of my land at Jengoteague in Somerset County I give to my son Bowman Littleton. To daughter Sarah Littleton 600 acres at Pocomoke. To Nathaniel Tunnell all my land at Accocomson in Accomack County. To Richard Jones, Jr. 200 acres in Accomack County as by the deed thereof, provided he pay accordingly. To William White, planter, 155 acres in Accomack County at the head of the Branches of Pungoteague upon the same terms as that of Richard Jones. All the rest of my lands not disposed of I give to my four daughters, their heirs and assigns forever, to be equally divided between them. Sons to be at age at 18 & daughters at 16. Daughter Esther to be kept at my sister Robins; daughter Sarah, at Mrs. Bridget Foxcroft's; daughter Elizabeth at Mrs. Anne Jenifer's & daughter Gertrude at Maj. Bowman's. Son Bowman at Mr. Richard Bayly's & Southy Littleton to be kept four years with his nurse Nicholas Tyler's wife - Thomas Teackle, Clerk, Col. William Kendall, Maj. Edmund Bowman, Capt. John Robins, Capt. Daniel Jenifer & Mr. Richard Bayly overseers of my will and to look to the education of my children. (Southy Littleton died in N.Y. State - Will probated in Albany 1679 - Certified copy recorded in Accomack.) That soon after the making of the said will the said Southy died of the premises seized. That the said Littleton had issue also Nathaniel, his eldest son and heir at law besides the other children all being since dead, and that the said Nathaniel has no issue now living except Esther Savage, who is now heir at law and has been so since the year 1720;

That Esther & Gertrude, daughters of Southy Littleton, were married and had issue, some of whom, both of Esther & Gertrude, are now in full life. That the husbands of the said Gertrude and Esther peaceably surveyed each 286 acres of the premises to the Eastward of that branch marked Matchepungo Beaverdam Branch in the plan;

That the said Sarah, another daughter of Southy Littleton, died without issue, her part of the premises became legally vested in the aforesaid Esther Savage as her heir at law, and that Elizabeth by her deed dated 21 Oct. 1741, conveyed her part of the premises to the said Esther Savage in fee, which deed is in these words, to-wit: "between Elizabeth Waters of Somerset County in the Province of Maryland of the one part, and Esther Savage of Northampton County in the Colony of Virginia, widow, of the other part" &c.

That the said Esther by her deed dated 10 July, 1759, conveyed all her remaining right in the aforesaid Littleton's patent unto the lessor of the plaintiff in fee, which deed is in these words, to-wit: I Esther Savage of Northampton County, in the Colony of Virginia, of the one part, and John Harman & Littleton Harman of Accomack County in the Colony of Virginia, planters, of the other part ------ whereas Southy Littleton the elder of Accomack County aforesaid devised "all the rest of my l and not disposed of I do give and bequeath to my four daughters Esther, Sarah, Gertrude and Elizabeth, to their heirs and assigns forever, to be equally divided between them, and the said Sarah dying without issue her part of the premises descended to the heir of Nathaniel Littleton, her eldest brother & heir at law, which is since descended to the said Esther Savage as his only surviving daughter & heir at law, and whereas the said Elizabeth, another daughter of the said Southy Littleton, then relict of a certain Richard Waters, by her indenture dated in or about the year 1737, conveyed her part of the premises to the said Esther, party to these presents in fee, and whereas the said Esther by her deed bearing date 15 Dec. 1755, sold to the said John Harman & Littleton Harman such part of the above mentioned land as is in that deed mentioned, supposing that she had conveyed her whole right of the premises to the said John Harman & Littleton Harman, &c.

That the said Esther also by another deed dated 15 Dec. 1755, conveyed unto the lessor of the plaintiff her right to 572 acres in fee within the red letters A.B.C.D.E; that the land granted within the black letters B.C.D.E. to be the plaintiff's pretentions, and that the defendants are in possession thereof under sundry conveyances from Edmund Scarburgh, to whom the same was granted by patent dated 12 Jan. 1746, and is included within the lines of Littleton's patent &c. 29 Jan. 1760 - p. 211

William Thrustout
vs. - Ejectment Proceedings.
James Rule

That Thomas Respess of Northampton County was seized of all the lands in the plan hereto annexed, and others in the whole to 750 acres, and that Edmund Allen was entitled to a ⅓ thereof in right of his wife; that the said Respess ordered Edmund Scarburgh, the county surveyor, to lay off 250 acres for his wife's dower; that the said surveyor laid out the land below the black line A.B. which was then marked, and supposed to contain 250 acres, but contained 215 acres, and that 250 acres will go up to the line C.D.

That there was a deed from Respess to Allen made soon after the said survey, dated 29 Aug. 1753 &c. 26 Feb. 1760 - p. 223

James Arbuckle and Tabitha Scarburgh, his wife,
vs. - Partition Suit.
Margaret Custis.

That the said James Arbuckle and Tabitha Scarburgh, his wife, in right of said wife, and Margaret Custis, together and undivided hold as daughters and coheirs of Henry Custis, late of Accomack County, dec., 630 acres on Matompkin, 840 acres at the head of Deep Creek and 400 acres at Pungoteague &c. 29 March 1763 - p. 231

Edward Bayly
vs. - Ejectment Proceedings.
John Shae

Edward Bayly being seized of sundry lands on Mossongo Creek by his last will duly probated in the year 1716, devised the premises and lands mentioned to his three sons, Edmund, John and Robert Bayly;

That at the death of the testator the said three brothers entered and were thereof possessed, and soon after the said John died intestate and without issue;

That the said Edmund afterwards by deed dated 5 May, 1724, conveyed to Daniel Shae, ancestor to the defendant, 133 ⅓ acres, part of the premises in question;

That the said Robert is since dead leaving issue, and that the said Edmund survived both the said John and the said Robert, and that the said Edmund is since dead and left issue his son Edward, the lessor of the plaintiff, his only son & heir at law.

That the said Edmund about three years after the execution of the said deed removed from Accomack County, Virginia, where he then lived, to Sussex County in the Province of Pennsylvania where he continued until his death, which is about 5 years ago;

That the said Edmund and Robert by their deed dated 30 Jan. 1724, sold to Daniel Shae in fee 267 acres, being part of the lands in question, by means whereof the said Daniel entered into and was seized thereof and died thereof possessed and left the aforesaid John his eldest son and heir at law, who entered

19

into the same and became seized thereof and is now so seized &c. 25 May 1762 -
p. 235

John Foster
vs. - Partition Suit.
Mary, Agnes & Elizabeth Sturgis, by Clement Parker their guardian appointed to
defend this suit.

That the said John Foster, Agnes, Mary and Elizabeth Sturgis together and
undivided hold 100 acres of land in the Parish of St. George, County of
Accomack, late the property of Jonathan Sturgis, dec., one half or moiety of which
belongs to the said John as purchaser from three of the said Jonathan's daughters
& coheirs, to whom the same descended at his death, to-wit: Bridget, Delilah &
Sinah, and the other half thereof doth belong to the said Agnes, Mary and
Elizabeth, the other three daughters and co-heirs of the said Jonathan Sturgis, dec.
30 Aug. 1763- p. 240

Thomas Trytitle
vs. - Ejectment Proceedings.
William Meers
That Bartholomew Meers, great grandfather of the defendant, was seized in
fee simple of the land in dispute & being so seized on or about the 16 Dec. 1692,
made his last will & thereby devised the said land to his son John in these words:
(abstract) To godson, John Rodgers 600£ tobacco & Caske out of a bill I have of
the said John Rodgers. To Samuel, the son of William Williams. To son
Bartholomew Meers my plantation where I now live on the south side of the
branch. To son John Meers all the land from the small branch southerly to
Richard Kellam's line. To son Richard all the land from the little branch north-
west. Should John and Richard die, reversion to my son Bartholomew. To sons
Robert and William my plantation at Occahannock where Nicholas Dun now lives.
Eldest son Bartholomew, To wife Mary and my children (except Elizabeth, now
the wife of George Freshwater) Wife Exec. Sons to be at age at 18 and daughters
at 16. Friends William Nock & William Burton overseers.

That after making the said will the testator died so seized, and that after his
death the said John Meers in the will mentioned entered into the lands aforesaid
and was so thereof seized, and being so seized about the first day of April 1729
by his deed conveyed the said lands to John Meers, his second son (land situate
near the head of Matchepungo Creek at a place called the Beaver Dam Branch,
containing 100 acres); That the said John Meers, the grandson of the testator,
Bartholomew, and son of the said John in the said will mentioned, by virtue of the
said deed entered into the said lands and was thereof possessed, and being so
seized in or about the year 1762 departed this life intestate, leaving issue the
defendant, William, who is his son and heir at law;

That the said John Meers, the grandfather of the defendant and son of the
testator, Bartholomew, on or about the 14 August, 1745, made his last will and

testament, and by said will devised the said lands to his said son John, and departed this life in the year 1747 afterwards;

That the lessor of the plaintiff is the eldest son and heir at law of John Meers the elder to whom the devise was made by old Bartholomew (Bartholomew Meers lessor of the plaintiff, eldest son of John who d. 1747) - 25 May 1762 - p. 245

Elizabeth Smith, infant, by Fairfax Smith her next friend.
vs. - Partition Suit.
Spencer Bagwell & Charles Bagwell

Robinson Smith, who claimed under Alexander Bagwell, late of the said County, dec., and the said Spencer & Charles, descendants of Henry Bagwell, late also of the said county, dec., together and undivided hold a certain tract of land containing 500 acres to be divided one moiety thereof to the said Elizabeth Smith and the other moiety to the said Spencer & Charles &c. 26 March 1765 - p. 256

Dunton & wife
vs. - Suit for Dower
Scarburgh

Isaac Dunton and Alice, his wife, who was the wife of William Scarburgh late of the said County, dec., vs. Edmund Scarburgh, eldest son & heir at law to William Scarburgh, dec. Suit for dower in 832 acres in Occahannock Neck - Thomas Hall appointed Guardian of the said Edmund Scarburgh to defend this suit. 25 June, 1765 - p. 259

Parker's Lessee
vs. - Ejectment Proceedings.
Henry Reid, Abraham Taylor & Jonathan Rowles, by Abel West his guardian.

That William Anderson was seized in fee of 400 acres of land lying on Pocomoke Branch & Deep Branch issuing into Pungoteague Creek;

That on the 23 July 1696 by his last will and testament he devised the aforesaid lands to Anderson Parker, his nephew and godson in these words, to-wit: &c. That by virtue of the said devise the said Anderson Parker entered and was thereof so seized, and on or about the 16 March, 1760, died and left William Anderson Parker, the plaintiff's lessor, his grandson and heir at law;

That Anderson Parker by his deed dated 3 June, 1701, conveyed the premises to John Rowles for 300 acres, by virtue of which deed the said Rowles entered into the said land and was thereof possessed, and the said Rowles and those claiming under his have been seized and possessed thereof until this time, &c. 28 June, 1763 - p. 261

Chandler's Lessee
vs. - Ejectment Proceedings.
Lewis

That Thomas Taylor, dec., by his last will and testament dated 8 Sept. 1702, devised the lands in question as follows: To my son David Taylor the plantation where I now live, being 100 acres, reversion to Thomas Taylor & heirs, reversion to the next children. To daughter Mary Taylor. Unborn child. To Peter Turlington the younger. To Jonathan James. Wife & children residuary legatees.

That the said Thomas at the time of his death left two sons, David & Thomas Taylor and four daughters, Mary, Joanna, Anne & Sarah, but Joanna, Anne & Sarah were not born at the making & publishing of said will, but that Joanna was in the womb at that time.

That Thomas died in the lifetime of the said David without issue, and that David also died without issue and left Joanna the now defendant the only surviving sister at the time of his death;

That the lessor of the plaintiff, William Chandler, is the heir at law to Anne, and that Caleb Niblet is the son of Sarah, and that David Taylor was possessed of the said lands by virtue of the said devise till about two years last past when he died in North Carolina, &c. 24 Sept. 1765 - p. 272

Hitchen's Lessee
vs. - Ejectment Proceedings.
Hall

That Catherine Moore being seized in fee of the premises in question by deed dated 7 Sept. 1726 conveyed the same to her son-in-law Thomas Stockly, of Sussex County, Delaware, being 200 acres in Jolly's Neck adjoining the land of Hancock Custis, and being a tract of land formerly belonging to John Bayly;

That soon afterwards the said Catherine died possessed of the premises after whose death George Philby, her eldest son & heir at law, entered into the premises and was thereof seized and possessed; the said Thomas Stockly being then and always afterwards until his death resident in the Province of Maryland or Pennsylvania;

That the said George Philby being so in possession by deed dated 7 March, 1737, conveyed the premises to Daniel Byrd, and that Daniel Bird [sic] by virtue of said deed entered into the premises and was thereof possessed, and by his deed dated 6 March, 1739, conveyed the same to George Philby the younger;

That the said George Philby the younger, by virtue of the said deed entered upon the premises and on the --- day of ---1749 devised the premises by his last will and testament to his wife Mary in fee simple, and afterwards departed this life, by virtue of which the said Mary entered into the premises and was thereof possessed, and afterwards was lawfully married to Gerard Hitchens who entered upon the premises and was thereof possessed by himself and tenants until about the year 1755 Thomas Stockly and Capewell Stockly, sons of Thomas Stockly, entered into this Government, having been always before that residents out of this Government, and entered into the premises aforesaid;

That the said Thomas Stockly and Capewell Stockly by their deed dated 27 April, 1755, conveyed the premises unto the defendant in these words, to-wit: "This indenture made this 27 April, 1755, between Thomas Stockly and Capewell Stockly of New Hanover, in the Province of North Carolina, Planters, on the one part and Daniel Hall of Accomack County in the Colony of Virginia, Planter, of the other part, &c."

That the said Mary, the devisee of the said George Philby the younger, is the feme lessor of the plaintiff and now in full life &c. 25 Oct. 1763 - p. 283

Margaret Allen, Infant daughter & Devisee of Edmund Allen, dec.
vs. - Partition Suit.
Henry Custis, Sr., heir of Robinson Custis, dec.

That the said Margaret and Henry together and undivided hold 735 acres of land and Marsh lying on the Jingoteague Island & Wild Cat Marshes aforesaid, and that there is due to the said Margaret ⅔ thereof and to the said Henry the other ⅓ thereof &c. 28 June 1786 - p. 288

Luker's Lessee
vs. - Ejectment Proceedings.
Jacob

That Anderson Parker was seized in fee of the lands adjoining and binding on the east part of the run or branch called Pungoteague Branch, being 400 acres, and being so seized by his deed dated 3 June, 1701, conveyed the same to John Rowles for 300 acres, being all that can be found of 400 acres given the said Anderson by Mr. William Anderson, dec., as will appear by his last will, and that by virtue of the said deed that said Rowles entered unto the said lands and on the 9 day of Aug. 1709, devised the same in fee to his son Jonathan Rowles, who entered into the premises, and on the 24 Sept. 1745, petitioned the County Court of Accomack for acre of land to be laid off on the opposite side of Pungoteague Branch belonging to John Lecatt in order to build a water grist mill; that the said acre was accordingly laid off for the purpose aforesaid; that in pursuance of the said order the said Jonathan did erect and build a water grist mill jointly (under their joint agreement) with the said John Lecatt, and after the death of the said John Lecatt the said John Rowles and Jonathan Rowles also jointly allowed and permitted the said Nathaniel Lecatt, son and heir of the said John Lecatt, to take a moiety of the profits thereof, and the said Nathaniel also paid one half of the repairs thereof and the said Jonathan the same;

That on or about the month of January, 1749, the said Jonathan died intestate and left John Rowles his eldest son and heir at law, who after the death of the said Jonathan entered into the said lands aforesaid with the mill aforesaid, and by his will dated 16 Jan. 1750, devised one half of the said mill to the said Nathaniel Lecatt in fee, who was then in possession of the tract of land from which the acre was taken, and in possession of ½ of the mill aforesaid;

That the said John Rowles last mentioned devised the other ½ of the mill to his son John Rowles.

That Anderson Parker departed this life sometime in the year 1760, leaving his grandson William Anderson Parker his heir at law, who commenced his suit of trespass & ejectment against Jonathan Rowles, grandson & heir at law of the last mentioned testator, John Rowles, for the land aforesaid conveyed by his grandfather Anderson Parker unto the first named John Rowles, as also for the mill aforesaid, sometime in the year 1763, and that on or about the month of July, 1765 the said William Anderson Parker recovered a judgment for the said lands and mill on the suit aforesaid, and in consequence of the said recovery was put in possession of the land & mill aforesaid.

That after he became possessed thereof the said William Anderson Parker by deed dated 26 Oct. 1765, conveyed the same unto Thomas Jacob, the now defendant (William Anderson Parker, and Mary his wife, of Sussex on the Delaware, in the Province of Pennsylvania); and that by virtue of the said deed the said Thomas Jacob entered into the said lands and was still in possessed thereof;

That the said Nathaniel Lecatt, by virtue of the devise of the said John Rowles, the last testator, entered into and became possessed of the moiety of the said mill and was so possessed thereof until the recovery so had as aforesaid, and further that the said Nathaniel by his last will and testament dated 6 March 1766, devised the moiety of the mill aforesaid to him devised, unto Luke Luker, the lessor of the plaintiff and that the said Nathaniel departed this life on or about the first of June, 1766, which will is in these words, to-wit: (abstract) To cousin Shadrack Lecatt; to friend John Reid; to friend John Luker ½ of the mill with all things thereunto belonging which my brother in law John Rowles gave my by his last will and testament, which mill Thomas Jacob now has in possession, and taken the same by force without consideration; Littleton Lecatt, Rachel, the wife of Robert Spiers & John Rowles resid. Legatees. &c. 29 July 1766 - p. 290

George Gilchrist, by Edward Rees, his guardian,
vs. - Partition Suit.
Southy Northam, John Northam, Zerobabel Northam & Nathaniel Beavans.

That the said George Gilchrist, Southy Northam, John Northam, Zerobabel Northam and Nathaniel Beavans together and undivided hold 200 acres of swamp land in the county aforesaid, whereof ⅓ belongs to the said George Gilchrist; to the said Nathaniel 50 acres; to the said Zerobabel 60 acres, and to the said Southy and John the residue &c. 27 Feb. 1769 - p. 298

Thomas Stringer
vs. - Ejectment Proceedings.
Hillary Stringer

Deposition of Sarah Joyne of Northampton County, age 86 or thereabouts, saith that she was formerly acquainted with Capt. Hillary Stringer of Northampton County, and she knew a son of his named John; that sometime after the death of the said Hillary Stringer and his wife, the said John married Margaret Teackle, a daughter of the Rev. Mr. Teackle of Accomack, and lived with her a year and upwards, and she believed that the said John died without issue; that the said John appeared to be a man from the time that his sister Ann married Capt. Willett of Northampton County, and that the said Ann was a great while married before her father and mother died; that the said Hillary Stringer departed this life sometime before his wife, at what particular time she cannot remember, but she remembers that the widow of the said Capt. Hillary Stringer, after her husband's decease, was at this deponent's mother's house, there having been an intimacy in the families as Col. John Stringer had brought up this deponent's mother, and she also says that the said John Stringer, the son of Hillary, did not marry as aforesaid until sometimes after his mother's death, but what age he was at the time of his marriage she cannot undertake to determine - Deposition dated 10 May 1769.

Deposition of William Harman, age 79 years and upwards, saith that about 30 years ago he saw a division of the 600 acres now in the possession of the defendants Hillary, Fereby and Elizabeth Stringer and William Ward made by Hillary Stringer, father to the aforesaid Hillary, and Thomas Stringer, his uncle, father of the aforesaid Fereby, and that he saw the sheriff put Hillary, the father, in possession of that part of the 600 acres now in the possession of the defendant Hillary, and saw the sheriff deliver the other part of the 600 acres to the aforesaid Thomas Stringer; that he heard John Stringer, father of the complainant, offer this deponent board timber on some part of a thousand distinct from this 600 acres aforesaid, but this deponent does not know that the aforesaid John had any right to lands about there &c.

Deposition of John Kellam, age 75 years - Same as above.

Deposition of John Sill, age 76 years & upwards - That he knew that Thomas Stringer, father of the defendant Fereby, lived near where William Ward now lives about 60 years ago, and that the said Thomas had possession of the whole 600 acres and leased part of it to several; that about 30 years ago he heard that a division was made of the said land by the aforesaid Thomas Stringer and Hillary Stringer and Hillary Stringer father of the defendant Hillary, and that he knew the said Hillary the father to lease the land where Hillary the defendant now lives to John Darby. - Depo. dated 28 Mary 1770

Jury impaneled and returned the following verdict.

That John Stringer, Gent: formerly of Northampton County was seized in fee simple of two tracts of land in the county of Accomack adjoining each other, containing by two several patents to William Taylor - Patent from Francis Morryson for 600 acres in Northampton at Accohannock Creek, the said land being formerly granted to the said Taylor by patent dated 21 May, 1651, and now renewed in his majesties name, dated 20 Oct. 1661; Patent from William Berkely for 1000 acres in Accomack, als. Northampton County in the woods between Occohannock Creek and Matxhapungo, adjoining 600 acres belonging to the said Taylor, &c., the said land formerly granted to the said William Taylor by patent dated 13 Oct. 1669, and now confirmed to the said Taylor, dated 25 Oct. 1673, which said two tracts were conveyed by one deed by the said William Taylor in fee to the said Stringer by deed dated 16 July 1674, the said land containing in the whole 1600 acres, and being so thereof seized on the 10 Feb. 1688, the said John Stringer made his last will and testament whereby he devised 600 acres, part of the said 1600 acres, and particularly the land now in question, unto his grandson, John Stringer, in fee tail, in these words: I will and bequeath unto John Stricker, my grandson, the son of Hillary Stringer, 600 acres of land lying and being at the head of Occohannock Creek, purchased by me from William Taylor &c. And the said testator by his said testator by his said will devised unto Hillary Stricker, another of his grandsons 600 acres of land, being part of 1600 acres so purchased of William Taylor, in these words: I give and bequeath unto my grandson Hillary Stringer 600 acres of land being part of 1000 acres of land also purchased from the aforesaid William Taylor, &c. And the testator likewise by his said will devised unto his third grandson, Thomas Stringer, the remaining 400 acres, the residue of the 1600 acres in the following words: I give and bequeath unto Thomas Stringer, my grandson & son to Hillary, the other 400 acres of land belonging to the 1000 acres so purchased from William Taylor, dec. &c.

That soon after the making and publishing of the said will the testator, John Stringer, departed this life so seized of said 1600 acres, which will was soon afterwards duly proved and recorded in Northampton County Court; that after the death of the said testator the said three grandsons, John, Hillary and Thomas by their father and guardian entered upon the said 1600 acres and were thereof severally seized; that the said John Stringer, the grandson, did attain to the age of 21 years and departed this life without issue, sometime in the year 1698; that soon after the death of the said John the said Hillary, his next eldest brother and heir at law to the first testator, entered upon the said 600 acres or some part thereof so devised to John, and was thereof seized in fee; that the said Hillary of Northampton, the devisee, by deed dated 3 Oct. 1704, purchased of Thomas Stringer of Accomack, his brother, the third grandson and devisee of John, the 400 acres devised as aforesaid to the said Thomas by their grandfather; that the said Thomas also by his deed dated 3 Oct. 1704, purchased of the said Hillary, the grandson, 300 acres said to be part of the 600 acres devised to John as aforesaid by his said grandfather, by virtue of which two several deeds the said Hillary entered upon the 400 acres conveyed to him by Thomas, and the said Thomas entered upon the 300 acres so as aforesaid conveyed to him by Hillary, and were thereof respectively seized;

That the said Hillary being so seized of the 400 acres conveyed to him by Thomas, of the 600 acres devised to him by his said grandfather, and of the residue of the 600 acres whereof his brother John had been seized, which he had not conveyed to his brother Thomas, on the 18 March 1721/2 made and published his last will and testament whereby he devised unto his second son John, who was the father and ancestor of the lessor of the plaintiff, his Accomack lands in these words: I devise, will, give and bequeath unto my son John Stringer all that my tract of land lying and being in the county of Accomack in Virginia, being 1000 acres more or less, as may more fully appear by the records of the said Court of Accomack , &c. That the said Hillary, the last named testator, soon after the making and publishing of his said will departed this life seized of the said lands in Accomack, and after his death his said will was duly proved and recorded in Northampton County, having left issue at his death two sons, Hillary, his eldest son and heir at law, father of the defendant Hillary, and the said John, his second son, father and ancestor of the said lessor of the plaintiff; that the said John after the death of the said Hillary, his father, entered upon the 400 acres which his father and testator and purchased of Thomas Stringer by deed of 1704, being part of the land devised to him, and was thereof seized and continued so seized until sometime in the autum[n] of the year 1750, when the defendant Ferriby, son and heir of the said Thomas, entered upon his seizen and took possession of the said 400 acres; that the said Hillary and Thomas, the two surviving grandsons of the first testator, and the defendants who claim severally under them have been uniformly in possession of all the residue of the said 1600 acres to this time, and the defendant Ferriby and those claiming under him have been continued in possession of the said 400 acres since his entry there in the year 1750.

That the said last named John Stringer departed this life sometime between the months of Feb. and April next following the entry of Ferriby on the 400 acres of land of which he had been seized, leaving issue the lessor of the plaintiff his eldest son and heir at law; <u>that</u> an infant of about three or four years of age

That the defendant Hillary through a course of regular descent is heir at law of Hillary the grandson mentioned in the first John Stringer's will; that the grandson Thomas held possession of the 600 acres which had been devised to the grandson John by the said first John Stringer, from the date of the death of the said grandson John until about 37 years past, when he gave up the possession of 300 acres thereof unto the father of the defendant Hillary, which was from thence held by the said father in possession till his death, and since that time the possession thereof has been in the said defendant Hillary until the commencement of this suit - 28 Feb. 1769 - p. 303

James Broughton & Anne, his wife
vs. - Partition Suit.
Elizabeth Wise Bayly, Sarah Wyatt, Susannah Bayly, Margaret Bayly & Charles Bayly Taylor.

That Elizabeth Wise Bayly, Sarah Wyatt, Susannah Bayly, Margaret Bayly & Charles Bayly Taylor and James Broughton and Anne, his wife, do hold together & undivided a certain tract of land in St. George Parish containing 845 acres with the appurtenances of the inheritance which was Charles Bayly, father of the said Ann Broughton, Elizabeth Wise Bayly, Sarah Wyatt, Susannah Bayly, Margaret Bayly and ---- Taylor, dec'd., mother of Charles Bayly Taylor, whose heirs they are &c. 23 Feb. 1773 - p. 337

LAND CAUSES - 1773 - 1805

Levin Merril & Rebecca, his wife
vs. - Partition Suit.
Anne Towles, Esther Towles & Betty Towles

That the said Anne Towles, Esther Towles & Betty Towles and the said Levin Merril and Rebecca, his wife, in right of said wife, do hold an undivided interest as daughters and co-heirs of Daniel Towles, dec., in 500 acres of land on the Seaboard side in Accomack Parish, whereof the said Daniel Towles died seized in fee. &c. 28 Sept. 1773 - p. 1

Henry Brooks, son & heir of Francis Brooks, dec.

vs. - Ejectment Proceedings.

Daniel Mifflin & Anne, his wife, daughter & heiress of John Walker, dec.

That Francis Brooks, dec., your orator's late father, did on the 8 day of October, 1742, borrow of one John Walker the sum of 12£ 1 s. and 3^d current money of Maryland, and 1450 £ of tobacco, and for security did by deed dated 8 Oct. 1742 mortgage to the said John Walker 200 acres of land on Muddy Creek until he, the said Francis or his heirs should repay the same to the said John Walker or his heirs; that the said Francis Brooks being a poor man soon after this indenture being acknowledged moved into Somerset County, Maryland, where he lived some small time and died in the year 17-- and the said land descended to your orator as son & heir of the said Francis Brooks; That your orator also being poor and never until very late knew what kind of title he hath in the premises, and residing altogether in the said Province of Maryland until very lately, when he came into the Colony and was informed of his claim to the equity of redemption to the mortgaged premises; that the said John Walker died in Accomack County in the year 17-- leaving the respondent, Anne, his only daughter and heir, who has since his death intermarried with the respondent Daniel Mifflin of the County aforesaid, Francis Brooks lived chiefly the latter part of his life with one William Floyd, with whom he died, whose mother the said Francis had married before the date of the said mortgage &c. 25 June, 1771 - p. 8

Charles Sneed, Sr.

vs. - Suit for recovery of a slave.

Robert Drummond

That a certain William Burton formerly of Accomack County, now dec., having a daughter then married to a certain John West, made his last will and testament in which he devised a number of slaves to his said daughter for life then to be equally divided between all her children; that the said Agnes West had nine children, one of whom named Katharine intermarried in her mother's lifetime with a certain Edmund Chambers and died before her mother and before any division could be made of said slaves; that after the death of the said Agnes the said Edmund Chambers obtained administration on the estate of his said wife, who was one of the said nine children, and a division was made among the complainants under the said Burton's will after a long and tedious litigation, and a slave named Lazar was allotted to the representative of the said Edmund's deceased wife without determining whether the right to the said slave vested in the son or the administrator of the deceased, as also the sum of 21£ 16 s. and 8^d for the proportion of the rent of the said slaves with interest from 23 Nov. 1766; that in consequence of the said partition and administration the said Edmund obtained possession of the said slave sometime in the year 1767 and sold him to your orator for a valuable consideration; that the said Snead held the said slave until sometime in the beginning of the year 1768 when he was spirited away and seduced from his service by Major Chambers, the son and heir of the said Catherine Chambers, one of the nine children aforesaid, and by a certain Jonathan Willett, and by them, after the said Willett had kept him in possession --- years sold to the respondent &c. Catherine Chambers left at her death Major Chambers, her only son and heir at law, and a daughter Agnes.

The defendant in his answer denies that the said Edmund Chambers had any right to any part of the slaves devised by William Burton, but only in right of his son, Major Chambers, one of the defendants; and that this will appear evident from a suit in chancery commenced in this Court by Jonathan Willet and Agnes, his wife, Garrat Topping and Scarburgh, his wife, Charles Crowson and Comfort, his wife, and Major West then plaintiffs vs. John West, Smith Bunting, Major Chambers, one of the present defendants, Thomas Goffigon & George Scott then defendants, in which it was decreed that the slaves devised to the said Agnes should be equally divided between the parties plaintiff and defendant, children and grandchildren of the said Agnes. Decreed that the plaintiff, Charles Snead, was a fair purchaser of Edmund Chambers whose property the said slave was, and that he recover the said slave Lazor of the defendant (Jonathan Willett m. Agnes West, Charles Crowson m. Comfort West, Garret Topping m. Scarburgh West, George Scott m. Susanna West, Thomas Goffigon m. Elizabeth West, Smith Bunting m. Anne West, Edmund Chambers m. Katherine West, daughters of John West & Agnes (Burton) West, who had nine children, the above named seven daughters and two sons, John and Major) 24 Sept. 1771 - p. 14

West's Lessee
vs. - Ejectment Proceedings.
Sturgis
That Anthony West on the 1st day of Feb. 1774 did grant, demise [devise?] and to farm lett to Thomas Den, his assigns &c. a tract of land containing 100 acres lately in the occupation of John Lyll, decd., to have and to hold the same from the 1st day of Feb. for the term of 10 years; that John West the elder, now dec., being seized of 1600 acres in fee simple made his last will in writing dated 6 Feb. 1702 & devised to his son Anthony West, his eldest son & heir at law, part of the said tract on Nandua Creek in fee, and afterwards in his said will devised to his said son Anthony's three daughters, Matilda, Mary and Jean "the Ridge land without the Neck where my son Anthony lives"; that after the death of the said John West, the devisor, the said Matilda, Mary and Jean entered upon the said land and about 60 years ago made partition thereof among themselves, ½ part being allotted to the said Matilda, adjoining to the head line of her father, Anthony's land; That the said Anthony departed this life sometime in the year 1717 seized of the land devised him by his father, leaving John West his eldest son & heir male by his wife Elizabeth, who entered upon the said land; that the said John West departed this life in the year 1773 seized and possessed of the said land, leaving Anthony West, the lessor of the plaintiff, his eldest son & heir male, who entered upon the said land and was, and yet is seized & possessed of the same; that the said Matilda intermarried with a certain Peter Hack who entered upon that part of the premises allotted to his said wife, which is the lands in question, and was thereof seized and possessed, and by their certain deed

29

conveyed the said Matilda's part of the premises to a certain ----- who by his deed reconveyed the same to the said Peter Hack; that the said Peter Hack departed this life in the year 1708 intestate, after whose death George Nicholas Hack, eldest son and heir at law of the said Peter, entered upon the premises and conveyed the same to a certain William Poulson who entered thereon, and by his deed conveyed the same to John Milby; that the said Milby entered upon the said premises, and at the time of his purchasing the same John West, father and ancestor of the lessor of the plaintiff before named, executed to the said Milby his bond in these words ----- not to disturb the said John Milby in the quiet and peaceable possession nor bring any suit of law against him for a tract of land bought of William Poulson by the said Milby, &c. That the said Matilda departed this life on the 17 Oct. 1742, and the line dividing the lands in question from the parts allotted to the two other sisters, Mary & Jean, has been kept up and processioned until this time. That Jane [sic], one of the sisters having departed this life sometime in the year 17--, John West, father of the lessor of the plaintiff, prosecuted a suit of ejectment against a certain Betty Jenkins, then in possession, and recovered the said Jane's part by a judgment in Accomack County April, 1756, entered upon the same and was thereof seized and possessed; that the other sister, Mary Scarburgh, having departed this life some few years afterwards, John Robins Downing, who had purchased her part surrendered the same unto the said last named John West, of which two several parts the said last named John West died seized & possessed, and the lessor of the plaintiff after his said father's death entered upon the said two parts as heir at law, and was and still is thereof seized and possessed. That John West, the father of the lessor of the plaintiff, was born on the -- day of --- 1696, and John Milby the obligee above named departed this life sometime about the commencement of this suit - 29 March 1774 - p. 31

Thomas Bayley & Anne, his wife
vs. - Suit for recovery of land.
Anne Buncle &c.

That Richard Drummond the elder, formerly of the county aforesaid, dec., grandfather of your oratrix, was in his lifetime seized and possessed of a very considerable quantity of land and personal estate; that the said Richard Drummond made his last will and testament dated the --- day of ---- 1730, and appointed his wife, the respondent Anne Buncle executrix, Capt. Hancock Nicless and his son Richard Drummond executors, and soon afterwards died so thereof seized and possessed, leaving issue at his death the aforesaid Richard the younger his eldest son and heir at law, father of your oratrix, whom he appointed one of his executors aforesaid, also George, William, Spencer, Elizabeth & Ann Drummond; that the aforesaid Ann, executrix, and the aforesaid Hancock & Richard, executors under the aforesaid Ann, executrix, and the aforesaid Hancock and Richard, executors under the aforesaid will, proved the same &c. That the said Richard the elder died seized of 1500 acres on Mesongo Creek in the county aforesaid, and by his last will and testament empowered his executors to dispose of the same for the payment of his debts; that 300 acres of said land sold by the executors, together with the personal estate of the testator, was more than sufficient to discharge the testator's debts; that Richard Drummond the younger after the settlement of his father's estate died leaving issue your oratrix, and another daughter called Elitia, who is since dead an infant and without issue; that Elizabeth, one of the daughters of the aforesaid Richard the elder, is also dead intestate and without issue; that the other daughter, Ann, is married to your respondent John Selby; that after the death of the aforesaid Richard the younger, father of your oratrix, who died on the --- day of ---, and after the death of Hancock Nicless on the --- day of ----, the said Ann Buncle, the respondent, then remaining sole executrix of the will of the aforesaid Richard the elder, under pretense that the personal estate of her former husband, Richard the elder, was sufficient to satisfy his debts, although she well knew to the contrary as the same were already satisfied and paid &c., did expose for sale the residue of the aforesaid 1500 acres, and it was so proceeded that Spencer Drummond aforesaid, now deceased, father of the respondents Betty, Spencer, Charles, Richard, Sarah & Ann Drummond, Jr., became the nominal purchaser thereof, to whom the said Ann Bundle as executrix conveyed the same. That the said Spencer Drummond departed this life --- as appears from the probate of his will, seized of the whole residue of the aforesaid 1500 acres; that soon after his decease the aforesaid George Drummond, dec., and the respondent William Drummond, by the suit in chancery commenced against the respondents Betty, Spencer, Charles, Richard, Sarah & Ann Drummond, Jr., devisees under the will of the said Spencer Drummond, dec., obtained a decree against the devisees under the will of the aforesaid Spencer, dec., that they should convey ⅓ of the said residue to the said George & William; that after the making of the said decree, which was on the 28 Nov. 1764, the Respondent, John Selby, who intermarried with the aforesaid Anne, one of the daughters of Richard Drummond the elder, complained of the fraudulent practice above set forth --- to quiet which complaint the said George and William made their joint deed bearing date 6 March, 1765, conveying to the said John Selby 249 acres of the said land. That soon after the said George Drummond made his will dated 9 May, 1765, and devised all his interest in the Mosongo land to his daughter, the respondent Anne Drummond, and soon after departed this life.

The joint and separate answers of Edmund Custis, who very lately intermarried with the defendant Elizabeth, to the bill of complaint of Thomas Bailey & Ann, his wife; That the residue of the 1500 acres so conveyed to the said Spencer Drummond was to be equally divided between the said Spencer and his brothers, William and George, but that the death of the said Spencer prevented the necessary conveyances being executed, by which means the said George and William were put to their suit in equity against his children and devisees to compel a conveyance agreeable to contract, after which the said John Selby, who intermarried with Anne, claimed in right of his wife her part of the residue of the said 1500 acres, which the said George and William by their joint deed dated 6 March 1765 conveyed to him; That the said William by his will devised his part of said land to one of his sons, but that his sons died without issue at the same time with their father, they all being unfortunately drowned together, all the testator's land descended to the defendant Elizabeth and her sister, Sarah, and that part of the said 1500 acres conveyed to him was allotted to the said Elizabeth - Answer dated 27 Sept. 1782.

The joint and separate answers of Henry Wilkins and Ann, his wife, defendants, to the bill of complaint of Thomas Bailey and Ann, his wife - That the said George Drummond made his last will and testament bearing date the 9 May 1765, and thereby devised all his interest in the Mesongo land to his daughter Ann, the defendant, and soon after departed this life &c. - Answer dated 23 Sept. 1782.

Deposition of John Drummond, age 20 year and upwards. .

Land surveyed and divided, and Thomas Bayly & Ann, his wife, put in possession of 450 acres of the aforesaid land, being for his full fifth part of the aforesaid land recovered, and for all the land which belonged to the aforesaid John Selby & Ann, his wife, as their share of the aforesaid land, the same being now conveyed to the said Thomas Bayly, &c. 25 July 1769 - p. 43, et seq.

Thomas Stringer
vs. - Ejectment Proceedings.
Hillary Stringer

Deposition of Elizabeth Benthall, aged about 75 years, taken 7 Aug. 1779, in Northampton County.

That she knew John Stringer, father of the plaintiff, when he lived in Savage's Neck, and heard him say he owned land in Accomack and should have lived on it but his wife craved to live near her mother, and he built on her land, and that the said land he owned in Accomack was given to him by his father; that she has heard her mother, who was sister to the plaintiff's great uncle, John Stringer, say that said John was older than her, and that her brother Hillary was also older than she was; that she has also heard her mother say she had two children before the death of the said John, and this deponent does not know that her mother ever had twins. That she heard that some of the Stringers in Accomack intended to take some land there that some of the Stringers own; and further saith that her mother said that her uncle John was older than her uncle Hillary.

Deposition of Jonathan Garrison, taken 7 Aug. 1779, in Accomack County, age 61 years and upwards. That about 45 years ago John Stringer, father of Thomas Stringer, at present of Northampton County, claimed 1000 acres of land in the county of Accomack, adjoining the lands of Jonathan Garrison, dec., father of this deponent; that his reason for knowing that the said John Stringer claimed said land at the time of this information, and further that he saw a tree deaded on said land and ground hoed upabout, which he understood by the information of the neighbors was done by Hillary Stringer, father of the said Hillary Stringer of Northampton, which he understood was done by way of taking possession of said land from said John Stringer, father of the said Thomas, whom he understands has brought suit for the said land.

Deposition of Jacob Savage, age 77 years and upwards, taken in Accomack County 7 Aug. 1779 - Same as above.

Deposition of Joseph Kellam, of lawful age, taken in Accomack County 7 Aug. 1779 0 That he knew Thomas Stringer, great uncle of both the plaintiff and defendant about 50 years ago &c. - Same as above.

Deposition of Smart Stringer, age 68 years & upwards, taken in Northampton County 7 Aug. 1779 - That said William Mears, Thomas Stringer and several persons from Accomack came to her husband John Stringer to buy staves off his land in Accomack, devised him by his father Hillery Stringer, &c. Suit instituted 30 June, 1762 - p. 52

John Brown Upshur, Infant, orphan of Caleb Upshur, dec., by John Upshur his
    next friend
vs. - Ejectment proceedings.
William Stockley
That the aforesaid Caleb Upshur in his lifetime was seized & in quiet possession of a plantation in Bradford's Neck in the county aforesaid and died thereof possessed, and the said land descended to the said John Brown Upshur, his son & heir &c. 29 March 1780 - p. 60

Janney
vs. - Order for Dower to be laid off.
Burdett
That Abel Janney and Elizabeth, his wife, who was the wife of William Burdett, late of Accomack County, dec., have recovered against Thomas Burdett, eldest son & heir at law of the said William Burdett, dec., their seizen of ⅓ part of and in 84 ¼ acres in Accomack County near the Court House - 10 Feb. 1786 - p. 88

William Barclay
vs. In Debt - Suit for sale of Land.
John Twiford, Infant, heir at law to James Twiford, dec.
That James Twiford, late dec., was in his lifetime indebted to your orator in the full sum of 44£ 3s. 5^d, and to secure the same did by deed of mortgage convey to your orator a tract or parcel of land in the Parish of St. George, containing 126 acres; that shortly after the said James Twiford departed this life leaving John Twiford his son & heir. 2 April 1788 - p. 103

Thomas Bayly and Anne, his wife,
vs. - Suit for Division of Land.
Major Rayfield & wife &c.
Whereas the said Major Rayfield and Mary, his wife, William Turner, William Willet & Garthery his wife & Jacob Taylor and the said Thomas Bayly & Anne his wife together and undivided hold six messuages and 354 acres of land at the head of Hunting Creek, and whereas one Finlay McWilliams was lately seized of and in the premises aforesaid as of fee, and being so thereof seized on the 25 March 1687 made his last will & testament and devised the said premises

by the description of the plantation where he then lived, supposed to contain 400 acres, to Finlay & Overton, the sons of the said Finlay McWilliams, and to their lawful heirs, remainder in case of death of either Finlay, the son, or Overton during their minority or without heirs, of the part of the said premises of him who should so die as aforesaid, to Sarah, the daughter of the said Finlay McWilliams the elder, and to her heirs forever, and the said Finlay McWilliams the elder being so seized afterwards died and the said Finlay the son and Overton entered into the said premises and were seized thereof, to-wit: the said Finlay of one moiety & the said Overton of one moiety undivided in their demesne as of fee tail, and being so seized the said Overton afterwards with intent to dock the entail of his moiety of the premises, sued forth a writ in the nature of a writ of Ad quod Damnum from the Secretarie's Office of the then Colony of Virginia, directed to the Sheriff of the County aforesaid, that he cause the value of the moiety of the said Overton in the premises to be enquired of &c., by virtue whereof &c. the said Overton became seized of the one moiety of the said premises in his demesne as of fee, and being so thereof seized, to-wit, on the 1 Feb. 1736, sold his moiety of the said premises to a certain George Scott, which said George Scott entered into the said premises and on the 3 Dec. 1747 sold the said moiety of the said premises to Richard Drummond; that the said Richard Drummond entered into the said premises and became seized of the one moiety thereof, and being thereof seized afterwards died leaving Anne his daughter & now wife of the aforesaid Thomas Bayly, whereby the said Anne entered into the said premises and being so seized the said Anne took to husband the said Thomas Bayly, whereby the said Thomas & Anne entered into the said premises and were seized of the one moiety thereof, and still are seized thereof in right of the said Anne as aforesaid; That the aforesaid Sarah, one of the daughters of the said Finlay McWilliams the elder, in the life of the said Finlay took to husband the said (blank) Courtney, and by his [sic] had issue Charles Courtney, and afterwards the said Sarah died and the said Finlay, the son, survived her, and afterwards the said Finlay the son being so seized died without issue & the said Charles Courtney, son & heir of the said Sarah, survived him and entered into the said premises and became seized of the one moiety thereof, and being so seized did on the 30 Jan. 1764, convey the one half of the moiety of the said Charles, being one fourth of the said premises, to a certain Abraham Turner, and the said Turner entered into the premises and became seized of the one fourth part thereof in fee, and being so seized afterwards died leaving the aforesaid Mary, now the wife of Major Rayfield his widow, and the aforesaid William Turner his son & heir, whereby the said Mary entered into the premises and became seized in right of dower of the one third of the one fourth part thereof, and the said Major Rayfield and Mary, his wife, are still seized thereof; and the said William Turner entered into the said other and became seized of two thirds of one fourth part thereof and still is thereof seized; and the said Charles Courtney being seized as aforesaid of the remaining one fourth part of the premises on the 31 Oct. 1764 made his last will and testament and devised the aforesaid remaining one fourth part of the premises to William Raleigh & Garthery Taylor; that the said Garthery entered into the premises and became seized of the ⅛ part thereof, and being so seized conveyed 25 acres of the said ⅛ of the premises to Jacob Taylor for and during the term of the natural life of the said Jacob; that the said Jacob entered into the premises and became seized thereof, and is still seized thereof, and the said Garthery being seized as aforesaid of the residue of the said ⅛ part of the said premises afterwards took to husband the aforesaid William Willet, whereby the said William Willet & Garthery entered into the said premises and were seized of the said residue of the said ⅛ part thereof, and still are seized thereof in right of the said Garthery; that the said William Raleigh entered into the premises and was seized of the ⅛ part thereof, and being so seized on the 30 July 1783, conveyed the same to the aforesaid Thomas Bayly - 31 Oct. 1786 - p. 106

Thomas Barry, Moses Dun & Rebecca, his wife, Robert Hezlet & Alice his wife vs. - Suit for the residue of the estate of James Barry
Lovin Joynes, surviving Ex'r. of James Barry, dec.

That a certain James Berry, alias Barry, late of the County aforesaid, in his lifetime, to-wit: 11 March 1782, made his last will & testament and left the remainder of his lands and personal estate to be sold, and after the payment of debts to be divided between his sisters Rebecca & Allah (Alice), daughters of William Berry of the Parish of Burt County of Donnegal in Ireland, and their heirs, if any, and "the eldest son of my uncle Thomas Berry or his heirs, of the same place," and in his said will appointed Levin Joynes, David Bowman & Alexander Stockly executors, and afterwards died; that his executors sold the said estate as directed in said will, and collected sundry debts due the said Berry, in the whole arising to a great amount; your complainants show that they are the persons entitled to the residue of the said estate, to-wit: that the said Thomas Barry, alias Berry, is the eldest son & heir at law of the said Thomas Berry in the said will mentioned as will appear by a certain attestation thereof under the hand and seal of John Coningham, Esq., Mayor of the City of Londonderry, in the Kingdom of Ireland, which is hereto annexed; that the said Rebecca, wife of the said Moses Dun, and that the said Alice, the wife of the said Robert Hezlet, are the sisters of the said James Berry dec. in the said will mentioned, as will appear by two other attestations thereof under the hand and seal of the said John Coningham, Esq., &c. 6 June, 1791 - p. 131

Arthur Downing & Sally, his wife
vs. - Partition Suit.
Martha Latchum

That Arthur Downing and Sally, his wife, daughter & co-heir & devisee of George Latchum, & Martha Latchum in her own right, own together and undivided a tract of land containing 100 acres in the parish of Accomack; that the said George Latchum on the 21 Aug. 1790, made his last will and testament & devised the premises aforesaid to his two said daughters, Sally & Martha - Will probated 27 July, 1791 - 3 Feb. 1795 - p. 132

Thomas Simpson Bayly & Anne, his wife, Isaiah Hickman & Sally, his wife &
    Zorobabel Core & Sinah, his wife
vs. - Writ of Partition.
Betsey Justice, Infant. Bridget Justice appointed her guardian to defend this suit.

    That a certain Ralph Justice, Gent: was in his lifetime lately seized of a tract
of land containing 250 acres situate near Guilford, that he made his last will and
testament & devised the said land to the said Anne, Sarah & Sinah & Betsy [sic],
being the daughters of the said Ralph Justice, and afterwards on the --- day of ----
1794 died, and the said Thomas Simpson Bayly and Anne, his wife, in right of
said wife, Isaiah Hickman & Sarah his wife, in right of said wife, Zorobabel Core
& Sinah his wife, in right of said wife, and the said Betsey Justice, are entitled to
the said tenement and tract of land &c. 12 March 1795 - p. 135

William Gibb & John Ker
vs. - Writ of Partition.
Nathaniel Burwell, William Bell, William Foster & John Drummond & Peggy
    Drummond, heirs of Sophia Drummond.

    That William Gibb & John Ker together hold undivided ¼ part of 436 acres
in the County of Accomack, the said Nathaniel Burwell as tenant in common of
½ of the said land, and William Bell, William Foster & John Drummond & Peggy
Drummond, heirs of Sophia Drummond, dec., as tenants in common of the
remaining ¼ part of the said land. Whereas a certain Col. John West was seized
of the said 436 acres, and being so seized in the lifetime made his last will &
devised the said tract of land to his four daughters & their heirs, & afterwards
died, and the said ___ (blank)_ entered upon the said land and were seized thereof
in fee, & whereas by divers descents and conveyances the undivided ¼ part of
Mary, one of the said daughters have come to the said William Gibb & John S.
Ker, as tenants in fee thereof, and 2/4 part of the said land have come to the said
Nathaniel Burwell as tenant by the Curtesy thereof, & the other ¼ part have come
to the said William Bell, William Foster & John Drummond & Peggy Drummond
as tenants in fee simple thereof &c. 3 May 1796 - p. 138

Edward Thornton, Infant, by William Warrington his guardian appointed to
    defend this suit
vs. - Writ of Partition
Henry Thornton

    Whereas one Henry Thornton, father of the said Edward & Henry, was lately
seized of 100 acres of land in the Parish of Accomack, and being so thereof seized
on the 2 Jan. 1782, made his last will & testament and devised the said premises
by the description of the place where he lived, to the said Henry, and being so
seized died, by virtue whereof the said Henry entered into the said premises - That
the said Edward Thornton, father of the said Edward & Henry, at the time of his
death had children to-wit: the said Henry & John & also his wife enscient who
after his death brought a posthumous child, the said Edward, who was unprovided

for by settlement, & neither provided for nor disinherited &c. 4 Nov. 1795 - p. 143

Spencer Waters
vs. - Writ of Partition.
Peggy Taylor, Betsy Taylor, John Taylor, Phamy Taylor & Wilson Taylor.

That William Taylor, late of the county aforesaid, was in his lifetime seized in fee of a tract of land containing 200 acres in the Parish & County of Accomack, and being so seized on the -- day of --- departed this life intestate leaving issue William Taylor, the said Peggy, Betsy, John, Phamy & Wilson Taylor his children & heirs who entered into the said 200 acres in their demesne as of fee; that the said William Taylor conveyed his 1/6 part of the premises to the said Spencer Waters by virtue whereof the said Spencer Waters entered into the premises and became seized thereof as of fee - 3 Nov. 1795 - p. 146

Mary Outten
vs. - Suit for conveyance of Land.
Edmund Custis, Garret Topping, John Joynes, Levin Joynes, Thomas Robinson Joynes, Susanna Joynes, Ann Smith Joynes & Sarah Joynes, children & heirs of Levin Joynes, dec., & John Wise Outten, son & heir of Abraham Outten, dec.

That a certain John Bradford, dec., being in his lifetime indebted to sundry persons in considerable sums of money, and among others to Edmund Custis, to Joynes & Snead & to Garret Topping, did on the 28 April 1783, make & execute his deed to the said Edmund Custis, Levin Joynes & Garret Topping, conveying to them the whole of his estate, real and personal, in trust to be sold for the payment of debts due the said Edmund Custis, Joynes & Snead & Garret Topping, in which was included the houses & lots then in possession of the said John Bradford, and on which he resided in the town of Port Scarburgh in the county aforesaid; that the said Edmund Custis, Joynes & Snead & Garret Topping did expose to sale the estate of the said John Bradford, and among the rest the said houses and lots; that at the said sale Abraham Outten, late husband of your oratrix, because the purchaser thereof; that the said Outten made considerable payments leaving a balance of £129:12:6 for which he gave a promissory note, but never got any conveyance from the said trustees; that on the 31 Dec. 1785, the said Abraham Outten departed this life leaving the said note wholly due; that the said John Bradford left a widow, Sarah Bradford who had been married to the said John before the conveyance to the said trustees; that Levin Joynes departed this life before any conveyance was executed for the said houses and lots, leaving children under age &c. William Gibb appointed guardian to John Wise Outten to defend this suit. 4 June, 1796 - p. 149

James East & Rachel his wife

vs. - Partition Suit.

John Turlington

That William Turlington was lately seized in fee of a certain plantation containing 120 acres in the Parish of St. George, adjoining the land of William Coleburn & others, and being so seized on the 3 Jan. 1785, made his last will & testament in which he devised the said plantation to his children, the said John and Rachel, now the wife of the said James East; that the said William Turlington afterwards died &c. Will probated 1 June 1785, and the said John Turlington & James East & Rachel his wife entered into the said plantation &c. Thomas Phillips, Sr. appointed guardian of John Turlington to defend this suit. 4 Nov. 1796 - p. 153

William Boggs & Sarah his wife, & Elizabeth Badger,

vs. - Partition Suit.

Spencer Kellam & Parker, his wife, & Henry White, heirs of Nathan White, dec.

That Nathan White, late of the County aforesaid was in his lifetime and at the time of his death seized in his demesne as of the fee of and in a certain tract of land containing 147 acres in the Parish of St. George, and being so seized on the -- day of --- 179- departed this life intestate, leaving a widow & the following children, Elizabeth, Sarah, Parker & Henry, by reason whereof the said William Boggs and Sarah his wife, in right of said Sarah, Elizabeth Badger, Spencer Kellam & Parker his wife, in right of said Parker, & Henry White entered into the said lands - Sheriff's return on summons "that the defendant Henry White not being found and having no place of abode within this county, that he gave Frances White, the tenant in possession of the premises due notice and a copy of the writ" &c. 2 May, 1796 - p. 156

Caleb Dix & Rachel his wife & Hepse Evans, daughters & co-heirs of William
  Evans

vs. - Partition Suit.

Edward Evans, Johannes Evans & Nancy Evans, children & heirs of John Evans,
  dec., who was a son & heir of the said William Evans.

That one William Evans was lately seized of & in a tract of land containing ---- acres in the Parish & County of Accomack, and being so seized had issue the aforesaid Rachel, the wife of the said Caleb Dix & Hepse Evans, his daughters, & the aforesaid Edward, Johannes & Nancy Evans, grandchildren by John Evans, dec., the son of the aforesaid William Evans, dec.; that the said William Evans died intestate in the year ----, his said daughters & grandchildren surviving him - 8 Feb. 1797 - p. 160

Charles Hope & John Teackle, Jr.
vs. - Ejectment Proceedings.,
James Moore, Infant son & heir of Robert Moore, dec.

That Thomas Hope sometime since dec., in his lifetime being eldest & heir apparent of George Hope, now also dec., who was then seized of a large tract of land at Kekotank in the County aforesaid, in the lifetime of his said father, to-wit: on the 9 Oct. 1771, purchased of him a part of the said entailed lands for the life of the said George Hope, which said entail according to the form of the gift pertaining to the said Thomas Hope after the death of the said George, his father; that the said Thomas Hope being rightfully seized as aforesaid of a part of the said tract, afterwards in the lifetime of his said father bargained with a certain Robert Moore for the conveyance of ½ of said land, which he had purchased as aforesaid of his father, in pursuance whereof the said Thomas executed a deed to the said Robert Moore dated 1 Nov. 1771, which either through ignorance of the parties or fraud on the part of the said Robert Moore, your orators know not which, but so it is that the said deed instead of being a conveyance of a moiety of the said lands from the said Thomas Hope to the said Robert Mason for the life of the said George Hope, hath been since discovered to be a conveyance of the fee simple of the said lands to the said Robert Moore, his heirs & assigns forever, entirely contrary to the bargain & agreement between the said Thomas Hope & Robert Moore; that the said George Hope afterwards on the -- day of --- 1778 died; that the said Thomas Hope then in his lifetime instituted a suit against the said Robert Moore suggesting the accident or fraud, and claiming a reconveyance of the said land or release of the apparent title therein; that shortly after the institution of the said suit the said Robert Moore died whereby the suit abated; that the said Thomas Hope threatened to renew his said suit against the son & heir of the said Robert Moore, but a certain Joseph Moore, the father of the said Robert Moore & grandfather of the said Robert Moore's heir, then guardian to the said heir, agreed with the said Thomas Hope in his lifetime to submit the title of his grandson in the said lands to arbitrators &c., who decided that the said land be given up to the said Thomas Hope; that your orator Charles Hope, being the eldest son & heir of the said Thomas Hope, after his death entered into the said lands & remained quietly possessed thereof until the -- day of 1793, when your orator conveyed the said land to your orator John Teackle, Sr. in few simple.
Deposition of John Moore, brother of Robert Moore, dec.
Deposition of Ann Hope, widow of Thomas & mother of Charles Hope.
27 Aug. 1794 - p. 164

John Carss & Peggy Carss by Thomas Ironmonger, their guardian - Petition for sale.

That John Carss, father of your petitioners, departed this life on the -- day of December, 1792, seized in fee simple of a certain tract of land containing 5 acres, being the land which the said John Carss purchased of Ambrose Willett & Susanna, his wife; that the said John Carss died intestate leaving a widow & your petitioners & no more - 29 March 1796 - p. 172

Edward Evans, Infant by Argil Bloxom, his guardian
vs. - Petition & Decree for sale of land.
Johannes Evans & Nancy Evans, Infants
That your orator & Johannes his brother & Nancy Evans, his sister, are all infants of tender age, being the children of John Evans late deceased, who was the son of William Evans, late dec.; that your orator & his said brother & sister are seized in their demesne as of fee by descent from their grandfather, the said William Evans, who died intestate since the death of their father, of 25 acres of land lying near Metompkin; that the buildings on the said land are old and in a condition almost ruinous; that the land is destitute of timber &c. and is also encumbered with the dower of the widow of the said William Evans dec., by reason whereof the said premises are entirely unprofitable to your orator & his said brother & sister &c. 20 Aug. 1797 - p. 173.

Richard Abbott, Infant
vs. - Petition & Decree for sale of land.
Elizabeth, Jane, John, Sarah & Margaret Abbott.
That Richard Abbott, father of your complainant, late deceased, was in his lifetime seized in fee of & in the reversion expected upon the estate of a certain John Abbott, of one undivided ⅓ part of 40 acres of land in the County aforesaid; that the said Richard Abbott died intestate leaving your orator, the said Richard Abbott, & Elizabeth, Jane, John, Sarah & Margaret Abbott, also infants of tender years; that since the death of the said Richard the said John Abbott, the tenant for life of the said 40 acres of land, hath also died, whereby the possession of the said undivided ⅓ part of the said 40 acres hath accrued to your orator and his said brother and sisters; that the other undivided ⅔ parts being also possessed by other two persons as tenants in common with the heirs of your orator's said father, &c. 1 April 1796 - p. 175

Rachel Broadwater & Robert Broadwater, Infants, by Rachel Broadwater, his next
    friend.
vs. - Petition & Decree for sale of land.
Hetty Broadwater.
That Caleb Broadwater, late deceased, died on the -- day of --- 179-, intestate, leaving your orator Robert Broadwater, Hetty Broadwater & Betsy Broadwater, all infants of tender years, and his widow the said Rachel Broadwater, your oratrix; that the said Caleb Broadwater at the time of his death was seized of a small piece of land containing 3 acres in the Parish & County of Accomack; that on the 10 May, 1795, your orator's sister, the said Betsy Broadwater, who was the daughter of the said Rachel, your oratrix; departed this life intestate, under age & without issue. 28 Aug. 1797 - p. 177

Richard Bayly

vs.- Partition Suit.

Nancy Bayly, Betsy Bayly, Edward Bayly & Charlotte Bayly

Whereas one Edmund Bayly was lately seized of & in a tract of land containing 750 acres in the Parish of St. George, and being so seized had issue, to-wit: the aforesaid Richard, Nancy, Betsy, Edward & Charlotte, & no more, and the said Edmund Bayly being so seized died intestate on the -- day of November, 1796. - 1 June 1797 - p. 178

Elisha Stephens

vs. - Partition Suit.,

Richard, William, Nancy & Hester Stephens

Whereas John Stephens, son of John & also grandfather of the said Hester by Southy Stephens, son of the said John, was seized in his lifetime as of fee of 100 acres of land in the Parish & County of Accomack, and in his lifetime, on the 21 April 1789 made his last will & testament and devised the said premises to all his children to be equally divided between them after the death of his wife who is lately deceased, and the said John afterwards departed this life (will probated 31 Dec. 1789) leaving at the time of his death his said children, John Stephens, Elisha Stephens, Richard, William, Molly & Southy then living that the said John Stephens the younger on the 12 March 1796, made his last will & testament & devised his land to his brother William Stephens & his heirs (will proved 1 Nov. 1796); that the said Molly Stephens on the 4 Jan. 1795, made her last will & testament and devised her land to her daughter Nancy Stephens (will probed 27 Jan. 1795); that the said Southy Stephens died intestate on the -- day of --- 1795 leaving issue his daughter the said Hester - 1 July 1797 - p. 182

Major Cole

vs. - Partition Suit.

John Cole & Sally Cole.

That Peter Cole was in his lifetime and at the time of his death entitled to 150 acres of land in the County & parish of Accomack, in his demesne as of fee expectant on the life estate of his father therein, and being thereto on the 29 Oct. 1791, made his last will & testament and afterwards on the -- Dec. 1791 died & devised to his brother John Cole ½ the said lands, to-wit: that ½ which lies next to Kekatank Branch, and to one other brother, to-wit: James Cole the other ½ of the said land; and whereas the said James Cole afterwards, to-wit: on the 15 July 1793 departed this life intestate, and infant under the age of 21 years, and without issue, leaving his father who was also the father of the said Major Cole, John Cole, Sally Cole, whereby the father of the said James became entitled to the share of the said James in the said lands, to-wit: ½ thereof, and whereas the said Major Cole, the father, departed this life intestate leaving the said Major Cole, John Cole & Sally Cole his only children, who became entitled to the said 150 acres of land &c. 1 Feb. 1798 - p. 185

41

Thomas Jenkinson, Jr. & Polly Jenkinson, Infant by Custis Jenkinson, their next friend.

vs. - Partition Suit.

Ralph Corbin, Thomas Jenkinson & Pamela, his wife, & Nancy Corbin.

That George Bonwill Corbin, late of the said County, was seized of and in 25 acres of land in the County & Parish of Accomack; and being so seized on the 7 June 1787, made his last will & Testament and devised the premises aforesaid by the description of all his land whereon he then lived, to his two sons, Ralph & Coventon Corbin, to be equally divided between them, and being so seized afterwards departed this life; that the said Coventon Corbin afterwards, to-wit: on the 8 Sept. 1793, departed this life an infant, under age, intestate and without issue, but leaving brothers & sisters, to-wit: the aforesaid Pamela & Nancy, sisters of the whole blood, the aforesaid Ralph, brother of the half blood on the side of the father, & the said Thomas & Polly Jenkinson brother & sister of the half blood on the part of the mother, by means whereof the said Thomas Jenkinson & Pamela, his wife, in right of said wife, Nancy & Ralph Corbin & Thomas & Polly Jenkinson entered into the said lands and became seized thereof in their demesne as of fee, to-wit: ½ to the said Ralph Corbin by virtue of the will of the said George B. Corbin, his father; 1/7 thereof as one of the co-heirs of the said Covington Corbin & brother of the half blood on the part of the father of the remaining ½ part to him pertaining, 2/7 to the said Pamela & Nancy Corbin, sisters of the whole blood of the said Covington Corbin of the remaining half part, & 1/7 part to the said Thomas & Polly Jenkinson, brother & sister of the half blood on the part of the mother of the said remaining 1.2 part - 5 June, 1798 - p. 188

Sarah Rodgers

vs. - Partition Suit.

Elizabeth Rodgers

That a certain John Rodgers died seized of ___ acres of land in the County of Accomack, and being so seized to-wit: on the 16 Feb. 1791, made his last will & testament (probated 27 Sept. 1791) by which he devised to his wife the whole of his land during her widowhood for the term of 7 years for the use of bringing up his small children, & ½ the said land during her widowhood or life. To his son James Rodgers ½ of my land after the said 7 years is out and the other ½ to his son John Rodgers, and for want of heirs to his brother Laban Rodgers, and so in like manner from Laban to Daniel & George. That after the death of the said John Rodgers the said Elizabeth Rodgers & James Rodgers by virtue of the devise aforesaid, entered into the said land and became possessed thereof, and the said James Rodgers being so seized of the ½ of said land on the 19 April 1795 made his last will & testament and devised to his wife all his lands & personal estate during her widowhood or marriage, and at her death or marriage to be divided between his son Reuben Rodgers, Richard Highland Rodgers and Martha Rodgers, and the said James Rodgers on the -- day of --- in the year last mentioned died, and the said Sarah by virtue of the devise made to her entered into the said

½ of the premises and became seized thereof, and the said Sarah says that she and the said Elizabeth together hold the said tenement or tract of land &c. 5 March 1798 - p. 192

Nancy Drummond, William Drummond & Leah Drummond, by Leah Drummond
    their next friend
vs. - Partition Suit.
Daniel Drummond
    That a certain William Drummond (ship carpenter) was lately seized of and in a tract of land containing 100 acres of land & marsh in the Parish of St. George, and being so seized on the -- day of February departed this life intestate leaving seven children, Daniel, Susanna, Patience, Robert, Nancy, William & Leah Drummond who entered into the said premises and became seized thereof, that Robert Drummond by deed dated 26 Oct. 1791, conveyed his 1/7 interest to the said Daniel Drummond; that the said Patience by her deed dated 18 March 1790, conveyed her 1/7 interest to the said Daniel Drummond; that the said Susanna, together with her husband, a certain Littleton Chandler, by deed dated 24 Feb. 1794, conveyed her 1/7 interest to the said Daniel &c. 9 Sept. 1795 - p. 195

William Coleburn & Betsy his wife & Charles Kellam & Nancy his wife
vs. - Partition Suit.
Molly James & Hetty James.
    That a certain William James, lately deceased, was in his lifetime and at the time of his death, seized of 200 acres of land on Kecotank branch, and being so seized on the 14 May 1796, made his last will & testament and devised the aforesaid land to the said Betsy, now the wife of William Coleburn, Nancy now wife of Charles Kellam, and the said Molly & Hetty James, and afterwards, on the 16 May 1796, the said William James departed this life &c. 7 Aug. 1798 - p. 198

Nock
vs. - Partition Suit.
Justice
    That Richard Justice dec., was lately seized of and in a tract of land containing 150 acres, another tract containing 150 acres, and another tract containing 86 acres, situate near Gargaphia, and being so seized had issue the aforesaid Rachel Nock, the mother of the said Anne, Sally, Amey & Richard Nock, who died in the lifetime of said Richard Justice, her said children surviving her, and also had issue the aforesaid Thomas, Nancy, William, Ralph & Samuel Justice, and the said Richard Justice being seized as aforesaid died intestate on the -- day of ---, the said Anne, Sally, Amey & Richard Nock, his grandchildren, & the said Thomas, Nancy, William, Ralph & Samuel, his children, surviving him - Benjamin Nock appointed guardian of Anne, Sally, Amey & Richard Nock to defend this suit. 8 Feb. 1797 - p. 201

John Gartner & Elizabeth, his wife, one of the daughters & co-heirs of William
    Bishop, dec.,
vs. - Partition Suit.
Nancy Bishop, Polly Bishop, & Henry Bishop, children & co-heirs of William
    Bishop, dec.

That William Bishop, dec. was lately seized of land containing 160 acres in
the County & Parish of Accomack, adjoining Muns Bishop, and being so seized
had issue the said Elizabeth, Nancy, Polly & Henry, his children, and being so
seized died in the year 1794 intestate, his children then being and still are alive;
that the said Elizabeth on the -- day of --- 1797 intermarried with the said John
Gartner, so that the said John Gartner & Elizabeth his wife, in right of said wife,
& Nancy, Polly & Henry Bishop together and undivided hold the said messuage
and tract of land &c. 7 March 1798 - p. 205

John Mehollums & Peggy, his wife,
vs. - Partition Suit.
Posey, Polly, James & Joyce Benston

That a certain John Savage Benston was lately seized of & in the 168 acres
of land in the Parish of St. George, and being so seized thereof on the -- day of ---
1795 departed this life intestate & under 21 years of age, leaving no children nor
father nor mother, but a brother & sisters of the whole blood, to-wit: the said
Peggy, now the wife of the said John Mehollums, and the said Posey (Rosey?),
Polly, James & Joyce, whereby the said land descended & passed to the said
Peggy, Posey, Polly   James & Joyce, brother & sisters of the said John Savage
Benston, dec. That the said Peggy afterwards, to -wit: on the --- day of --- 1797,
intermarried with the said John Mehollums &c. 7 March 1798 - p. 209

John Snead
vs. - Partition Suit.
Isaac, William & Thomas Snead.

That one William Snead (B.S.) was lately seized of and in 37 ½ acres of land
in the Parish of St. George, adjoining the land of Bowden Snead, and being so
seized had issue the aforesaid John, Isaac, William, Thomas & Agnes and no
more, and that being so seized the said William Snead on the -- day of --- 1789
departed this life intestate, his said children then being living; that the said Agnes
Snead afterwards, on the __ day of ___ 1794, died an infant, intestate & without
issue, so that the said John, Isaac, William & Thomas together and undivided hold
the said land &c. 22 Feb. 1799 - p. 215

Zorobabel Kellam & Bridget his wife
vs. - Partition Suit.
William B. Addison.

That Nathan Addison was lately seized of and in 500 acres in the Parish of
St. George, and being so seized had issue the aforesaid Bridget and William his
children, and no more, and afterwards to-wit: on the --- day of --- 1788, died

intestate, whereby the said lands descended to the said Bridget & William Bradford; that the said Bridget, to-wit: on the -- day of --- 179- intermarried with the said Zorobabel Kellam &c. 6 Feb. 1799 - p. 219

Charles Leatherbury
vs. - Partition Suit.
Thomas Leatherbury &c.

That one Charles Leatherbury, father of the said Charles & of the said Thomas, Nancy, John, Susanna & Perry Leatherbury, was lately seized of & in a tract of land containing 636 acres on Onancock, and being so thereof seized to-wit: on the -- day of ---, 17--, departed this life intestate, leaving the said Charles, Thomas, Nancy, John, Susanna & Perry his children, and no more, who entered upon the said land and became seized thereof according to law - 3 March 1800 - p. 225

Daniel Baker & Nancy his wife,
vs. - Partition Suit.
William Copes.

That one Joshua Copes was lately seized of and in a tract of land containing 100 acres, situate in the County and Parish of Accomack, and being so seized had issue the aforesaid Nancy & William Copes, his children, and no more, and being so seized the said Joshua, to-wit: on the -- day of --- 1789, died intestate and that his said children were then and still are living, whereby the said land descended to the said Nancy & William Copes, who entered upon the same and became seized thereof; that on the __ day of __ 179_ the said Nancy intermarried with the said Daniel Baker &c. 4 Sept. 1799 - p. 228

Selby Dunton & Catherine, his wife,
vs. - Partition Suit.
Thomas Jenkins & Sally Broadwater..

That whereas one William Broadwater was lately seized of 160 acres of land in the Parish of Accomack, and being so seized in the year 178- made his last will and testament, and devised the aforesaid premises to his three children, viz: James Broadwater, the said Catherine, now the wife of the said Selby Dunton, & the child his wife was then pregnant with, to-wit: the said Sally Broadwater; that the said James, Catherine & Sally entered upon the said lands and became seized thereof; and that afterwards, to-wit: on the -- day of --- 1800, the said James Broadwater conveyed his undivided ⅓ part of the said premises to the said Selby Dunton, and the said Selby Dunton by deed dated -- day of --- 1800 conveyed one undivided ⅓ part of the premises to the said Thomas Jenkins, by virtue whereof the said Thomas Jenkins entered into the premises and because seized thereof, to-wit: ⅓ undivided part thereof &c. 2 Aug. 1800 - p. 232

Nancy Shield

vs. - Partition Suit.

James Wharton & Sally, his wife &c.

That one William S. Shield, brother of the whole blood of the said Nancy Shield, Sally Wharton, John Shield & James Sheild, was lately seized as of fee in and to 200 acres of land in the Parish of St. George, and being so seized departed this life on the -- day of --- 179- without issue, but leaving his aforesaid brothers & sisters of the whole blood, and no more, who entered upon the premises and became seized thereof - 8 Oct. 1799 - p. 235.

William Dunton & Mary, his wife.

vs. - Partition Suit.

Catherine (Caty) Coleburn

That a certain Thomas Coleburn was lately seized of and in 150 acres of land in the Parish of Accomack, and being so thereof seized on the -- day of ---, 1791, departed this life intestate leaving three daughters, Mary, the wife of the said plaintiff, Cate Coleburn & Ann Coleburn, who entered upon the said lands and became seized thereof; that shortly after September 179(6?) the said Ann Coleburn departed this life intestate and without issue, and her undivided ⅓ descended to Mary, the now wife of the plaintiff, and Cate Coleburn &c. 2 Aug. 1800 - p. 239

Thomas Bayly

vs. - Partition Suit.

Mary, Richard & John Turner.

That whereas one Major Rayfield & Mary his wife, in right of said wife, were seized of and in a tract of land containing 100 acres in the Parish of St. George; that on the -- day of August, 1796, in the lifetime of her said husband, the said Mary died leaving issue the said William Turner, the father of the aforesaid Mary Turner, and John Turner, Dianna, the wife of William Bull, and Peggy, the wife of Levi Ames, children by her first husband, Abraham Turner, and also Sarah Delastations an infant grandchild born of her daughter Ritta, then deceased, who was also a child of the said Abraham Turner, and leaving by her last husband, the said Major Rayfield, the following children: William, Elizabeth, Major & Mary, whereupon the lands descended to the above said children and grandchild of the said Mary Rayfield, liable to a tenancy by the curtesy of the said Major Rayfield who survived his said wife; that afterwards, to-wit: on the -- day of Sept. 1797, after the death of the said Mary Rayfield the elder, Mary Rayfield the younger, one of the children of the said Major & Mary Rayfield, died an infant & without issue; that on the 4 day of October, 1797, the above named William Bull & Dianna, his wife, & Levi Ames & Peggy, his wife, conveyed their rights and interests in the premises to the said Major Rayfield the elder; that on the 21 May 1798, the said Major Rayfield the elder conveyed the interests so purchased by him to Thomas Bayly; that on the -- day of --- 1799, the said Major Rayfield the elder died, and the said Thomas Bayly thereupon entered into, the premises in consequence of the rights by him so purchased; that Elizabeth, William and Major Rayfield, children,

children of the said Major the elder and Mary, his wife, upon the death of the said Major entered into the premises and afterwards, on the 7 Oct. 1799, conveyed all their interest and rights in the premises to the said Thomas Bayly, by virtue whereof the said Thomas Bayly entered and became possessed thereof, and afterwards, on the 22 July, 1802, Sarah Delastations, the daughter of Ritta and grandchild of Mary Rayfield, the elder, conveyed to the said Thomas Bayly all her right and interest in said land, so that he, the said Thomas Bayly and the said Mary Turner and John Turner, heirs of William Turner, together and undivided hold the said messuage & lands &c. Stephen Drummond appointed guardian to the infant defendants to defend this suit. 1 Nov. 1802 - p. 243.

Joseph Gibb & Esther, his wife, Betsy Wheelton, Elisha Wheelton, John Johnson
    & Sally his wife & Charles Wheelton & James Wheelton
vs. - Partition Suit.
George Wheelton, Nancy Wheelton & William Wheelton.

That one Elisha Wheelton was lately seized of and in a tract of land containing 200 acres in the Parish of Accomack, and being so seized had issue, to-wit: the said Esther Gibb, Betsy Wheelton, Elisha Wheelton, Sally Johnson, Charles Wheelton, George Wheelton, Nancy Wheelton & William Wheelton, and no more; that being so seized the said Elisha on the -- day of --- departed this life intestate, his said children then living, whereby the said land descended to the aforesaid children of the said Elisha Wheelton who entered into and became possessed of the same &c. 2 March 1801 - p. 247

John Eyre & Ann, his wife, Littleton D. Teackle & Elizabeth, his wife
vs. - Partition Suit.
Arthur Upshur.

That one Abel Upshur, Esq., was lately seized as of fee of and in a tract of land called Upshur's Neck, supposed to contain 2400 acres, lying on Matchepungo Bay & Matchepungo River, and being so seized in his lifetime and issue the said Ann, now the wife of John Eyre, the said Elizabeth, now the wife of the said Littleton D. Teackle, and the said Arthur Upshur, and the said Abel Upshur being so seized afterwards, to-wit: on the -- day of March, 1790, died, whereby the said land came and descended to the said Ann, Elizabeth & Arthur as the children and co-heirs of the said Abel Upshur, dec. Edmund Bayly appointed guardian to the infant defendant, Arthur Upshur, to defend this suit. 3 March 1801 - p. 252

John S. Ker
vs. - Partition Suit.
Nancy Ker, Margaret Ker, John Ker & David Bowman & William Seymour, a
    committee of Hugh Ker an insane person.

That Edward Ker the elder was lately seized of and in a tract of land containing 250 acres in the Parish of St. George, and being so seized in his lifetime, to-wit: on the __ day of __ 17__ made his last will and testament, and devised the premises aforesaid to his four sons, George, John S., Hugh & Edward

47

Ker, to be equally divided; that by virtue thereof the said George, John S., Hugh & Edward Ker entered into the said premises and were seized thereof; that the said George Ker on the -- day of --- 179- died intestate, leaving a widow Sarah Ker and three children, to-wit: Nancy, John & Margaret, and no more, whereby the interest of the said George Ker in the said premises descended to the said Nancy, John & Margaret; that the said Edward Ker the younger on the -- day of --- 179- died intestate leaving no children nor father nor mother, but brothers and sisters and their descendants, to-wit: the said John S. Ker and the said Hugh his brothers of the whole blood, Elizabeth Seymour & Isabella Bowman his sisters of the whole blood, and Edmund Scarburgh, Jr., Margaret Coward, Alice Bayly & Edward, William & Elizabeth Scarburgh his nephews and Nieces, children of Jane Scarburgh, dec., his sister of the whole blood, Margaret, William, John & George Edward Christian his nephews & Nieces, children of Catherine Christian, dec., his sister of the whole blood, John & Margaret Revell, his nephew & niece, children of Ann Revell, dec., his sister of the whole blood, the said Nancy, Margaret & John Ker, his nephew & nieces, children of the said George Ker, dec., his brother of the whole blood, and Smith Snead, his nephew, the only child of Margaret Snead, dec., his sister of the whole blood, whereby the interest of the said Edward the younger in the said land descended to his brothers & sisters & nephews & nieces aforesaid, who entered in the same and became seized thereof as of fee, and being so seized on the 29 July 1800 the said John S. Ker, Samuel Coward & the said Margaret, his wife, the said Edmund Scarburgh, Jr., the said Hugh Ker, William Seymour & the said Elizabeth, his wife, David Bowman and the said Isabella his wife, Thomas Bayly and Alice his wife, presented their bill in chancery against the said Edward, William & Elizabeth Scarburgh, Margaret, William, John & George Edward Christian, John & Margaret Revell, Nancy, Margaret & John Ker & Smith Snead for the sale of the said Edward Ker, Jr's. part, which sale was ordered and Edward's part purchased by John S. Ker, so that the said John S. Ker, Nancy, Margaret & John Ker and the said David Bowman & William Seymour, committee as aforesaid of the said Hugh Ker, in right of the said Ker, hold together and undivided the said tract of land - George Parker appointed guardian to the defendants Nancy, Margaret & John Ker, infant defendants, to defend this suit. 4 March 1801 - p. 256

John Revell, Jr.
vs. - Partition Suit.
Margaret & Edward Revell.

That one Edward Revell, father of the said John, Margaret & Edward, was lately seized of and in the premises aforesaid as of fee, being a tract of land containing 1200 acres in the Parish of St. George & ½ of a water grist mill on Pungoteague Creek in the aforesaid Parish, and being so seized on the -- day of Dec. 1791, departed this life intestate, leaving four children, to-wit: the said John and Margaret and Leah by one marriage, and the said Edward Revell, Jr., by another marriage, who entered into and became seized of the said land subject to the dower of the widow of the said Edward, Sr., and afterwards, to-wit: on the 23

Aug. 1793, the said Leah departed this life an infant under the age of 21 years, intestate and without issue &c. John S. Ker appointed guardian to the defendant Margaret & Thomas Parker guardian to the defendant Edward, who are infants, for the purpose of defending this suit - 23 March 1803 - p. 262

John Savage (of Abel)
vs. - Partition Suit.
William Savage (of Abel) & Abel Savage (of Abel)
    That one Abel Savage, father of the said John, William & Abel, was upon the 28 Jan. 1793, seized as of fee of and in a tract of land containing 150 acres in the Parish of Accomack, and being so seized on the day and year aforesaid, made his last will and testament & devised 75 acres to be laid off from the North side of the said land to the said William, and the remaining 75 acres to that said John Savage, and being so seized on the -- day of --- 179- departed this life, and the said William & John Savage entered upon the said lands and became seized thereof; that at the death of the said Abel Savage the elder, he left the following children then born, to-wit: the said John & William, also Jacob, Nancy, & Sally Savage and grandchild Abel, son of his deceased son Parker Savage, also a widow, to-wit: Nancy Savage, who at the time of the death of the testator was enceinte of a child which was born after the death of the said testator, to-wit: the said Abel the defendant, which said Abel being unprovided for &c.; that the said Abel according to the act in such cases made and provided, succeeded to this same position of his father's estate as he would have been entitled to had his father died intestate, to-wit: to one undivided 1/7 part thereof - 29 Aug. 1803 - p. 267

John Finney
vs. - Partition Suit.
Elijah Nock, Jr., Joseph Conquest & Mary, his wife, & Shadrack Taylor & Comfort his wife.
    That one James Nock was lately seized of and in a tract of land containing 81 ½ acres as of fee, situate in Accomack Parish, and afterwards, to-wit: on the -- day of --- died, being of full age and without issue, leaving the aforesaid John Finney his brother of the half blood, and the aforesaid Elijah Nock and the aforesaid Mary, the wife of Joseph Conquest, and the said Comfort, the wife of the said Shadrack Taylor, his brother and sisters of the whole blood who survived him and entered into the lands and were seized thereof as of fee - 1804

William Sharpley & Esther, his wife,
vs. - Partition Suit.
Daniel, Joshua, Betsey, Polly and Nancy Wheelton.
    That one Joshua Whealton [sic], Sr., now dec., was lately seized of and in 145 acres on Chincoteague Island, and being so seized had issue Esther, now the wife of the said William Sharpley, and also the said Daniel, Joshua, Betsey, Polly & Nancy Wheelton; that the said Joshua Wheelton, Sr., on the -- day of ---- died leaving his said children surviving him, who entered into the said premises and

were seized thereof as of fee as co-heirs of the said Joshua Wheelton - 28 Oct. 1804 - p. 280

Joseph Collins & George Collins
vs. - Partition Suit
William Collins, Custis Collins & David Collins
That one Anne Marshall, sister of the said John, George, William, Custis & David Collins, was lately seized of a tract of land containing 460 acres at Chincoteague, in the Parish of Accomack, and being so seized on the -- day of --- 1792, died without issue, and the said land descended to her said brothers, who entered upon and became possessed of the same. Elisha Vernelson appointed guardian of the infant defendants to defend this suit - 1 Aug. 1803 - p. 275

William Ewell & Sally, his wife,
vs. - Partition Suit.
Betsey, Susanna & Jesse Dickinson.
That one Jesse Dickinson, Sr., was lately seized as of fee of 500 acres of land at Pocomoke, and being so seized on the -- day of ---, 1788, departed this life intestate leaving five children, to-wit: Thomas Dickinson, the said Sarah, now the wife of William Ewell, and the said Betsey, Susanna and Jesse Dickinson, Jr., who entered upon the said lands and became seized of the premises; that on the -- day of --- 1803, the said Thomas Dickinson departed this life intestate, at full age leaving no child nor father or mother, but brothers & sisters, all of the whole blood, who entered into and became seized of the said 1/5 share of the said Thomas, dec. Thomas Fletcher appointed guardian to the infant defendants to defend this suit. 28 July 1805 - p. 284

Thomas Leatherbury & Charles Leatherbury,
vs. - Partition Suit.
John, Susanna & Perry Leatherbury.
That Nancy Leatherbury was lately seized of and in one messuage, one orchard, one garden & 66 acres of land upon the waters of Onancock Creek, and being so seized on the -- day of --- 1802, departed this life intestate & under age, leaving no child nor father nor mother, but brothers and sisters of the whole blood, viz: the said Charles, Thomas, John, Susanna & Perry Leatherbury, who with the said Nancy were all children of a certain Charles Leatherbury, dec., from whom the said premises descended, who thereupon entered upon and became seized of the premises - 28 July 1803 - p. 288

Richard Bloxum
vs. - Partition Suit.
Major Bloxum
That a certain Richard Bloxum, dec., father of the said Richard & Major was in his lifetime seized of two tracts of land containing 290 acres, in the Parish of Accomack, and being so seized on the 1 Feb. 1786 made his last will & testament

in which he devised the said premises to his wife Margaret S. Bloxum during her widowhood, then the land where he lived to be divided between his two sons, Major Simpson Bloxum & Richard Bloxum; that the said Richard Bloxum, Sr., afterwards departed this life; that the said Margaret S. Bloxum died on the --- day of --- 1802 &c. 7 June, 1803 - p. 291.

William Smith & Adah, his wife,
vs. - Partition Suit.
Jenny Mears
    That Coventon Mears, late deceased, was in his lifetime seized of 200 acres of land in the Parish of St. George, and being so seized on the -- day of --- 1796 died intestate leaving two daughters, to-wit: Adah & Jenny, whereupon the said Adah & Jenney entered into the said premises; that afterwards on the -- day of --- the said William Smith intermarried with the said Adah and became seized of one moiety thereof in right of the said Adah &c. 13 Sept. 1804 - p. 295

Daniel Baker & Susanna Baker
vs. - Partition Suit.
Esther Baker &c.
    That one John Baker, father of the said Daniel & Susanna Baker, and also of the said Esther, Henry, Finney & Viola Baker, was lately seized in fee of a tract of land containing 90 acres in the Parish of Accomack, and being so seized on the 23 March 1804, departed this life intestate leaving the said children and no more, and also a widow, to-wit: Molly Baker, whereupon the said Daniel, Susanna, Esther, Henry, Finney & Viola Baker entered upon the said lands and became seized thereof subject to the dower of the said Molly Baker &c. Levin Bloxom appointed guardian of the infant defendants to defend this suit. 27 Sept. 1804 - p. 298

Maria Wishart, by Arthur Whittington, her guardian,
vs. - Partition Suit.
James Wishart.
    That one Joshua Wishart, father of the said James and Maria, was lately seized in fee of a tract of land containing 700 acres at Assawoman, in Accomack County, and being so seized on the -- day of --- 1804 died intestate leaving the said James & Maria his only children who entered into and became seized of the said premises. Elias Taylor appointed guardian of the infant defendant to defend this suit - 5 June 1805 - p. 301

William Watts
vs. - Partition Suit.
William Hickman &c.
    That one John Hickman was in his lifetime seized of a tract of land containing 30 acres in the Parish of Accomack, and being so seized on the -- day of --- 17--, departed this life intestate, leaving issue John Hickman, Parker

Hickman and the said William & Polly Hickman all his children, and also a widow, to-wit: Sarah who hath since intermarried with the said Elisha Vernelson, which said issue entered upon the premises and became seized of one undivided ¼ part each as of fee, subject to the dower of the widow who was the mother of the said issue of John Hickman; That John Hickman, one of the said issue, on the -- day of --- 1803 departed this life without issue, and of full age, leaving his brothers & a sister of the whole blood, to-wit: the said Parker & William & the said Polly & his mother, the said Sarah, who entered into the said premises; That on the -- day of --- 180- the said Parker by his deed conveyed his interest in the said premises to the said William Watts &c. - 1 August 1805 - p. 204

William Shrieves &c.
vs. - Partition Suit.
Bonwell
    That one Bartholomew Shrieves late of the county aforesaid, dec., was seized as of fee of 100 acres of land in Accomack County, Parish of Accomack, near the head of Deep Creek, and being so thereof seized on the -- day of --- 1805, departed this life intestate, leaving the following children, William, Milby, Mary, the wife of the said John West, Esther Singleton, Susanna Shrieves & Sarah Shrieves, and also grandchildren to-wit: the said John & Elizabeth Bonwell, being children of Dolly Bonwell, dec., a daughter of the said Bartholomew Shrieves, which said children & grandchildren entered into and became seized of the said premises &c. John Custis (B.S.) appointed guardian to the infant defendants, John & Elizabeth Bonwell, to defend this suit. 12 Oct. 1805 - p. 309 (Susanna Shrieves not a party to this suit, but allotted her 1/7 share in the division)

Thomas West & Leah, his wife &c.
vs. - Partition Suit.
Preeson Baker &c.
    That one Elias Bundick was lately seized as of fee of and in 100 acres in the Parish of Accomack, and being so seized on the -- day of --- 1805 departed this life intestate, leaving the aforesaid Leah, wife of the said Thomas West, Tabitha, the wife of the aforesaid William Hinman, Patience, the wife of the aforesaid William Baker, and the aforesaid Keziah his sisters, and also the aforesaid Preeson Baker, Tabitha Baker, Richard Baker & Rachel Baker, infants, his nephews & nieces, being the children of Rachel Baker, another sister of the said Elias Bundick, and the said Sally Bundick his niece, being the daughter of Levin Bundick brother of the half blood of the said Elias Bundick - John Nock appointed guardian to the infant defendants to defend this suit. 28 Oct. 1805 - p. 313

William Grinnalds & Nancy, his wife &c.
vs. - Partition Suit.
Richard Bundick &c.
    That Richard Bundick, Sr. was lately seized as of fee of and in two tracts of land & Marsh containing 300 acres, situate in Accomack Parish, and being so

seized on the 13 March 1805 died intestate, leaving children, to-wit: the said Nancy Grinnalds, wife of the said William Grinnalds, Betsy Vessels, wife of the said Arthur Vessels, & Richard Bundick, and also grandchildren, to-wit: the said Tabitha Taylor, wife of the said James Taylor, William Bundick, Betsy Bundick, and Sally Bundick, children of one George Bundick, a deceased son of the said Richard Bundick, Sr., who entered into and became possessed of the said premises. Tabitha Bundick appointed guardian of Betsy & Sally Bundick, two of the infant defendants to this suit. 7 Aug. 1805 - p. 317

Samuel Baker, by Jemima Baker his mother & next friend
vs. - Suit for his share of his father's estate.
William Baker & Hezekiah Baker.

That Hezekiah Baker, late deceased, having issue the following children, Hezekiah Baker, William Baker, Stephen Baker, Grace Baker, now the wife of John Baker, & Betsy Baker, and also his wife, the said Jemima Baker being enscient, on the 13 April 1790, made his last will and testament, & being seized of a tract of land containing 100 ½ acres, near Gargaphia Church, and also personal estate to a considerable amount, disposed of the same among his children then born, and also made provision by his said will for the child unborn; that the said Hezekiah Baker afterwards, to-wit: on the 3 May 1797, the child of which his said wife was escient at the time of making the said will being then born, and Grace, one of the daughters of the said Hezekiah Baker late dec. being then dead, leaving lawful issue, made a codicil to his said will wherein he then took notice of the said occurrence & made such provisions relative to the same, that afterwards, on the -- day of January 1804 your orator aforesaid was born & afterwards, to-wit: on the -- day of --- 1804 the said Hezekiah Baker, the father, departed this life &c. 27 Nov. 1804 - p. 321

DISTRICT COURT RECORDS - MAY 1794 TO OCTOBER 1797

Copes' Lessee
vs. - Trespass & Ejectment.
West & Copes

That Thomas Copes, grandfather of the lessors of the plaintiff, was on the --- 1741 seized in fee simple of 440 acres of land; that the said Thomas Copes duly made and published his last will and testament in the year 1741, in the following words: Dec. 4, 1741 - My will is that my son Southy Copes shall have 200 acres of land where John Sterling now lives; daughter Mary; wife & Peter Parker Copes Ex'rs. That 140 acres of land, being the land in question, is part of the 440 acres of which Thomas Copes died seized and also part of the 200 acres devised to Southy Copes; Thomas Copes, the devisor, had at the time on his death two sons, Thomas Copes, father of the lessors of the plaintiff, who was eldest son & heir at law to the said devisor, and Southy Copes his youngest son who was devisee of the lands in question. The said Thomas Copes, eldest son of the devisor Thomas Copes, departed this life on the -- day of March 1785, having first made his last will & testament in these words following: I, Thomas Copes, Sr., &c. To sons Hancock & Levin Copes my plantation where I now live to be divided between them; to grandson Thomas Simpson; wife to have use of residue of estate for life then to be divided between two sons & grandson; wife & sons Ex'rs. Dated 19 Jan. 1784 - Probated 1 June, 1785 - Hancock Copes heir at law, Edmund Bayly his guardian - Susanna Copes qualified. The aforesaid Southy Copes entered on the lands in question and continued in possession thereof under the aforesaid will of Thomas Copes the elder until the death of the said Southy, who died on the -- day of May, 1790. The lessors of the plaintiff and devisees of the lands mentioned in the will of Thomas Copes the younger, & the interest of the testator in the lands in question included within the devise so as aforesaid made to the lessors of the plaintiff - 17 May, 1798 - p. 41

Thomas, a negro
vs. - Suit for freedom - Appeal from Judgment of Northampton Court.
Roberts.

That Ann Mifflin being seized in her demesne as of fee of and in a certain tract of land in the County of Northampton, and also of sundry slaves annexed thereto in fee tail, of which slaves the said Thomas was one, on the -- day of --- intermarried with Humphry Roberts, father of the defendant, Edward Roberts, whereby the said Humphrey [sic] & Anne, in right of the said Anne, became seized of the said land and slaves in fee; that at the commencement of the last war between Great Britain and America, in the year 1775, the said Humphrey, being a Briton born and then resident in Virginia, sought the protection of the British Government and removed to and remained within the Territories of Great Britain from the year 1775 aforesaid to the conclusion of the late war, but without engaging in hostilities against America further than the peaceable citizens of the country at war are presumed to; that during the whole time of the late war the aforesaid Anne, the wife of the said Humphrey Roberts, together with the aforesaid defendant Edward Roberts, and her two daughters, her children by the aforesaid Humphrey Roberts, remained and resided within the State of Virginia; that the said Anne afterwards in the life of the said Humphrey, to-wit: on the 7 Jan. 1782, executed a deed to a number of slaves whom the said Thomas is one, in the following words: Whereas John Roberts of Northampton County, Virginia, being possessed of a number of negroes as slaves, and through adverse circumstances permitted by divine Providence under the present calamitous dispensation to overtake us, whereby I am separated from my husband and one child, thereby in my own experience have to witness the grievous hardship of being forcibly separated from those near connections whereunto the African slave has for a long series of time been subjected by the oppressive practice of making them slaves, which I am fully persuaded is inconsistent with Christianity & totally derogatory to the Injunction of Jesus Christ our Holy Lawgiver --- in which my eldest son Charles Mifflin of the City of Philadelphia being under the former laws heir to all those negroes after my decease, and now willing to unite with me herein &c. Emancipation Deed dated 25 March 1782 - "I do certify that the above and foregoing is a true transcript of the manumission of Anne Roberts & Charles Mifflin on the Manumission Book of Records for the monthly meeting of the people called Quakers of Duck Creek, in Kent County and State of Delaware, folio 63, 64, 65 of said Book - Warner Mifflin - Recorded 26 Day of 6 month 1792. That soon after the peace concluded on by a treaty between Great Britain & America, to-wit: in the year 1783, the said Humphrey Roberts returned to this State and took possession of the whole of the said negroes in the said deed mentioned, including the said Thomas, and being so seized by his deed dated --- gave and granted the said Thomas as a slave to the said Edward Roberts, the defendant, by virtue whereof the said Edward Roberts, the defendant, took possession of the said Thomas &c. 18 Oct. 1793 - p. 91

Marshall
vs. - Partition Suit.
Marshall
    That Nehemiah Marshall, dec., father of the defendant Nancy Marshall, an infant, was at the time of his death, which happened on the 14 Feb 1784, seized in his demesne as of fee of the premises in the declaration mentioned; That the same Nehemiah died intestate leaving two children, viz.: George Beavans Marshall & the defendant Nancy Marshall and a widow Tabitha Marshall, mother of the said George Beavans & Nancy; That on the 7 Oct. 1787 the said Tabitha, the widow of the said Nehemiah, intermarried with Stephen Marshall by whom she had issue Polly & Leah Scarburgh Marshall; that after the marriage aforesaid, and the birth of the plaintiffs, to-wit: upon the 2 March 1792, the said George Beavans Marshall, the son of the said Nehemiah, departed this life an infant under the age of 21 years, seized in his demesne as of the fee of the premises in the declaration mentioned, but whether the plaintiffs have lawful right to have partition of the premises in the declaration mentioned as their defendant, or the defendant to hold the same in severalty, we of the jury doubt &c. 21 March 1794 - p. 154

Severn Major, of Shelburne in the Province of Nova Scotia, but at present of the City of New York, in the State of New York - Will dated 9 Jan. 1797 - Wife Abigail - Severn Major lived in Accomack County in the Parish of St. George in 1791 - pp. 227 et seq.

Americus Goodrich, lessee of John Poolman & others,
vs. - Ejectment Proceedings
Francis Shamtitle
    Jury impaneled and returned the following verdict:
    That Joshua Foster of the County of Accomack, being seized of the lands in the declaration mentioned in fee, and also possessed of sundry slaves & a considerable personal estate, and having issue Absalom Foster, his only son & heir apparent & Betty, Peggy & Sinah, three daughters, also two grandsons, to-wit: Joshua Foster, a son of the aforesaid Absalom Foster & Joshua Hickman, the

eldest son & heir apparent of the aforesaid Peggy, by Custis Hickman, her husband, on the 5 Aug. 1773, made his last will & testament as follows: (abstract) To son Absalom plantation where I now live during his natural life, then to the equally divided between my two grandsons Joshua Foster, son of the said Absalom, and Joshua Hickman, son of my daughter Peggy Hickman. To Custis Hickman. Land purchased of Jemimah Booth, lying over the road, to return whence it came after the crop is taken off. Jemimah Booth to have my negro wench Lisha as long as she lives in the station she now is in, but if she marry or suffer her children or anybody else to abuse the said wench, then to return to my estate to be divided between the rest of my children hereafter named. Daughters Betty, Peggy & Sinah reside legatees. That after the making of the said will the said Joshua departed this life on the -- Aug. of the same year, seized & possessed as aforesaid, which said will was proved on the 1 day of Sept. 1773 and admitted to record; That after the death of the said Joshua Foster the said Absalom Foster entered into the premises in the declaration mentioned and was possessed thereof, and afterwards Joshua Hickman, one the grandsons before mentioned, on the __ day of April, 1786, died an infant, intestate and without issue, leaving Custis Hickman, his father aforesaid, Peggy Hickman, his mother aforesaid, and several sisters then living; that afterwards the said Absalom Foster being still possessed of the premises as aforesaid, together with his wife, Charity, to-wit: on the 23 March 1787, conveyed 50 acres of land, being part of the said premises, to John Boisnard; that the said Absalom Foster and his wife Charity, on the 20 Feb. 1792, demised, granted and to farm lett the residue of the premises in the declaration mentioned to the said John Boisnard, for and during the term of 10 years commencing the 1 Jan. then last past, and afterwards, to-wit: on the -- Oct. 1792 the said Absalom Foster died intestate leaving issue William Foster, his eldest son, Leah Foster, Joshua Foster, Sally Foster, George Foster, Samuel Foster & Betty Foster. We also find that Joshua Foster, son of the said Absalom, and grandson of the said Joshua Foster the testator as aforesaid, to-wit: on the -- Oct. 1794, died intestate and without issue, leaving his said brothers and sisters then living &c. 9 May 1795 - p. 364

DISTRICT COURT RECORDS
OCTOBER 1797 TO MARCH 1809

John Lugg, lessee
vs. - Trespass & Ejectment Proceedings.
Peter Lugg.

Jury impaneled and returned the following verdict:

That the said T. Copes was on the 16 Dec. 1720 seized in his demesne as of fee of and in the premises in the declaration mentioned, together with and contiguous to other lands forming in all one tract of 500 acres; that the said T. Copes being so seized on the day and year aforesaid made his last will & testament in writing, and shortly afterwards, died without having altered said will, which said will was probated on the 4 April 1721; that T. Copes the second, son & heir at law of the aforesaid T. Copes the first, afterwards entered into the whole of the said tract of land and was seized thereof under the will of the said T. Copes the first, and that afterwards the said T. Copes the second, being seized as aforesaid, on the 4 Dec. 1741 made his last will and testament and died without having altered said will; that T. Copes the second at the time of his death left issue T. Copes, the third, his eldest son and heir at law, and Southy Copes his second son named in his will aforesaid; that the said Southy Copes by virtue of the said devise upon the death of his said father in the name of the whole, entered into ---- acres, part of the premises in the declaration mentioned, and continued seized thereof to the time of his death, to-wit: on the -- May 1790 in manner hereafter expressed; we also find that the said T. Copes the third, entered into the residue of the cleared land of the said tract whereof the said Thomas the second was seized as aforesaid, and continued seized thereof to the time of his death on the -- April 1785; and we find that no line was ever run between the lands whereof the said Southy Copes and the said T. Copes, third, were seized as aforesaid; We further find that the lands whereon John Starling is mentioned in the will of the said T. Copes the second to have lived, are the same whereon Patrick Clarke in the will of T. Copes the first is mentioned to have lived, and composed a part of the premises in the declaration mentioned; We find that the said T. Copes the third in his lifetime, on the 15 Jan. 1784, made his last will and testament, and afterwards, died without having altered said will, which said will was probated on the 1 June, 1785; That the lands mentioned in the will of T. Copes, third, and devised to Hancock and Levin Copes, his sons, comprehend the whole of the lands, as well as those whereof the said Southy Copes was possessed as aforesaid as those whereof the said Thomas Copes, third, was possessed as aforesaid; that the said Hancock & Levin Copes upon the death of the said T. Copes, the third, entered into the lands whereof the said Thomas Copes, third, was seized at his death, and claimed the reversion of those lands whereof the said Southy Copes was possessed as aforesaid; that the said Hancock Copes on the 24 March, 1795, made his last will and testament and on the -- April, 1795, died without having altered said will, which said will was probated 29 Sept. 1795; That John Custis Copes mentioned in the will of the said Hancock Copes, is the same John Custis Copes who is the lessor of the plaintiff; We find that the aforesaid Southy Copes on the 25 May, 1790, made his last will and testament and afterwards died without having altered said will, which said will was probated 29 June, 1790; That Thomas Copes the fourth, the son of the said Southy Copes, and Comfort Copes his daughter, the devisees in the said will mentioned, entered in the premises upon the death of the said Southy Copes and were seized and possessed thereof according to their several rights & titles; that the said Thomas Copes, fourth, being seized and possessed as aforesaid on the -- Dec. 1793, died intestate and without issue, leaving four sisters, to-wit: Comfort, the wife of Scarburgh West, Leah Parker Copes, Ritter Copes and Catharine Copes, the defendants in this present action who, as heirs of the said Thomas Copes the fourth, entered into the lands thereof he was seized and possessed as aforesaid, and are still thereof seized &c. 15 May, 1797 - p. 9

Americus Goodright
vs. - Ejectment Proceedings.
Francis Shamtitle

Jury impaneled and returned the following verdict:

That Levi Watson being on the -- day of --- 1776 seized in his demesne as of fee in 13 acres of land, being the premises in the declaration mentioned, and of other visible property or estate, on the day and year aforesaid made his last will & testament in these words (abstract) To my sister Rosey Watson 13 acres of land adjoining the place called Bell Haven, and £2:15:0 that is due for the rent of the said 13 acres, and £6:12:0 in the hands of Thomas Addison, and I do appoint my brother in law Churchill Ames executor - Dated 20 Dec. 1776. That afterwards, to-wit: on the -- day of --- 1778, the said Levi Watson died without issue leaving William Watson his brother & heir at law; That William Watson died intestate on the -- day of --- 1778 leaving Benjamin Watson, the lessor of the plaintiff, his only son & heir at law; that Rosey Watson, sister of the said Levi Watson, entered upon the premises in the declaration mentioned by virtue of the will of the said Levi Watson; that the said Rosey Watson was on the -- day of --- 17-- duly and legally married to Littleton Addison, and afterwards, to-wit: on the 26 March, 1782, the said Littleton Addison & Rosey, his wife, of the County of Northampton, conveyed by deed to Amos Underhill, of the county of Accomack, the said 13 acres of land; That Amos Underhill & Rachel, his wife, on the 26 April 1786, by deed conveyed to James Henry the aforesaid 13 acres; that the said James Henry entered upon the premises and was thereof seized as the law requires, and on the 12 Feb. 1787 made his last will and testament in the following words (abstract) To his wife, Susannah, the lot of land & house where I now live forever, negroes, stock, household furniture &c. To mother Sarah Darby, widow of John Darby, dec. of the State of Maryland, negro Rachel during her life & then to dispose of as she sees fit. To brother Isaac Henry my watch, and to his son Hugh Henry my sleeve buttons; to my cousin Handy Harris wearing apparel; to sister Nancy Polk. To sister Elizabeth Henry, relict of William B. Henry. Which said will was probated on the 27 Feb. 1787; That Susannah Henry, by virtue of the said will, entered upon the premises in question, and on the -- day of --- 17-- intermarried with Benjamin Stratton, and on the 15 April 1789 the said Benjamin Stratton & Susannah, his wife, of the County of Northampton, by deed conveyed to James Powell of Accomack the aforesaid 13 acres; that the said James Powell by virtue of the said deed entered upon the premises and was thereof seized as the law requires, and being so seized made his last will & testament in these words: (abstract) To dau. Nancy Wainhouse Powell; to dau. Hannah Powell; To dau. Mahala Powell "my desire is that my executors shall move the houses that I built of my lot on the point adjoining Bell Haven if they find I shall loose the lot," which said will was probated 25 Dec. 1797; that the defendants, children of the said James Powell, entered upon the premises in question under the will of their father, and were and still are seized thereof as the law requires; that Rosey Addison aforesaid, sister of the said Levi Watson, died on or about the -- day of --- 1795 - 19 May, 1799 - p. 140

Moses Griffith

vs. - Boundary suit.

Nathaniel Bishop & Nancy, his wife, Thomas Clay & Sally, his wife, Nathaniel
    Freshwater, by John Wise, their attorney, & Polly, Susanna & Christopher
    Freshwater, Inf'ts. by Nathaniel Freshwater, their guardian, heirs of William
    Freshwater.

Deposition of Nathaniel Goffigon, of Northampton County:

That sometime past he happened at the house of Benjamin Griffith with his
surveying instruments, and in conversation with Moses Griffith, the present
plaintiff, he presented to this deponent a transfer from several persons made to a
certain Jerom Griffith, said to be the ancestor of the said Moses Griffith, of the
tract of land called the Griffiths, the precise quantity of land mentioned in said
instrument this deponent does not remember, however the bounds & courses were
expressed in the said instrument, and knowing the dispute which had long
prevailed concerning the same, he, this deponent, had a curiosity to see which of
the disputed lines did coincide nearest the description of said transfer, in order to
effect which he repaired to a known corner tree --- and took the bearings of the old
line, which after making what he thought necessary allowance for variations for
upwards of 100 years it answered the old line very near by reversing the course,
he then took the bearings of the present line which the deceased William
Freshwater established, that he found not to answer the course described in said
instrument within twenty degrees and upwards &c. 22 Oct. 1798 - p. 180

Aminidab Seekright, lessee of Ezekiel Beach, Robert Savage & Tamer, his wife,
    James Ashby & Susannah Ashby by John Wise, their attorney,

vs. - Ejectment Proceedings.

Ferdinando Dreadnaught

That Ezekiel Ashby was in his lifetime and at his death seized in his demesne
as of fee of and in the lands & appurtenances in the declaration mentioned, which
were contiguous to other lands of the said Ezekiel, and being so seized on the --
day of --- 1764 made his last will & testament; that on or about the 15 April 1764
the said Ezekiel Ashby died without having altered said will, which said will was
probated 24 April 1764; that the aforesaid Ezekiel Ashby died possessed of
several slaves & personal estate including the legacies in his said will mentioned
to amount of £370:7:8 ½; that John Ashby in the said will mentioned after the
death of the said Ezekiel entered into the lands in question and was thereof seized
at the time of his death; that William Ashby was the eldest son and heir at law of
the said Ezekiel Ashby; that the said William Ashby died on or about the -- day
of --- 1767 intestate and without issue; that John Ashby aforesaid was the second
son of the said Ezekiel Ashby and heir at law of said William Ashby; that said
John Ashby made his last will & testament and afterwards died without having
altered said will on or about the -- day of Jan. 1792, leaving children to-wit: John
Ashby, the defendant, Sarah, Samuel, Ezekiel, William, David & Elizabeth, which
said will was probated 1 Feb. 1792; that upon the death of the said John Ashby the
elder, John Ashby, his son, the defendant, entered upon the lands in the

declaration mentioned and become and still is possessed thereof; That the lands in the declaration mentioned are the same lands mentioned in the will of said Ezekiel Ashby and called and known by the name of Fox Ridge, and contains 70 acres, and is the same land conveyed by a certain James & Elizabeth Longo to the said Ezekiel Ashby; that the lessors of the plaintiff, to-wit: James, Tamer & Susanna, are children of the said Ezekiel Ashby and part of the children mentioned in the residuary clause of the said Ezekiel's will; that Ezekiel Beach, one other lessor of the plaintiff, is the son and only child of Mary, one other child in the said resid. clause mentioned; Sarah, one other of the children named in the said resid. clause died on the -- day of --- 1769, an infant, intestate & without issue; that Ezekiel, another of said children in said resid. clause mentioned, died on or about the -- day of --- 1794, having first made his last will & testament, which was probated 30 Jan. 1797; That afterwards, to-wit: on or about the -- Jan. 1796, David Ashby, one other of the said children in the said resid. clause mentioned, died having first made and published his last will & testament, which said will was probated 25 Jan. 1796; that George Ashby, one of the sons of Ezekiel Ashby the elder died on or about the -- day of --- 1794, after having made his last will & testament , which was probated 23 Feb. 1795; that Sarah Ashby, widow of Ezekiel the elder, & mentioned in said will, died intestate and without having married a second time on or about the -- day of --- 1795, leaving property of her own acquiring after the death of the said Ezekiel her husband, and of the estate of said Ezekiel Ashby bequeathed to her by his said will during life or widowhood, to amount of $114:8:5 &c. 15 May 1797 - p. 222

Usher, Roe & Co. of Baltimore Town
vs. - In Debt - Suit for sale of land.
Elizabeth D. Burdett, heiress of Thomas William Burdett - William Wallop appointed her guardian to defend this suit.

That William Burdett in his lifetime, to-wit: 12 Feb. 1776, in the county aforesaid by his certain writing obligatory, acknowledged himself to be bound to the said Usher Roe & Co. in the sum of £275:2:4 Pennsylvania currency of the value of £220:1:9 Virginia money, and for the payment of which the said William Burdett bound himself and his heirs by the said writing, yet the said William Burdett in his lifetime and the said Thomas William Burdett since the death of the said William in his lifetime, and the said defendant since the death of the said Thomas William Burdett, hath not yet paid the said sum &c.

Answer of Elizabeth D. Burdett: That she cannot deny the action of the plaintiff, nor but that the writing aforesaid is the deed of one William Burdett, her grandfather, nor but that she detains the aforesaid sum from the plaintiff, nevertheless, the defendant says that she hath not any lands or tenements by heredity descent from the said William Burdett, her grandfather in fee simple, except two undivided third parts of one messuage and two lots of ground at the Town of Drummond in the county of Accomack, one of the said lots containing about 3 acres and the other 30 feet in length and 20 feet in ---, which ⅔ parts of said messuage & lot are of the yearly value of ----£ and except the reversions of the other undivided third parts of said messuage & lots, which said undivided third parts Daniel J. Marshall and Tabitha, his wife, who was the wife of the said Thomas W. Burdett, who was heir of said William Burdett, held for the term of the life of the said Tabitha in right of the said Tabitha as her dower, and are of no value during the life of said Tabitha -- and except the reversion of one messuage and lot of ground containing about ¼ acre with the appurtenances in the said Town of Drummond, which said messuage & lot last mentioned, Elizabeth Jenny, who was the wife of the said William Burdett, holds for the term of her life as her dower --- That the said Tabitha and also the said Elizabeth Jenny are still surviving, and in full life - &c. 24 Nov. 1798 - p. 227

John Din, lessee of Isaac Nottingham
vs. - Trespass & Ejectment Proceedings, on an appeal from a judgment of the Court of Northampton 11 June, 1799.
John Simkins
    Jury impaneled & returned the following verdict.
    That a certain Isaac Nottingham, father of the lessor of the plaintiff, was on the -- day of Jan. 1761, seized & possessed as of fee of and in the premises in the declaration mentioned, and being so seized upon the day and year aforesaid at the Parish of Hungars, County of Northampton, contracted with a certain William Ward that he the said William Ward & Mary, his wife, should hold and enjoy the said premises during the term of their natural lives, and executed a certain obligation to the said William Ward that he, the said Isaac Nottingham, would when required, execute a deed conveying the said land to the said William Ward & Mary his wife, for and during their respective lives; that the said Isaac Nottingham on the -- day of --- 1768 departed this life intestate leaving Robert Nottingham his eldest son & heir at law, also children Benjamin, Peggy, Anne, Molly & Isaac, the lessor of the plaintiff; that Robert, Benjamin, Peggy & Anne were children by a first wife, and Molly & Isaac, the lessor of the plaintiff, were children by a second wife of the said Isaac Nottingham the elder; Robert Nottingham, eldest son of Isaac Nottingham the elder, immediately upon the death of the said Isaac Nottingham, the father & elder, entered as heir at law to the said Isaac the elder, and was seized of all the lands whereof the said Isaac the elder died seized, except the dower lands of the mother of the lessor of the plaintiff, but whether the said Isaac Nottingham the elder died seized of the lands in question or not we leave to the court: That the said Ann, Peggy & Robert all departed this life intestate and without issue in the lifetime of the said William & Mary his wife, and afterwards, to-wit: on the 30 March 1777 the said William Ward departed this life, and afterwards, to-wit: on the -- day of --- 1778, the said Benjamin also departed this life; We also find an obligation with the condition thereto annexed dated 29 Feb. 1782, signed by Mary Ward & William Simkins the elder in these words, to-wit: Know all men &c., and that afterwards by virtue of the said obligation & condition the said William Simkins the elder entered into the premises and was seized thereof and continued so seized until the death of the said Mary Ward; that after the death of the said Benjamin, to-wit: on the 15 Nov. 1784,

the said Mary Ward also departed this life; that upon her death Robert Nottingham, cousin of the said Benjamin, to-wit: a con [sic] of a certain Michael
Nottingham, only brother of the whole blood of the said Isaac Nottingham that
elder, entered into and took possession of the premises in the declaration
mentioned, and by his deed, together with his wife Sally, dated 8 Dec. 1788,
conveyed the same to William Simkins, Jr., in fee simple; that the said Mary
Nottingham departed this life the -- day of --- 1798; that by virtue of the said deed
from Robert Nottingham & wife to William Simkins, Jr., he the said William
Simkins, Jr., entered into and was possessed of the said premises and by is will
dated __ day of __ 1796, devised the same to be sold by Coventon Simkins, by
virtue of which devise the said Coventon Simkins sold and conveyed the same to
the defendant, &c. 21 May, 1802 - p. 331

Arthur Emmerson, assignee of John Teackle
vs. - In debt.
Robert Pitt, William Pitt, Jabez Pitt & John Pitt, heirs of Jabez Pitt.
    Robert Pitt died between 1800 and 1802 - Charles Stockly appointed
guardian to the other defendants to defend this suit - 20 Dec. 1800 - p. 367

John Goodright, lessee of Mary Richard &c.
vs. - Ejectment proceedings
Richard Thrustout
    Jury impaneled and returned the following verdict.
    That a certain Finla McWilliams the elder was in his lifetime seized as of fee
of and in a certain tract of land supposed to contain 400 acres, of which the
premises in question is part; that being so seized on the 25 March 1687, made his
last will & testament and shortly afterwards died without having altered said will;
that the said will was probated 16 Nov. 1687; that Finla McWilliams the younger
& Overton, the sons of the said Finla McWilliams the elder, entered into the land
devised them and were of their several parts respectively seized according to their
several estates in the said will specified; that Overton McWilliams, one of the sons
of the said Finla the elder, died leaving issue, which still survived at the time of
the death of the said Finla the younger; that the said Finla the younger lived till
1762 and then died intestate and without issue, having seized at the time of his
death of that part of the tract of 400 acres which his father, the said Finla the elder,
had devised to him as aforesaid; that immediately after the death of the said Finla
the younger, Charles Courtney, being the heir at law and the eldest son lawfully
begotten of the body of Sarah, the daughter of the said Finla the elder, entered into
the lands whereof the said Finla the younger had died seized as aforesaid, claiming
title as heir of the said Sarah, who was then dead, under the will of the said Finla
the elder; We also find that Mary, the wife of Abraham Turner, and only daughter
and heir of the said Overton McWilliams, entered at the same time with the said
Charles Courtney into the said lands whereof the said Finla the younger died
seized as aforesaid, claiming title thereto as heir both of the said Finla the younger
and the said Finla the elder; we find that the title to the said lands whereof the said

Finla the younger died seized being in contest between the parties as aforesaid, the following deeds were respectively executed between them: A certain indenture from the said Charles Courtney to the said Abraham Turner, dated 30 Jan. 1764, & one other indenture from the said Abraham Turner dated the day and year aforesaid; we find that the said parties after the execution of the said deeds, to-wit: on the said 30 Jan. 1764, entered respectively into the lands in the said deeds respectively specified to them and remained possessed thereof; that the said Abraham Turner died on the -- day of April, 1769 leaving issue two sons, Richard & William & three daughters, Ritter, Dina & Peggy, having previously made his land will & testament; that Richard Turner, one of the said children of the said Abraham Turner, on the -- day of --- 1774, died an infant & without issue, and that William Turner, the younger of the two sons survived his said brother and arrived at lawful age in the year 1781; that Mary, the widow of the said Abraham Turner, having afterwards married with a certain Major Rayfield, remained on the lands which the said Charles Courtney had conveyed to the said Abraham Turner, and which are the premises in question, until the said William Turner, the younger of the two sons of the said Abraham Turner, had come to lawful age; that the said William Turner after coming to lawful age, to-wit: in the year 1781, entered upon the premises claiming title as heir of his said father whom he pretended held under the deed of the said Charles Courtney, and cleared a few acres of woodsland and built a house thereon and made other improvements; that on the -- day of Aug. 1796, in the life of her said husband, Major Rayfield, the said Mary Rayfield died leaving issue the said William Turner, Dina, the wife of William Bull and Peggy the wife of Levi Annis, children of the first husband, Abraham Turner, and also Sarah Delastacion, an infant grandchild born of her daughter Ritter, then dec., who was a child of the said Abraham Turner, and leaving issue by the said last husband, Major Rayfield, the following children: William[,] Betty, Major & Mary Rayfiled; that Mary Rayfield, one of the children of the said Mary and Major Rayfield, after the death of her said mother, to-wit: on the 1 Sept. 1797, died an infant and without issue; We find that Major Rayfield, the husband of the said Mary the elder, continued in possession of the lands at the death of his said wife, claiming to hold the same as tenant by the curtesy; that the before named William Bull & Dianna his wife, & Levi Annis & Peggy his wife, on the 4 Oct. 1797 conveyed their right & interest in the said premises to the said Major Rayfield the elder; That Major Rayfield the elder by deed dated 21 May 1798 conveyed the said right & interest so purchased to the defendant Thomas Bayly; that on the -- day of --- 1799 the said Major Rayfield the elder died, and the said defendant Thomas Bayly entered into the premises claiming to hold part thereof in consideration of the right & interest conveyed to him by the said Major Rayfield aforesaid; that William, Elizabeth & Mary Rayfield, children of the said Major Rayfield the elder, entered into the premises and afterwards, to-wit: 7 Oct. 1799, by their deeds conveyed their interest and rights in the said premises to the said Thomas Bayly, the defendant, by virtue whereof the said Thomas Bayly entered into and became seized & possessed thereof according to the tenor of said last mentioned indenture; that William Turner aforesaid, after the death of his mother, died leaving issue the following children, Mary[,] Richard & John, Lessors of the plaintiff &c. 17 May 1799 - p. 407

Jeremiah Fairclaim
vs. - Ejectment Proceedings.
Peregrine Poorclaim
     That William Bradford being seized in fee simple of 400 acres of land, by deed dated 27 July 1727, conveyed 400 acres, of which the premises in the declaration mentioned are a part, to his son Bayly Bradford, by virtue whereof the said Bayly Bradford entered into and became seized thereof; that the said Bayly Bradford being so seized on the 8 July 1745 sued out of the Secretary's Office a writ in the nature of a writ of ad quod demnum directed to the Sheriff of Accomack County, by virtue of which said writ the Inquisition was taken by the Sheriff of the said County on the 16 Nov. 1745, and returned into the Secretary's Office; that on the 24 June 1746 the said Bayly Bradford by his deed conveyed 100 acres, part of the said 400 acres, and which are the same lands in the declaration mentioned, to Whittington Addison & Joanna Mary, his wife, by virtue whereof the said Addison & wife entered into the said lands and were possessed thereof; that on the 27 Feb. 1753, the said Whittington Addison & wife conveyed the said 100 acres to Fisher Bradford; that the said Fisher Bradford entered into the said lands & was possessed thereof; that on the 1 April 1761, the said Bayly Bradford executed a deed to the said Fisher Bradford; that the lands in the declaration mentioned are a part of the lands mentioned and described in the last mentioned deed, and that the said Bayly Bradford at the time of the execution of the said last mentioned deed was not in possession of the lands in the declaration mentioned, nor had been possessed thereof at any time since the before mentioned conveyance to the said Whittington Addison & Joanna Maria, his wife; that the lessor of the plaintiff is the heir at law to said Fisher Bradford; that the said Fisher Bradford remained in possession of the said lands in the declaration mentioned from the time of his entry until his death, and that upon his death Nathaniel Bradford, his son & heir at law entered into and became possessed of the said land, and continued possessed until the -- day of --- 17-- when the same was recovered by an ejectment in the Court of Accomack County by the heirs of the said Bayly Bradford under whom the defendant now claims. 15 Oct. 1800 - p. 447

John Den
vs. - Ejectment Proceedings.
Richard Fen.
     That a certain Isaac Melson was in his lifetime seized as of fee of & in the premises in the declaration mentioned; that being so seized on the 5 Jan. 1784 he made his last will & testament; that the said Isaac Melson departed this life without having altered his said will, which said will was probated 1 June, 1785; that Levin Melson in the said will mentioned was the eldest son & heir at law of the said Isaac Melson, the testator; that the said Levin Melson survived his father & on the 31 March 1795, made his last will & testament and departed this life

without having altered his said will, which was probated on 29 June 1795; That Betty Melson, one of the daughters of the before mentioned Isaac Melson, died an infant and without issue in the lifetime of the said Isaac, & that Caty Melson & Polly Melson, two other of the daughters of the said Isaac Melson, dec., having survived their said father, died in the full of the year 1788, infants & without issue; that the whole of the personal estate of the said Isaac Melson, dec., amounts only, as appears by the account of sales returned by the administrator, to the sum of £42:9:10; that Rachel Melson, the widow of the said Isaac Melson, dec., in his said will mentioned, continued in her state of widowhood until the -- day of --- when she intermarried with the said Mathew Phillips, the lessor of the plaintiff, & is now in full life; that Nanny Melson, the widow of the said Levin Melson, is the defendant in this present suit; that the said Isaac Melson at the time of his death left two daughters not mentioned in his said will, to-wit: Peggy Wyatt, who is now living, and Susannah Smith who has died since the death of the said Isaac Melson, leaving issue who are yet alive &c. 19 May 1802 - p. 460

Timothy Trytitle
vs. - Ejectment Proceedings.
Henry Holdfast.
    Jury impaneled and returned the following verdict:
    That Benjamin Floyd, the elder, being seized as of fee of and in a certain tract of land containing by estimation 150 acres, of which the lands in the declaration mentioned are a part, with the water grist mill in the said declaration mentioned, lying in the Parish of St. George and County of Accomack, and having three children, to-wit: Elizabeth, one of the lessors of the plaintiff, by one venter, also Benjamin and Polly Floyd by a second venter, and being so seized on the 20 Nov. 1801 made his last will & testament, and afterwards, to-wit: on the -- day of --- 1802, the said Benjamin Floyd the elder departed this life leaving the said will in full force, which said will was probated 27 Dec. 1802; that by virtue of the said will the said Benjamin Floyd the younger, and devisee of the said lands and mill in the said will mentioned, immediately after the death of the said Benjamin the elder, entered into the said lands and mill and became seized thereof and being so seized on the -- day of --- 1803 departed this life an infant, under age and without issue, and leaving Elizabeth, the lessor of the plaintiff, his sister of half blood on the part of his said father, and the defendant his sister of the whole blood, and his mother a certain Molly Floyd, &c. 18 Oct. 1803 - p. 491

Peggy Scott & George Fisher, alias George Scott,
vs. - Ejectment Proceedings.
Rachel Gleeson &c.
    That Henry Scott, Sr., of the county of Northampton, dec., was in his lifetime and at the time of his death, seized of the premises in the declaration mentioned as of fee, and being so seized by his last will & testament duly probated in the Court of Northampton County, bearing the date 19 Jan. 1731, did devise the said premises to his son Henry Scott in these words: I give to my son Henry Scott 110

acres of land, it being the land whereon my son Joseph now dwells, to him and the heirs of his body lawfully begotten forever - wife Deborah Scott to have use of whole estate during her widowhood, and in the event of her marriage to be divided equally between his wife and five children, Joseph, Henry, Daniel Scott, Abigail Barker and Rachel Parsons - To son Joseph 250 acres, being the plantation where I now dwell. To son Daniel 120 acres, being part of the land bought of Jestition Pettit. To grandson William Scott, son of Joseph Scott, provided he stay with his grandmother if she lives till he reach the age of 18 years. To granddaughter Agnes Pettit, dau. of John Pettit. To dau. Tabitha Lingo, Codicil: To son Joseph my right of 100 acres which fell to me by the death of my brother John Scott during his natural life, and upon his decease to my grandson William Scott, son of Joseph Scott. To granddaughter Amey Scott, dau. of Daniel Scott. To William Barker all that I lent him except one small gun; That after the death of the said Henry, which happened on the -- day of --- 1731, his said son Henry entered into the lands aforesaid and became seized thereof, and being so seized by deed dated 2 March 1761, conveyed to a certain Caleb Scott, eldest son & heir in tail of the said Henry Scott, 110 acres of land; that the said Caleb Scott died on the -- day of --- in the lifetime of his father, Henry Scott, and previous to the execution of the writ of ad quod damnum herein mentioned on the premises, leaving issue four children, to-wit: Peggy Scott, one of the defendants, Patience, Nancy & Betsy Scott, all of whom were at the time of the death of the said Caleb Scott under age; the said Nancy Scott died on the -- day of --- 1784, an infant without issue; that the said Patience Scott died in the year 1784 an infant without issue; the said Betty Scott died on the -- day of --- 1787 under age & leaving a natural son, George Fisher, alias George Scott the other demandant; that on 19 Dec. in the 10th year of the reign of George the Third, King of Great Britain &c., the aforesaid Henry Scott, the younger, being in possession of the premises, sued out a writ of ad quod damnum according to law for docking the entail of the premises in the declaration mentioned; that on the 15 Aug. 1770, the aforesaid Henry Scott, the younger, conveyed the said 110 acres of land to a certain John Harmanson; that on the -- day of --- 1770, the said John Harmanson entered into the premises, and being so seized on the 13 Feb. 1771 conveyed the said premises to a certain Teackle Robins, by virtue of which said deed the said Teackle Robins entered on the premises and became seized thereof, and being so seized on the 21 July, 1774, made his last will and testament, which said will is duly probated in the County Court of Northampton, whereby he authorized his executor, John Robins, to sell & convey the premises in fee simple for the purpose of paying his debts; that on the 12 Aug. 1777, the said John Robins together with Elizabeth Robins, the widow of the said Teackle Robins, conveyed the said premises to Thomas Dolby, Sr., by virtue of which deed the said Thomas Dolby entered upon the premises and being so seized on the 10 Feb. 17--, together with his wife, Rachel, conveyed the said premises to John Gleeson, Sr., by virtue of which deed the said John Gleason entered into the said premises and being so seized on the -- day of --- 180- duly made his last will & testament and devised the premises to the present tenants, Rachel, James & Thomas Gleeson in fee simple, which said will was duly proved in the County Court of Northampton County; that upon the death of the said John Gleeson the said tenants entered into the said premises and became seized thereof; &c. 24 June, 1802 - p. 514

LAND CAUSES - SUPERIOR COURT RECORDS - 1806 to 1827

Simon Seekright, lessee of Thomas Jarvis & Anne Senior, his wife, &c.
vs. - Ejectment Proceedings
Timothy Thrustout

That Thomas Bell was seized of the premises in the declaration mentioned, situate in Northampton County, and being so seized on the -- day of --- 1791 departed this life intestate leaving two children, to-wit: Peggy Bell and William Bell, and a widow Sarah Bell, the mother of the said two children; that upon the death of the said Thomas Bell the said Peggy and William and their said mother, entered in the lands and became lawfully seized, thereof; that on the -- day of March 1792, the said Peggy departed this life an infant and without issue, whereby her said brother William became seized of the whole of the said lands subject to the dower aforesaid; that the said Sarah, the widow aforesaid, intermarried with Michael Dunton, the defendant, the -- day of --- 1792; that the said William departed this life on the -- day of --- 1802 seized as aforesaid of the premises, an infant & without issue, but leaving Anne Senior Jarvis, the wife of the said Thomas Jarvis, his aunt, being the sister of his said father Thomas Bell, also the said Thomas Jacob and Mary, the wife of the said Nathaniel Nottingham, the son & daughter of Mary Jacob, dec., another sister of the said Thomas Bell, and Susanna, the wife of the said Severn Nottingham and the said Sally Bell, cousins of the said William Bell, being children of Robert Bell, dec., who was a brother of the said Thomas Bell, the father of the said William Bell, and leaving his said mother also; that on the 2 March 1803, the said Sarah, mother of the said two children of Thomas Bell, with Michael Dunton her husband, the defendant, conveyed such part of the said land as the said Sarah might be entitled to, to Littleton Kendall, the said Sarah & Michael being at the time in possession of the said lands, by virtue of which deed the said Littleton Kendall became seized thereof; that on the 2 March 1803, the said Littleton Kendall reconveyed the said interest and title therein to the said Michael & Sarah Dunton, by virtue of which the said Michael & Sarah entered upon the lands in the declaration mentioned and became seized thereof, and continued so jointly seized until the death of the said Sarah on the -- day of --- 1803, and since her death the defendant hath continued seized or possessed of the land under the deed aforesaid &c. 18 Oct. 1803 - p. 5

William Nock & Elizabeth, his wife
vs. - Ejectment Proceedings.
Joseph Powell.

That Joseph Powell, the defendant in this cause, being seized in his demesne as of fee in the premises in the declaration mentioned, being 200 acres called Powell's Pocomoke Land, on the 25 July 1801 conveyed the same to his sisters

Agnes Powell & Elizabeth Powell, alias Nock, and the whole and sole estate of the mother, Sary Powell, given them in her last will & testament &c. 14 May 1805 - p. 25

Taylor's Lessee
vs. - Ejectment Proceedings.
Taylor.

That John Taylor, deceased, father of the lessor of the plaintiff, was in his lifetime seized as of fee of and in the land and tenements in the declaration mentioned, and being so seized on the 9 April 1779, made his last will & testament in these words: (abstract) To wife Sophia Taylor all my land where I now live until my son George Taylor comes to lawful age, and then to return to George Taylor. To wife all the household goods that she brought with her from her father's &c. To son Thomas Taylor. To son Peter Taylor; to son William Taylor; to dau Sophia Custis; that said will was proved 25 May 1779; that the said John Taylor at the time of his death left issue by his first marriage William Taylor, his eldest son & heir, Thomas B. Taylor, the lessor of the plaintiff, and Peter Taylor, and a daughter Sophia Custis, sons and daughter of the first venter, and George Taylor a son of the second venter, to whom the lands in the said will mentioned were devised when he should come to lawful age; that Sophia Taylor, the widow of the said John Taylor, entered into the said lands after his decease and was possessed therewith according to the said will till the said George Taylor came to lawful age; that the said George Taylor came to lawful age the -- day of --- 1789, and then entered upon the said land and was seized thereof subject to the dower of the said Sophia; that the said George Taylor being so seized died on the -- day of December, 1804, leaving issue Polly Taylor, Sally Taylor, & Betsy Taylor, to whom he devised said lands by his will; that the said William Taylor, the eldest son and heir at law of the said John Taylor died intestate and without issue on the -- day of --- 1781, leaving the said Thomas B. Taylor, the lessor of the plaintiff, his eldest brother and heir at law, who after the death of the said George entered upon the possession of the defendants into the said land, subject to the dower of the said Sophia, claiming the reversion thereof as undisposed of by the will of the said John Taylor deceased - 14 May 1805 - p. 30

John Day, lessee of Mitchel S. West, by Thomas M. Bayly his attorney,
vs. - In Custody &c.
Ned Wright

John Day complains of Ned Wright in custody &c. for that, to-wit: that whereas Mitchell West, Salathiel West, Susey West & Hepsy West, co-heirs of Salathiel West, dec., and by deed dated 1 May 1806, demised & granted and to farm let to the said John Day one messuage and 1 plantation containing 50 acres, to have and to hold from the 1 May 1806, for the term of ten years &c. It appearing to the Court that William Lecatt, tenant in possession, is an infant, Capt. William Lecatt is by the Court appointed his guardian to defend this suit. &c. 14 Oct. 1806 - p. 36

Richard Coleburn &c.

vs. - Partition Suit.

David Nottingham, &c.

That David Nottingham, Sarah Nottingham, Nicholas Bull & Elizabeth, his wife in right of said wife, and Richard Coleburn, together and undivided hold one messuage & 114 acres of land in the Parish of St. George, County of Accomack &c. That Abel Nottingham was lately seized of and in the land aforesaid, and being so seized had issue David Nottingham, Sarah Nottingham, . . . (blank) . . .& Elizabeth Nottingham, now Elizabeth Bull, the wife of the aforesaid Nicholas Bull, and no more, and being so seized to the -- day of --- died intestate, his said children then living, whereby the said land descended to the said David Nottingham, Sarah Nottingham, ----- Nottingham and Nicholas Bull and Elizabeth, his wife, in right of said wife; that afterwards, to-wit: on the -- day of --- Nicholas Bull and Elizabeth his wife conveyed to Richard Coleburn all their right, title & interest to their ¼ part of said land; that on the -- day of --- the said --- Nottingham died intestate and without issue, whereby his ¼ part of the said land descended to David Nottingham, Sarah Nottingham and Nicholas Bull & Elizabeth his wife, &c. 17 June 1804 - p. 40

Phillips Lessee

vs. - Ejectment Proceedings.

Churn & wife.

That Stephen Harrison was in his lifetime seized & possessed as of fee of & in the premises in the declaration mentioned, which had descended to him from his father, James Harrison, dec., and being thereof seized departed this life on the night between the 23 & 24 day of December, 1790, an infant under the age of 21 years and without issue, leaving one sister of the whole blood, to-wit: the now female defendant, and a brother of the half blood by the side of his mother, to-wit: Abel Phillips, the lessor of the plaintiff, and no other brother or sister or mother; that upon the death of the said Stephen Harrison the female defendant, Nancy, entered into the said premises and afterwards intermarried with the other defendant, William Churn, and that they are now in possession thereof; that at the death of the said Stephen Harrison, the lessor of the plaintiff, Abel Phillips was an infant, & that he arrived at age the 11 day of March, 1801 - 20 May, 1808 - p. 64

Mears' Lessee

vs. - Ejectment Proceedings

Robinson Savage

Order to take depositions of William Johnson, Sr., John Summers, Sr., James Evins, Elizabeth Freeman, Joshua Freeman, John Speer, Sr. & George Lash, witnesses on behalf of the plaintiff, and residents of the County of Surry in the State of North Carolina - Verdict for the defendant. 18 Oct. 1803 - p. 67

Hinman's Lessee

vs. - Ejectment Proceedings

Bull

That Peter Fitzgerald was in his lifetime and at the time of his death, seized of and in the premises in the declaration mentioned, and being so seized died upwards of 50 years ago leaving issue Frances Hinman, the lessor of the plaintiff his only child & heiress at law. That upon the death of the said Peter Fitzgerald the said Frances entered into the said premises and became seized thereof, and afterwards intermarried with a certain Bayly Hinman who afterwards, to-wit: on the 28 Oct. 1784, together with the said Frances, conveyed to William Barclay the said premises containing 60 acres, but it does not appear that the said Frances was examined privily & apart from her husband touching the said indenture as the law requires, by virtue whereof the said William Barclay entered into the premises and became possessed thereof; that the said William Barclay being so seized on the 12 Jan. 1799 conveyed the said premises to Benjamin Potter, by virtue of which the said Benjamin Potter entered into and became seized thereof; that the said Benjamin Potter & Elizabeth, his wife, on the 29th Sept. 1801, conveyed the premises to John Bull, Jr., the defendant; that Bayly Hinman, the husband of the said Frances, died on the -- day of --- in the year 1800, and that the said Frances is now living in the State of Delaware where she was residing with her said husband at the time of his death, and that she has continued ever since to reside in the said State of Delaware &c. 2 Oct. 1809 - p. 74

Taylor & wife

vs. - Suit for the recovery of land.

Powell.

That the said Joseph Powell was seized of a messuage of land as of fee, and being so seized by his certain deed dated 21 Nov. 1805, sold to Elishe Garrett, the ancestor of the plaintiffs, William R. Taylor & Bridget, his wife, & Susan Garrett, who are of full age, and Nancy, Samuel, Charles, Elisha & Sally Garrett (Sally Garrett their next friend), heirs of Elisha Garrett; that the said Elisha Garrett often required the said Joseph Powell that he would warrant to him, the said Elisha Garrett, the messuage, which he has ever since refused to do &c. 7 Dec. 1809 - p. 81

Phillips

vs. - Partition Suit.

Churn & wife.

That one Stephen Harrison was lately seized of and in the premises aforesaid, and being so seized on the 24 Dec. 1790 departed this life intestate, an infant under the age of 21 years and without issue, leaving a sister of the whole blood, to-wit: Nancy Churn, since deceased, late wife of the defendant, William Churn, and a brother of the half blood, to-wit: the plaintiff, Abel Phillips, whereby the said premises descended & passed to the said William Churn in right of the said Nancy, since deceased, & Abel Phillips, that is to say ⅔ part thereof to the said

William Churn and Nancy his wife, in right of said wife, and the remaining ⅓ to the plaintiff, Abel Phillips, who thereupon entered into the same & became seized thereof, and being so seized afterwards, on the 24 Aug. 1810, the said Nancy died intestate leaving children, to-wit: the defendants Betsy, Adah, Molly, Caty, James & George Churn, and her said husband William Churn, which said William Churn entered and became possessed of two undivided parts thereof as tenant by the curtsey, with reversion to the children of the said Nancy &c. 15 Sept. 1810 - p. 90

Bunting's Lessee
vs. - Ejectment Proceedings
Bunting
 That Elizabeth Jenkinson and was seized and possessed in fee tail of and in the premises in the declaration mentioned; that being so seized she intermarried with a certain Jonathan Bunting about the year 1747, by whom she had issue George Bunting, the defendant, her eldest son & heir, Esme Bunting, the lessor of the plaintiff, and sundry other children; the said Jonathan Bunting & Elizabeth his wife, on the 23 Feb. 1762, conveyed to their son Esme Bunting the land where they then lived, containing 281 acres upon Warner's Creek, with reversion to their son Hollowell Bunting, reversion to their son Severn Bunting, reversion to their heirs at law; that the said Esme Bunting, the lessor of the plaintiff was then an infant of tender years, being of the age of two years, and that the said Jonathan Bunting & Elizabeth his wife, still had and kept the possession of the said premises after the execution of the said deed; that the said Jonathan Bunting & Elizabeth Bunting being still in possession of the said premises on the 28 June, 1786, in consideration of love & affection for their son George Bunting, conveyed all the tract of land whereon they then lived, containing 251 acres, reserving the use of same during their natural lives, to George Bunting, their eldest son & heir in tail, the defendant, who was then of full age, and part of the sam premises aforesaid, and delivered the possession of all the said premises to the said George which lie to the North of the branch called Middle branch, and still kept and had the possession of the remainder part of the said premises from the branch called the Middle branch Southwardly to the Creek called Crooked Creek, and which said deed intended being for 251 acres was acknowledged on the 27 June, 1786, that the said Jonathan Bunting & Elizabeth his wife & Esme Bunting, the lessors of the plaintiff on the 28 June, 1786, conveyed to Samuel Wilson of Somerset County in Maryland, 30 acres of land in Jolly's Neck in Accomack County, adjoining the land there the said Jonathan & Betty Bunting then lived; that the said Jonathan & Elizabeth continued possessed of the land from the branch called Middle branch Southwardly to the Creek called Crooked Creek to the death of the said Jonathan, which happened on the -- day of --- 1795; that after the death of the said Jonathan Bunting the said Elizabeth Bunting remained in possession of part of the said land aforesaid until her death which happened on the -- day of Jan. 1809; that on the 12 Feb. 1808, the said Elizabeth Bunting duly made and published her last will & testament; proved on the 26 June, 1809, in the following words (abstract) To son George Bunting the plantation where I now live and

thereon George Bunting, Jr. lives, containing by estimation 251 acres. To son Severn; to son Jonathan; to dau. Phamy Downing; son George Ex'r., and which said lands devised to the said George Bunting, the defendant, are the same lands comprised in the said deed to Esme, the lessor of the plaintiff and George Bunting, the defendant; that upon the death of the said Elizabeth the said George Bunting, the defendant, entered into that part of the premises from the branch called Middle branch Southerwardly to the Creek called Crooked Creek, and became seized thereof, and has continued and is now possessed of all the premises in the declaration mentioned being 251 acres.

And at another day, to-wit: at a Superior Court of Law held for Accomack the 8 day of Oct. 1811, it appearing to the Court that the defendant, George Bunting was dead, this suit abated as to him, and George Bunting and Elijah Bunting, devisees of the said George Bunting, dec., came voluntarily into Court and entered themselves defendants in this cause;

And at another day, to-wit: at a Superior Court of law held for Accomack County 8 May, 1812, came the parties by their attorneys and agreed that the following additional facts be added to those already in the cause heretofore stated, which with them are to be taken in lieu of a special verdict: To strike out of the said cause the following words, viz: that Elizabeth Jenkinson was seized & possessed in fee tail general of and in the premises in the declaration mentioned, and insert that Thomas Jenkinson being seized in his demesne as of fee of and in the lands in the declaration mentioned duly made his last will & testament on the 17 Jan. 1720/21, and having departed this life the said will was proved on the 2 June, 1724, which said will is in these words, to-wit: (abstract) To son Thomas Jenkinson during his natural life, one point of Marsh commonly called the little Island, and after his death to fall to my son Moses Jenkinson; to son Thomas also that point of land he is now settled upon, commonly called plator's point, upon condition that the said Thomas give us much of his land that he purchased of Sacker Parker to join upon the tract of land I shall give my son Moses Jenkinson; to wife Elizabeth the use of whole estate during her natural life, and if she marry to have no more of my moveable estate than the law allows, and my son John Jenkinson shall take possession of my now dwelling house with 107 acres, being the ½ of my 374 acres situate in Jolly's Neck; to son Moses Jenkinson the remaining part of my tract of land being 187 acres; to son Jesse Jenkinson; dau. Frances Jenkinson; dau. Mary Jenkinson, dau. Neome Jenkinson; dau. Catharine Jenkinson; dau. Elizabeth Jenkinson; daughters to be at age at 18, sons at 21. Friend & brother in law Ralph Corbin Ex'rs. Wife Exec. That afterwards Moses Jenkinson and John Jenkinson entered into and were possessed of the lands devised to them by the said will of their father; that on the 5 July 1738, Moses Jenkinson conveyed to Daniel Stewart 187 acres lying near Pocomoke at the head of Crooked Creek, which was devised to the said Moses by the last will & testament of his father, Thomas Jenkinson, dec.; that the said Daniel Stewart entered on the said lands and became possessed thereof, and being so possessed on the 27 Jan.1740, together with Comfort his wife, conveyed the said premises to George Douglas in trust for Hugh McBright & John Jenkinson, and was to be reconveyed to the said Hugh McBright & John Jenkinson in fee in such manner as by a bond and condition thereof from the said Moses Jenkinson to the said Daniel Stewart was mentioned; that on the 26 May 1741, 117 acres of the said land was conveyed to the said Hugh McBright, and on the same date the remainder of the said land was conveyed to the said John Jenkinson; that the said John Jenkinson entered into and became possessed of the premises, and on the -- day of --- 1744 departed this life intestate leaving Elizabeth Jenkinson, who afterwards intermarried with Jonathan Bunting, his heir at law who entered into the premises in the declaration mentioned and became possessed thereof &c. 2 Oct. 1809 - p. 96

Edwards Lessee
vs. - Ejectment Proceedings.
Groten
Jury impaneled and returned the following verdict.

That a certain Richard Wells being seized in fee of and in the premises in the declaration mentioned departed this life in the year 1790 intestate, leaving issue Elizabeth Wells his only child, which said Elizabeth upon the death of her said father entered into the said premises and became seized thereof; that the said Elizabeth being so seized departed this life the 23 Dec. 1802 under age of 21 years, intestate and without issue; that the mother of the said Elizabeth died in the lifetime of her father, the said Richard Wells and left no other child besides the said Elizabeth; that the said Elizabeth had at her death no kindred whatsoever on the side of her father; that she had no grandfather, grandmother or uncle nor any issue of a brother or sister on the part of her mother, but that she left an aunt on the part of her mother, to-wit: Molly Groten, the defendant, who was sister of the whole blood to the mother of the said Elizabeth, also a cousin, to-wit: Peggy Edwards, the lessor of the plaintiff who is the daughter of Esther Edwards: an aunt on the part of her mother, being a sister of the half blood to the mother of the said Elizabeth; that the said Peggy Edwards, the lessor of the plaintiff, is a bastard child of the said Esther Edwards; that the said Esther Edwards & Molly Groten were children of the same mother but had different fathers; that the said Esther Edwards was a bastard child and was born in 1773 &c. 17 Oct. 1804 - p. 112

Wyatt's Lessee
vs. - Ejectment Proceedings.
Hyslop
That William Lingo being seized in fee of the premises in the declaration mentioned on the 28 Jan. 1749/50 duly made & published his last will & testament in these words (abstract) Wife Hannah to have the use of all my lands & plantation where I now live and all my moveable estate during her life or widowhood, and at her death or marriage I give to my son William Lingo the plantation where he now lives, together with 65 acres of land adjoining thereto; to son John Lingo the plantation where he now lives, together with 60 acres of land adjoining; to son Littleton Lingo that land and plantation where I now live;

balance of estate to be divided between all my children at the death or marriage of my wife. Wife Hannah Exec. That immediately after the death of the said William Lingo his son, Littleton entered upon the premises in the declaration mentioned and became seized thereof, and being so seized on the 25 Sept. 1770, duly made and published his last will & testament in these words (abstract) To wife Elizabeth all my lands & tenements during her widowhood, and at her death or marriage to my beloved brother Caleb Lingo, and after his death to his son Littleton Lingo; wife to have the use of all my moveable estate during her widowhood, and at her marriage ½ of said estate to be at her disposal and the other ½ to be equally divided between my brother John Lingo & Caleb Lingo. Brother John Lingo & Capt. John Coleburn Ex'rs. That upon the death of the said Littleton Lingo his widow, the said Elizabeth Lingo, and his brother Caleb Lingo entered upon and became seized of the premises aforesaid; that Littleton Lingo the younger departed this life under the age of 21, without issue, on the -- day of April 1787, leaving his father the said Caleb then living; that the said Caleb Lingo on the 16 Jan. 1789 duly made & published his last will & testament as follows: (abstract) I appoint Thomas Ames & Abraham Taylor my executors. To Thomas Ames land where I now live to rent out as long as Joice Lewis lives, and after her death I give the said land to my son Thomas Lingo during his life, and at his death to return to my grandson Robert Taylor. To son Thomas Lingo, dau. Sarah Lingo & dau. Leah Lingo and Robert Taylor the rest of my land to be equally divided between them as long as Joice Lewis lives. To dau. Lusy Lingo 50 acres of land on the head of Machapungo, and she shall never inhabit as long as Littleton Wyatt lives; that immediately after the death of the said Caleb Lingo his said daughter Lusy Lingo entered upon and became possessed of the premises aforesaid; that the said Lusy departed this life intestate in the year 1811 leaving the lessors of the plaintiff her only children and heirs at law; that the said Lusy Lingo intermarried with a certain Littleton Wyatt about the year 1792; that previous to that marriage Elizabeth Wyatt, one of the lessors of the plaintiff, was born but was recognized by her father after that time and during his life; that Littleton Wyatt, the said lessor of the plaintiff, was born subsequent to said intermarriage; that the said Littleton Wyatt the elder departed this life about he year 1800, leaving the lessors of the plaintiff his only children and heirs at law; that Director Watson was a daughter of William Lingo, who was the son of William Lingo the first testator above mentioned; that the said Director Watson, of Northampton County; on the 1 July 1791, conveyed to Littleton Wyatt of Accomack a piece or parcel of land being the land formerly belonging to Littleton Lingo, dec., and all the estate, right, claim, interest &c. of her the said Director Watson in and to the said premises &c. 4 May 1813 - p. 127

Toby Tryright, lessee of Bezelel Watson, William Crowson & Polly his wife, Susy W., George & Betty Martin

vs. - Ejectment Proceedings.

Ann Welch, Elizabeth Welch, Margaret R. Welch, William Welch & Sarah Welch, infant children of Elizabeth Welch by Raymond Riley, their guardian, Elizabeth Young, infant child of Thomas Young, John Riley & Susannah, his wife, Euphemia Finney, Henry Parker, William Parker, Levi Rodgers & Euphima, his wife, Jesse Dickerson, Susannah Dickerson, James White, William Ewell, Raymond Riley, Dennis Clayton & Susannah, his wife, Elijah Boggs & Nancy his wife.

That Matthew Fletcher was seized in fee on and in the premises in the declaration mentioned, and being so thereof seized on the 22 Jan. 1750, made his last will and testament, to-wit: (abstract) To Bezelel Watson 125 acres of land adjoining Harrison's land; to my brother in law Daniel Watson 125 acres of land adjoining upon Robert Heath's land; Brother in law Bezelel Watson & Littleton Scarburgh Major Ex'rs. That Daniel Watson, one of the devisees in said will mentioned, departed this life on the -- day of Oct. 1811, intestate, leaving the lessors of the plaintiff his only children and heirs at last that the present defendants are the tenants in possession and heirs at law to the said Matthew Fletcher, and that they entered upon and became seized of the premises upon the death of the said Daniel Watson. 4 May 1813 - p. 136

Watson & wife's lessee

vs. - Ejectment Proceedings - On an appeal from a judgment of the County Court of Accomack rendered in favor of William Tunnell & Elizabeth his wife, against the said lessees.

Elizabeth Tunnell &c.

Jury impaneled and returned the following verdict:

That Selby Simpson was in his lifetime and at the time of his death, seized in fee of the lands in question, and on the 20 March 1795, duly made and Published his last will & testament as follows: (abstract) To wife whole estate until my daughter Betsey arrives to lawful age or marries, and then an equal division to be made of the said extate bet. my wife & daughter and unborn child; should both my children die under the age of 21 and without heirs, wife to hold & enjoy my whole estate forever. That the unborn child mentioned in said will was born about 5 or 6 months after the death of the testator, and departed this life on the -- day of July 1796, under age, intestate, unmarried and without issue, that Betsy Selby, the daughter & devisee of the testator, and one of the lessors of the plaintiff, was under the age of 21 and was unmarried and without issue at the time of the death of the infant child, and that the said Betsy Selby intermarried with John Watson, the lessor of the plaintiff, on the 29 July 1806; we also find that the said Betsy was born on the -- day of Feb. 1792; that from the evidence of John Burton, the witness and writer of said will, that it was his impression that the testator intended to make an equal division of his estate, both real and personal, between the said Elizabeth, his wife, and his daughter Betsy, in case his said wife had not been pregnant, but that the said testator did not tell him so, and that the testator declared that in case his said daughter and unborn child should die he did not wish any of his brother ever to have or enjoy any part of his said estate &c. 5 May 1809 - p. 142

Wright's Lessee
vs. - Ejectment Proceedings
Dix

That Southy Simpson late of Accomack, being seized in fee of 120 acres of land, being entitled to the reversion expectant on the death of Rhoda Copes, the wife of Peter Parker Copes, formerly the wife of Thomas Simpson, in another 100 acres, which said tract with the aforesaid 120 acres by deed dated 14 July 1755 the said Southy Simpson & Comfort, his wife, conveyed to John Dix, the elder, and the said John Dix, pursuant to said deed entered upon and became possessed thereof; that on the 14 July, 1756, the said John Dix & Leah, his wife, conveyed to McWilliams Wright the reversion in the 100 acres held by Copes & wife; that the aforesaid Rhoda Copes departed this life --- and on the 1 day of May, 1769, Thomas Teackle, then surveyor of Accomack County, at the request of the parties made a survey in these words, Accomack County &c.; that immediately thereafter by virtue of the deed aforesaid the said McWilliams Wright entered upon and became seized of all the lands now held by the lessor of the plaintiff included in the survey up to the line now dividing from the lands of the defendants; that being so seized the said McWilliams Wright departed this life in the year 1786, having first duly made & published his last will & testament in these words: (abstract) To wife Elizabeth the use of my plantation where I now live and the use of all my moveable estate during her widowhood, and at her death or marriage I give to my son Elijah Wright my plantation where I live, and for want of heirs to my son Abel Wright; to son Jacob Wright the plantation he lives on and 60 acres of land during his natural life, and at his death to my son George Wright; to son George Wright the remaining part of that tract of land, being 40 acres; moveable estate to be divided between my daughter Elizabeth Wright, son Abel Wright, Son Henry Wright, dau. Rachel Wright, dau. Sinah Wright and dau. Leah Wright. Wife Elizabeth & son Elijah Ex'rs. That Jacob Wright shortly after entered upon the said 60 acres devised him by the said McWilliams Wright and became seized thereof; that George Wright, the lessor of the plaintiff, immediately after the death of the said that McWilliams Wright entered upon & became possessed of the balance of said land, that Jacob Wright, departed this life 1798, and immediately thereafter the said George Wright entered upon and became seized of the said 60 acres of land of which the said Jacob Wright died possessed; that the land held by the said George Wright the lessor of the plaintiff, really contains only 86 acres, 34 perches, and that the land in the declaration mentioned and the other lands held by the defendants are part of the tract of 220 acres conveyed by Simpson to Dix as aforesaid; that John Dix the elder, and Leah, his wife, on the 11 Feb. 1795, conveyed to their son John Dix, Jr., 80 acres of land being the land where the said John Dix, Sr. then lived, reserving to themselves the whole of the land during their

76

natural lives; That John Dix the younger, by virtue of said deed entered upon and became seized of the premises therein mentioned; that the said John Dix the younger departed this life in the year 1812, having first made & published his last will & testament as follows: (abstract) To son John Savage Dix the plantation where I now live, he paying 400£ to Julius Pettit Dix & Levi D. Dix. To son James Henry Dix the mortgage which I hold on the land of John West, he paying 300£ to Julius Pettit Dix & Levi D. Dix, and should either of my sons die without issue my surviving sons to divide the same. The money arising from the two plantations to be equally divided between my two sons Julius Pettit Dix and Levi D. Dix. Bal. of estate to be divided between James Henry Dix, John Savage Dix, Julius Pettit Dix & Levi D. Dix and Demarris Dix & Dianna Pettit Dix. By virtue of which will the defendant entered upon and became seized of the lands devised to him &c. 4 Oct. 1810

Warner's Lessee
vs. - Ejectment Proceedings.
Mason.

That William Warner the elder was seized in fee of and in the premises in the declaration mentioned, and being so seized duly made & published his last will & testament as follows: (abstract) To son George Warner ½ my shop tools & fine hat; to dau. Nancy Bishop 10£; to dau. Elizabeth Nock $1.; to my dau. Elizabeth Nock's four children, William, George, Nancy & Lewis, the sum of 7£ 10 s.; to my son Isaac Warner's children by name Jacob, George & Nancy the sum of 10£ and to my son Isaac's child by name Solomon I give $1.; to son William my seaside plantation during his natural life & then to his heirs, and for want of heirs to my son Isaac's two sons Jacob & George, one of them to set a price on the whole of it and give or receive ½ of that sum from the other; to wife Elizabeth plantation where I now live during her widowhood or until my youngest child, Polly, arrives to lawful age, and at the marriage or death of my wife, or then my said daughter arrives to lawful age, my said plantation to be divided in equal quantities between my there daughters, Lucretia, Hepsey & Polly; dated 20 June 1803. That after the death of the testator, William Warner, Jr., the devisee in the said will mentioned, entered upon the premises and became seized thereof; that the said William Warner, Jr., on the 25 Feb. 1812, made his last will & testament as follows: (abstract) Land I purchased of George Willett containing 17 ¾ acres to be sold to pay my debts; to nephew Lewis B. Taylor my gun, watch & clothing; to niece Sally B. Taylor all my wife's clothes; to Bagwell Taylor in lieu of which I owe him, my sorrel colt, cattle - To sister Hepsey Hickman; to sister Polly Warner the balance of my estate provided she does not choose my brother George Warner for her guardian, and if she will relinquish all claim against my estate on account of my being her guardian, and should she die before lawful age or marriage estate to be divided between my nephew Lewis B. Taylor, niece Sally B. Taylor & my sister Hepsey Hickman after the death of her present husband Revel Hickman, Parker Barnes & Bagwell Taylor Ex'rs; That the said William Warner, Jr., departed this life in the year 1812 without issue, never having had any issue; that by virtue of that by virtue of the devise in the said will of William Warner, Jr., the said Charles Mason & wife, in right of said wife, who is the devisee under the will of the said William Warner, Jr., entered into the premises and are now seized thereof; that the said Jacob & George Warner are the same Jacob & George mentioned in the will of William Warner the elder &c. 6 May 1814 - p. 188

Wright's Lessee
vs. - Ejectment Proceedings.
Dix.

That Southy Simpson late of Accomack County being seized in fee of 120 acres of land, and being entitled to the reversion expectant on the death of Rhoda Copes, the wife of Peter Parker Copes, formerly the wife of Thomas Simpson, in another 100 acres which formed one tract with the aforesaid 120 acres, by deed dated 14 July 1755 conveyed the aforesaid 220 acres to John Dix the elder, and the said John Dix pursuant to the said deed entered upon the premises and became seized thereof; that on the 14 July 1756 the said John Dix the elder conveyed to McWilliams Wright the reversion in the 100 acres held by Copes & wife; that the aforesaid Rhoda Copes departed this life in the year ----, and on the 1 May 1769 Thomas Teackle, then surveyor of Accomack County at the request of the parties made a survey in these words: Accomack County &c.; that immediately thereafter by virtue of the deed aforesaid, the said McWilliams Wright entered upon and became seized of all the lands now held by the lessor of the plaintiff included in the said survey up to the line now dividing from the lands of the defendants, which is the line A.B.; that being so seized the said McWilliams Wright departed this life in the year 1786, having first made his last will & testament; that Jacob Wright shortly thereafter entered upon the 60 acres devised him by the said McWilliams Wright, and became possessed thereof; that George Wright, the lessor of the plaintiff, immediately after the death of the said McWilliams Wright, entered upon and became seized of the balance of the said land; That Jacob Wright departed this life in the year 1798, and immediately thereafter the said George Wright entered upon the said 60 acres of land of which the said Jacob died seized and because possessed thereof; that the land held by the said George Wright the lessor of the plaintiff, really contains only 86 acres, 34 perches; that the land in the declaration mentioned and the other lands held by the defendants are part of the tract of 220 acres conveyed by Simpson to Dix as aforesaid; that John Dix the elder on the 11 Feb. 1795, duly executed a deed in these words: This indenture &c.; that John Dix the younger by virtue of said deed entered upon the premises and became seized of the premises therein mentioned; that the said John Dix the younger departed this life in the year 1812, having first made his last will & testament, by virtue of which said will the defendant entered upon and became seized of the lands devised to him &c. 4 Oct. 1810 - p. 202

William Weelburn, assignee of John H. Anderson, Cashier of the Bank of
    Somerset,
vs. - In debt.
John Marshall, James Marshall, George Marshall, Peter Marshall & Josiah
    Marshall, inf't children & heirs at law of James Marshall, dec., by Hepsee
    Marshall, widow of the said James Marshall, their guardian. 31 May 1810 -
    p. 215

Metcalf's Lessee
vs. - Ejectment Proceedings.
Edmunds.
    That Mark Metcalf being seized as of fee of the lands in the declaration
mentioned, duly made & published his last will & testament in these words:
(abstract) Plantation whereon Thomas Metcalf now lives, lying at the head of the
creek containing 100 acres to be rented out till my son John Metcalf comes to the
age of 21 years, and the money to be put to the use of schooling all my children,
& to my son John the said plantation then he comes to the age of 21 years, and for
want of heirs to my son William Metcalf; to son Thomas Metcalf 100 acres where
I now live when he comes to the age of 21 years, and for want of heirs to my son
Samuel Metcalf when he comes to the age of 21 years; to wife Sarah Metcalf the
plantation where I now live till my son Thomas comes to the age of 21 years; to
daughter Elizabeth Metcalf; Jesse Kellem & Thomas Bagwell Ex'rs.; that the said
will was probated on the 25 Jan. 1796; that after the death of the said Mark
Metcalf, Thomas Metcalf, his son & devisee, entered into the lands in the
declaration mentioned and was seized thereof; that the said Thomas Metcalf on the
12 Nov. 1810 conveyed the said land to Thomas Edmunds, defendant; that the
said Thomas Metcalf was upwards of 21 years of age when he executed the said
deed; that the said Thomas Metcalf departed this life in the year ---- intestate &
without issue, he never having had a child; that Samuel Metcalf, the lessor of the
plaintiff, is the same Samuel Metcalf mentioned in the will of the said Mark, and
was more than 21 years of age when the lessor of the plaintiff commenced this
suit, &c.
    At a further Court held 9 May, 1817, came the parties and agreed. In
addition to the above facts we do also agree that Sarah Metcalf after the death of
the said Mark Metcalf, entered into the lands in the declaration mentioned, and
was possessed thereof according to her right until the death of the Sarah Metcalf,
which was on the -- day of --- 1804; that after her death as aforesaid, and after the
said Thomas became of the age of 21 years, he became seized and possessed
thereof; that the said Thomas Metcalf departed this life on the -- day of --- 1813;
That Mark Metcalf died on the -- day of --- 1795 - 7 May, 1816 - p. 223

Kellam's Lessee
vs. - Ejectment Proceedings.
Shoomaker.

That Major Hornsby in his lifetime and at the time of his death was seized and possessed of the lands in the declaration mentioned as of fee, and being so seized on the 5 Aug. 1809, made his last will & testament in these words: (abstract) My plantation at the head of Deep Creek which I purchased of Tully Snead to be rented out for the term of 2 years from the end of the present year, and the profits to be applied to the payment of my debts, at the end of the said 2 years, I give my daughter Leah Kellam 86 acres, part of said tract, to be laid off so as to leave 14 acres of woodsland supposed to be the residue thereof; to my said dau. during her life, and at her death to her dau. Sidney and her heirs. To wife Susanna the residue of my estate during her life or widowhood in lieu of dower for the purpose of raising & supporting my children; at my wife's death or marriage I give to my daughter Molly Rose the land I bought of Salathiel Fitchett, containing 30½ acres, and that I bought of John Poolman containing 18½ acres, which lands adjoin the lands where I live; to dau. Rosey the land where I live including 50 acres given me by my father, 49 acres I bought of the Bagwell Hargis & 7 7/8 acres I bought of Jacob Bird & ⅔ of the swamp lands I purchased of Keely Bonwell; to dau. Betty the land called Foster's purchased of James Wise, containing 95 acres & 16¼ acres bought of Dr. John Boisnard, and the remaining ⅓ of the swamp land; to dau. Sukey the lands lying on the road called Town road purchased of the executors of Thomas Snead, and those purchased of Edward & Mary Bell, containing in all 70 acres; the balance of the Deep Creek tract, containing 14 acres to my dau. Sukey. To dau. Sally slaves, she to have a home with my dau. Rosey in case of the death or marriage of her mother. To grandson Jacob Major Ross; John Wise Ex'r.; which said will was proved 28 Aug. 1809; that after the death of the said Major the lands in the declaration mentioned was rented out until the 1 Jan. 1812, when the defendant Leah, the daughter of the said Major & his devisee, entered and was possessed thereof; that Revel Kellam, one of the lessors of the plaintiff, departed this commonwealth on or about the 25 December, in the year 1805, being at that time under suspicion of murder, and continued absent until the 15 July, 1814; that at the death of the said Major Hornsby the said Leah had living an only child named Sidney, who was the daughter of the said Revell by the said Leah; that the said Revell & the said Leah were duly married about six years before the departure aforesaid of the said Revell from the Commonwealth; that the said child Sidney departed this life on or about the -- day Dec., 1809, an infant, under age, unmarried and without issue; that the defendant Leah intermarried with the defendant William Chandler on or about the 25 Jan. 1810; that the said Leah the defendant is the same Leah who with the said Revell is made a plaintiff, but without her consent or application; that the said Leah & William are now living together as man and wife, and that the said Revell is now removed out of the limits of this Commonwealth. &c. 3 Oct. 1814 - p. 231

Haley's Lessee
vs. - Ejectment Proceedings.
Haley.

That William Haley the elder, late of the County of Accomack, was in his lifetime and at the time of his death, seized as of fee or and in the lands in the declaration mentioned; that being so seized he duly made and published his last will and testament on the 24 Nov. 1799 as follows: (abstract) To son James Haley all my land & for want of heirs to my son William Halley; wife & Jesse Kellam Ex's.; that the said William Halley departed this life on the -- day of Nov. 1813; that at the date of the making the said will the said William Halley the elder had four children living, viz: James Halley & William Halley (the last of whom is the defendant to this action) and Leah Halley and Benjamin Halley; that after the date of the said will, and before the death of the said William Halley he had three children born, viz: George Halley who was born Sept. 1800; Jesse Halley, one of the lessors of the plaintiff, who was born 11 March 1805, and John Halley, the other lessor of the plaintiff who was born 9 Nov. 1809; that the said James Halley departed this life before his aforesaid father in the year ---- without having married; that at the time of the death of the said William Halley the eldest he left six children living, viz: the said William Halley, the defendant, Leah Halley, Benjamin Halley, George Halley and Jesse & John Halley, the lessors of the plaintiff; that the lessors of the plaintiff are not provided for in any way by any settlement made by their said father, but that immediately upon the death of the said William Halley the elder, the defendant entered upon and became seized of the lands in the declaration mentioned and continued seized thereof &c. 7 Oct. 1816 - p. 241

Twiford, lessee
vs. - Ejectment Proceedings
Copes.

Jury impaneled and returned the following verdict:

That a certain T. Copes on the 16 Dec. 1720 was seized in his demesne as of fee in the premises in the declaration mentioned, together and contiguous to other lands forming in all one tract of 500 acres, and being so seized on the day and year aforesaid made his last will & testament, which said will was proved on the 4 April 1721; that T. Copes the second, the son & heir at law of the aforesaid T. Copes the first, entered into the whole of the aforesaid tract of land and was seized thereof, and being so seized on the 4 Dec. 1741 made his last will & testament; that T. Copes the second at the time of his death left issue T. Copes the third his eldest son & heir at law, and Southy Copes his second son named in his will aforesaid; that the said Southy Copes by virtue of the said devise upon the death of his said father, in the name of the whole, entered into --- acres, a part of the premises in the declaration mentioned and continued seized thereof to the time of his death on the -- day of May 1790; that the said T. Copes the third entered into the residue of the cleared lands of the said tract whereof the said T. Copes the second was seized as aforesaid, and continued seized thereof until his death on the

-- day of April 1785; that a line was never run between the lands whereof the said Southy Copes and the said T. Copes the third were seized; that the lands whereon John Starling is mentioned in the will of T. Copes the second to have lived are the same whereon Patrick Clark in the will of T. Copes the first is mentioned to have lived, and composed a part of the premises is the declaration mentioned; that the said T. Copes the third on the 19 Jan. 1784, made his last will & testament which was proved 1 June 1785; that the lands mentioned in the will of the said T. Copes third, and devised to Hancock & Levin Copes, his sons, comprehended the whole of the lands as well those whereof the said Southy Copes was possessed as aforesaid as those whereof the said Thomas Copes third was possessed as aforesaid; that the said Hancock Copes & Levin Copes upon the death of the said Thomas Copes third entered into the lands whereof the said Thomas Copes third was seized at the time of his death, and claimed the reversion of those lands whereof the said Southy Copes was possessed as aforesaid; that the said Hancock Copes afterwards, on the 24 March 1795, made his last will & testament, and died on the -- day of April, 1795, which will was proved 29 Sept. 1795; that John Custis Copes mentioned in the will of the said Hancock Copes, is the same John Custis Copes who is the lessor of the plaintiff; that the aforesaid Southy Copes on the 25 May 1790 made his last will & testament which said will was proved 29 June 1790; that Thomas Copes the fourth, the son of the said Southy Copes, and Comfort Copes, his daughter, the devisees in the said will mentioned, entered into the premises upon the death of the said Southy Copes and were seized and possessed thereof according to their several rights; that the said Thomas Copes the fourth being so seized, on the -- day of Dec. 1793, died intestate, without issue, leaving four sisters, Comfort, the wife of Scarburgh West, Leah Parker Copes, Ritter Copes & Catharine Copes, the defendants in the present action who are heirs of the said Thomas Copes the 4th, who entered into the lands whereof he was seized, and are still thereof seized, &c. That Comfort Twiford, one of the lessors of the plaintiff, is the same person who was Comfort West, the wife of Scarburgh West; that Ritter Copes who was a defendant in the suit above mentioned is now dead without issue, and that Catharine Copes who was one of the defendants in the suit is the same Catharine Lamden, one of the lessors of the plaintiff who has intermarried with John Lamden, a lessor of the plaintiff; that Leah Copes another of the defendants in the suit above mentioned is now dead leaving James Boisnard her only child and heir at law, she having intermarried with John Boisnard who is now dead. 22 Oct. 1817 - pp. 248 et seq.

Bagwell's Lessee
vs. - Ejectment Proceedings.
Bagwell.
     Jury Impaneled & returned the following verdict:
     That Thomas Bagwell, late of the County of Accomack, being aged upwards of 21 years, on the 5 Nov. 1810, made his last will & testament, which said will is as follows: (abstract) To wife Peggy Bagwell all the plantation and tract of land on which I now live, containing 100 acres, for the term of her natural life; to my

half sister Sarah Poulson the house in which she now resides with three acres of land for the term of her natural life; to wife Peggy the remainder of the said tract, a part of which is given to my said sister Sarah Poulson as aforesaid, the whole tract supposed to contain 25 acres, during her natural life; upon the death of my said wife I give my brother Isaiah Bagwell the aforesaid tract of land containing 25 acres upon condition that he or his heirs shall within 1 year from the death of my wife pay or secure to be paid to George Poulson, the son of my said sister, Sarah Poulson, the sum of $100. which sum I give to the said George Poulson; To my brother Isaiah and his heirs the plantation where I now live at the death of my wife, & for want of issue to my brother George Bagwell & his heirs; To brother Isaiah my land on Cedar Island; to wife Peggy the store house & lot of land supposed to contain 9 acres called Stewart's Store, lying on the Westward side of the seaside County Road near the head of Watchaprigue. To brother George P. Bagwell & his heirs land adjoining Southy Bloxom &c., supposed to contain 90 acres, excepting thereout a piece of about 5 acres which I lend to Moses Landon & Esther his wife during their joint lives, or the life of the survivor of them, and at the death of the said Moses & Esther to go to my brother George P. Bagwell & his heirs; to wife Peggy the term of service which Moses Landon has to serve agreeable to the deed of Manumission on record; to sisters Elizabeth Jones Wise, wife of George E. Wise of Nansemond, and Sarah Poulson 50£. To Eliza Poulson son of George Poulson 3£; to nephew William Bagwell; brothers Isaiah & George Bagwell Ex'rs.; that the said Thomas Bagwell departed this life in May, 1816; that subsequent to the date of the said will and before the death of the said Thomas Bagwell, viz. on the 7 Sept. 1815, the said Thomas Bagwell purchased the land in the declaration mentioned of a certain William Long; that at the death of the said Thomas Bagwell he left no children nor father nor mother living, but leaving two brothers of the whole blood, viz: Isaiah Bagwell and George P. Bagwell, lessors of the plaintiff, and two sisters of the half blood, viz: Elizabeth J. Wise and Sarah Ashby, wife of Robert Ashby (p. 275), lessors of the plaintiff; that after the death of the said testator the defendant Margaret entered upon the lands in the declaration mentioned, and that she and her husband (Jesse Elliott - p. 277) the other defendant continued possessed thereof &c. 6 May, 1877 - p. 264

Ironmonger's Lessee
vs. - Ejectment Proceedings.
Lilliston
    Jury impaneled and returned the following verdict:
    That Jacob Dunton being seized in fee of the land in the declaration mentioned, on the 4 Sept. 1762 duly made & published his last will & testament as follows: (abstract) To wife Elizabeth Dunton ½ of all my land &c. during her widowhood, and at her death or marriage to my daughter Elizabeth Dunton all the land lying on the North-east side of a branch or Gully running close along the side & through my plantation, & for want of issue to my daughter Esther Ironmonger, and should both die without issue to my three youngest daughters to be equally divided between them & their heirs forever; to son Benjamin Dunton all my land

not already given, also the ½ which I lent my wife during her widowhood and should he die without issue then I give the said land to my four youngest daughters, Esther, Rachel, Bridget & Susey; To Elizabeth, Jacob & Annaritta, the children of John Lilliston, dec., and also to Sarah Dunton, the daughter of Robert Guy, 24£ current money to be equally divided between them, the said money to be paid them by my executors as they come to lawful age or marry; wife Exec. son Benjamin Ex'r. which said will was proved 26 Jan. 1763; that immediately after the death of the said Jacob Dunton, Benjamin Dunton entered upon the said lands and took possession thereof; that being so seized the said Benjamin on the 20 April 1786, conveyed unto Jacob Lilliston the land in the declaration mentioned; that the said Jacob Lilliston entered upon the said land and was possessed thereof according to his right, and being so seized on the 2 Nov. 1804, made his last will & testament which was proved on the 24 June, 1805, as follows: (abstract) To son Isaac Lilliston 60 acres of my land where I live; to son John Lilliston all the remaining part of my land where I live (both under 21) and in case of the death of both my sons without issue I give the whole of the land to my daughter Eleanor & her heirs; To wife Susannah; to dau. Isabel; wife & Matthias Outten Exrs.; that by virtue of the said devise the lands in the declaration mentioned came into the possession of his two sons, the defendants, who entered and are now possessed thereof; that Benjamin Dunton above mentioned departed this life on the -- day of --- 1800 unmarried and without issue; that the lessors of the plaintiff, Esther Ironmonger & Bridget Walker are two of the daughters of the said Jacob Dunton mentioned in his will; that Rachel the daughter of the said Jacob Dunton departed this life of the -- day of --- 1770, intestate & unmarried & without issue; that Susey, the other daughter of the said Jacob is now dead leaving issue. 8 May, 1817 - p. 285

Martin
vs. - Suit for Land.
Adah &c., negroes.

That John West, Sr., Gent. being seized in fee of a certain tract of land situate in the County of Accomack, upon the 6 Feb. 1702, duly made & published his last will & testament, in which said will he bequested to the three daughters of his son Anthony West, viz: Matilda, Mary Scarburgh & Jean West, the Ridge land without the Neck where my said son Anthony lives to be equally divided between them, which said will was probated on the 3 Aug. 1703; that Matilda, Mary Scarburgh & Jane West, devisees under the said will, entered upon the land to them devised and made partition thereof between themselves; that Matilda, one of the said devisees, intermarried with a certain Peter Hack, who together with the said Matilda conveyed their ⅓ part of said land to John Osborne by deed dated 6 Aug. 17--; that the said Peter Hack departed this life on the -- day of --- 1708, intestate, leaving George Nicholas Hack his eldest son & heir at law who entered upon the said land and by deed dated -- March 1732 conveyed the said land to William Poulson, and that the said land by several conveyances came to the possession of John Sill who by his will dated 1773 devised the said land to Americus Sturgis;

that by virtue of the said will he entered upon the said land and continued to hold the same until the year 1783 when he was evicted by virtue of a judgment of the Court of the County aforesaid in an ejectment brought against him by a certain Anthony West, the heir at law of the said John West, Sr., the testator aforesaid; that the said Americus Sturgis departed this life about the year 1795, intestate, leaving the demandant Famey Sturgis, only sister & the demandant Ned Martin a nephew & the only issue of Molly, another sister, his next of kin; that the said Anthony West immediately after the recovery in the aforesaid ejectment entered upon and became seized of the land so recovered, and continued seized thereof until his death in the year 1795; that the said Anthony West before his death, viz: on the 3 Feb. 1795, duly made his last will & testament; that the land in the court mentioned is a part of the 500 acres on Andua Creek devised to the said Abel West in said will; that immediately thereafter the said Abel West entered upon and became seized of said land and continued seized thereof until his death in the year 1816; that the said Abel West on the 22 May 1816 made his last will & testament; that the land in the court mentioned is a part of the land devised in said will to all the negroes who properly belonged to the said Abel West, lying above the Neck and supposed to contain 500 acres; that the tenants are a part of those negroes and entered upon the land in the court mentioned immediately after the death of Abel West, and continued seized thereof - 7 April 1818 - p. 324

Carlton & wife's lessee
vs. - Ejectment Proceedings.
Cropper.
　　Jury impaneled & returned the following verdict:
　　That John Allen the elder, late of the County of Accomack, was on the 6 Nov. 1764, seized as of fee of a tract of land supposed to contain 300 acres, and being so seized on the 6 Nov. 1764 made his last will & testament as follows: (abstract) To my three sons, Stephen, Edmund & John Allen 300 acres of land to be equally divided between them; to wife Esther Allen all the said plantation during her life or widowhood to bring up her children; wife Exec., which said will was probated 28 April 1767; that Esther Allen, the widow of the said John Allen the elder, immediately after the death of the said John Allen, entered upon and became possessed of the said tract of land and continued seized thereof until her death sometime in the year 1774; that Stephen Allen in said will mentioned, who was the eldest son of the said John Allen the elder, departed this life in the year 1771 intestate, unmarried & without issue; that immediately after the death of the said Esther Allen, Edmund Allen & John Allen the younger in said will named, entered upon the said land and became seized thereof; that the said Edmund Allen & John Allen were twins, but the said Edmund Allen was the first born; that the said Edmund Allen left this Commonwealth on the -- day of Dec. 1780 being still seized of the said land, and being then upwards of 21 years of age, and departed this life on the 25 Dec. 1789 intestate & without issue; that at the time of his death the said Edmund Allen left neither father, mother, brother nor sister, nor their descendants living except the lessors of the plaintiff, Margaret & Tabitha who

85

were the only children of his deceased brother John Allen, who departed this life on the 7 March 1788; that immediately after the departure of the said Edmund Allen from this Commonwealth as aforesaid, the said John Allen entered upon and took possession of the said tract of land; that the said John Allen being so seized on the 7 June, 1785, conveyed the said land to Jabez Pitt, attorney for the County of Accomack in these words: This Indenture &c., between Capt. John Allen, Seaman, of the one part & Jabez Pitt, Attorney for the County of Accomack in the State of Virginia of the other part, &c.; that the said Jabez Pitt, Attorney, entered upon the said land and became seized thereof, the said tract in said deed being expressed to contain 290 acres; that on the 25 Sept. 1786, the said Jabez Pitt & Hannah his wife, reconveyed 145 acres of the said land to the said John Allen, being that part thereof which the said John Allen claimed from his brother, Edmund Allen who has been absent for about 6 years and is supposed to be dead; that immediately thereafter the said John Allen took possession of the said 145 acres in the declaration mentioned and held the same until the 25 Sept. 1787 when he, together with Margaret, his wife, conveyed the said 145 acres to John Cropper, Jr., of the same place; that immediately thereafter the said John Cropper entered upon the said land and has continued seized thereof until his death; that the said Jabez Pitt on the 21 Aug. 1786, being seized of 145 acres of said tract purchased by him from the said Allen as aforesaid, and being that part which he had not reconveyed to the said John Allen, together with his wife conveyed to Littleton Armitrader 100 acres of the said land; that immediately thereafter the said Littleton Armitrader entered upon the said land, and on the 8 Aug. 1788, the said Littleton Armitrader and Elizabeth his wife, conveyed to John Cropper, Jr., 20 acres of the said land, and that the said John Cropper immediately entered upon & became seized of the said 20 acres and continued possessed thereof until his death; that on the 23 Dec. 1800, the said Littleton Armitrader & wife conveyed to John Cropper, Jr. two tracts of land, one containing 25 acres of woods land, and the other containing by estimation 60 acres where the said Armitrader then lived and which constitute one tract which the said Littleton Armitrader purchased of Jabez Pitt & Hannah his wife, and that the said John Cropper immediately entered upon and became possessed of the said land and continued seized thereof until his death; that on the 12 Oct. 1787, that said Jabez Pitt being seized of 45 acres, being the remainder of the land purchased of John Allen, conveyed the said 45 acres to the said John Cropper, Jr.; that the said John Cropper immediately entered upon and became seized of the said 45 acres of land and continued seized thereof until his death; that Margaret Allen, one of the lessors of the plaintiff, married in the year 180- John Carlton, another of the lessors of the plaintiff; that at the time of the institution of this suit the said Margaret Carlton was 24 years of age, and Tabitha Allen, another lessor of the plaintiff, was about 22 years of age; that the said John Cropper departed this life on the 15 Jan. 1821, being seized of the land aforesaid and having first made his last will & testament, to-wit: (abstract) To wife Catherine Cropper during her natural life all that plantation and tract of land where I now live called Bowman's Folly, personalty; to my three sons, John Washington Cropper, Thomas Bayly Cropper and Covington Hanson Cropper, personalty; dau.

Margaret Pettit Bayly; whole estate not before given, including Military Lands in the States of Kentucky & Ohio to be sold for payment of debts & the residue to be divided between my children or the descendants of such as may be dead, except Margaret Pettit Bayly; Bowman's Folly to be sold at the death of my wife; Richard D. Bayly, John G. Joynes & Thomas R. Joynes Ex'rs.; that Catherine Cropper, Sr., is the widow of the said John Cropper, and the other defendants are the children and grandchildren of said John Cropper &c. 3 Oct. 1810 - p. 348 (Elizabeth W. Cropper, John W. Cropper, Catharine B. Cropper, Thomas B. Cropper and Covington H. Cropper, children & devisees of John Cropper, dec., infants; Margaret D. P. Wise, Henry A. Wise & John C. Wise, children of Sarah Wise & devisees of said John Cropper, dec., infants - Richard D. Bayly appointed their guardian to defend this suit.)

Removed from Accomack Court to the Superior Court of Northampton, and the following record received from said Court.

That John Allen, the elder, was seized in fee simple of a tract of land situate in Accomack, containing by estimate 300 acres, and being so seized on the -- day of --- 1764, duly made & published his last will & testament; that the said John Allen left three sons his only children, to-wit: Stephen, John & Edmund Allen; that Stephen, one of his said sons & devisees departed this life on the -- day of --- 1771 intestate & without issue; that Edmund Allen, another of said sons left this Commonwealth upon the -- day of Dec. 1780 as second lieutenant on board of an American privateer; that at the capture of St. Eustaces on the 3 Feb. 1781, the said Edmund Allen was taken prisoner by the British and carried to the City of London in Great Britain; that the said Edmund Allen was the elder brother of the said John, they being twins, and was living in the fall of 1781; that John Allen, the only other brother of Edmund Allen, departed this life upon the 7 March 1788, intestate, having issue Peggy & Tabby Allen his only children & co-heirs; that upon the -- day of --- 1808, the aforesaid Peggy Allen intermarried with a certain John Carlton, one of the lessors of the plaintiff; that the said John Allen on the 7 June, 1785, conveyed to Jabez Pitt 290 acres of land, being the aforesaid tract supposed to contain 300 acres; that the said Jabez Pitt on the 21 Aug., 1786, conveyed to Littleton Armitrader 100 acres, part of the aforesaid tract; that on the 25 Sept. 1786 the said Jabez Pitt & wife conveyed 145 acres, being one moiety of the aforesaid tract, to John Allen; that Jabez Pitt on the 12 Oct. 1787 conveyed to John Cropper, the now defendant, 45 acres being the balance of the aforesaid tract - That on the 8 Aug. 1788 the said Littleton Armitrader conveyed to the said John Cropper 20 acres, being part of the said tract; that on the 23 Dec. 1800 the said Armitrader & wife conveyed to the said John Cropper 60 acres, and by the said deed conveyed to him 25 acres which had been previously conveyed by the said Trader to said Cropper, but which conveyance had never been recorded, being the balance of the said 100 acres; that upon the 26 Sept. 1787 the said John Allen & wife conveyed to the said John Cropper 145 acres, being a moiety of the aforesaid supposed 300 acres; by virtue of which said several conveyances the said John Cropper is now seized of the whole of the said tract of land supposed to contain 300 acres, but which from the said several conveyances appears to contain but 290 acres; that the witness who stated that he saw Edmund Allen in London first communicated that information and the evidence he has this day deposed, in the summer of 1809, but it appears the facts to which the witness deposed were accidentally discussed in the course of conversation on another subject; that there was no intimation of any claim to this land or any intention to commence this suit made to the witness at that time - 19 Oct. 1813

Watson
vs. - Ejectment Proceedings
Mears (John Mears, of Modest John)
That Matthew Fletcher, formerly of the County of Accomack, was in his lifetime and at the time of his death, seized in fee of a tract of land containing by estimate 250 acres, and being so seized on the 22 Jan. 1750, made his last will & testament in these words: (abstract) To Bezelell Watson 125 acres of land &c. to my brother in the law Daniel Watson 125 acres of land &c. Brother in law Bezelell Watson & Littleton Scarburgh Major Exrs.; That the said will was duly proved 26 March 1751; that immediately after the death of the said Matthew Fletcher, Bezelell Watson in said will named, entered upon and became seized of the 125 acres of land devised him in said will, and held the same until his death; that the land in the Court mentioned is a part of the 125 acres devised to and held by the said Bezelel Watson; that the said Bezelel Watson departed this life intestate on the -- day of --- 1772, leaving the demandant, William Watson, his eldest son & heir at law; that immediately after the said Bezelel's death a certain Henry Fletcher entered upon and became seized of the said 125 acres devised to the said Bezelel Watson, the said Henry Fletcher claiming the same as heir at law to the said Matthew Fletcher; that the defendant is in possession of 18 acres 2 Rods & 38 Perches of land in the bounds mentioned, agreeable to survey made in this cause, which land is claimed by the defendant under the said Henry Fletcher; that the said Henry Fletcher and those claiming under him have held possession of the said land from the death of the said Bezelel Watson to the present time &c. 11 Set. 1820 - p. 371

Same parties plaintiff vs. John Riley & Susey, his wife - 4 Sept. 1820 - p. 376

Same parties vs. Thomas Young - 4 Sept. 1820 - p. 381

Same parties vs. William Thomas, Henry &Walter Finney - 4 Sept. 1810 - p. 386

Coxon's Lessee
vs. - Ejectment Proceedings
Gunter
That Richard Bull the elder being seized of the 30 acres of land in the declaration mentioned, and also other lands mentioned in his will, and being so seized on the 19 June, 1796, made is last will & testament, proved 27 June, 1797, as follows: (abstract) I lend to my wife Bridget Bull during her natural life or

88

widowhood, my whole estate, and at her death or marriage all the land to the south of a line to be run on my plantation, containing 95 acres &c. to my son Teackle Bull; daughters Molly, Betsy & Sally Bull; to son Tobias Bull 50 acres adjoining his brother Teackle; to son Richard Bull 50 acres adjoining Tobias; granddaughters Kitty Bonwell & Nancy Bloxom; dau. Peggy Bayly; sons Teackle & Tobias Ex'rs.; That after the death of the said Richard Bull his widow, Bridget Bull, entered upon the said 50 acres of land and was possessed thereof until her death which took place in the year 1807; that Tobias Bull died intestate on or about the month of -- in the year 1801, leaving Margaret Coxon, the lessor of the plaintiff, his widow, & Jesse Bull his son and Scarburgh Bull his daughter his only children and heirs at law, having left no grandchildren or their descendants; that Jesse Bull, the son of the said Tobias Bull, died in the year 1805, an infant and without issue; that the said Scarburgh Bull, the daughter of the said Tobias Bull, died on or about the -- day of Nov. 1808, an infant and without issue; that the said Margaret Coxon was the mother of the said Jesse & Scarburgh Bull; that immediately after the death of the said Scarburgh Bull the heirs of the said Richard Bull the elder entered on the said 50 acres of land in the declaration mentioned and became possessed thereof, and made partition among themselves in a friendly way, viz: Abel Bull, the son & heir of Teackle Bull, who was then deceased, and was a brother of the whole blood of Tobias Bull, Peggy Bayly, Molly Bonwell, Sally Bonwell and Hetty Bonwell, sisters of the whole blood of the said Tobias Bull, and Richard Bull, brother of the whole blood of the said Tobias Bull; That Laban Gunter, one of the defendants in possession of about 31 acres of land, part of the 50 acres in the declaration mentioned, which said 31 acres he purchased by several deeds from the brothers & sisters of the whole blood of the said Tobias Bull; that the remainder of the said 50 acres is still held by the defendants Thomas Edmunds & James Belote, who purchased of the brothers & sisters of the said Tobias Bull, and the defendant Peggy Bayly; that at the death of the said Scarburgh Bull she left a brother of the half blood named William H. Coxon, who is the son of the lessor of the plaintiff, by her deceased husband William H. Coxon, to whom the lessor of the plaintiff had been married after the death of her first husband, Tobias Bull, and said Scarburgh left no other brother nor sister nor any descendant of a brother or sister; that upon the death of the said Bridget Bull, the guardian of the said Scarburgh Bull entered upon the lands in the declaration mentioned and held the same until the death of the said Scarburgh Bull &c. 18 Oct. 1820 - p. 392

Bagwell Lessee
vs. - Ejectment Proceedings.
John Downing.

That John Bagwell, the elder, late of this County in his lifetime and of the time of his death, was seized in fee simple of a tract of land containing 150 acres, and being so seized on the 25 April 1795, he duly made his last will & testament as follows: (abstract) To wife Ann Bagwell all my lands & all my other estate till my son Henry Bagwell comes to the age of 14 years, to bring up my two sons, she to give my sons John Young Bagwell & Henry Bagwell sufficient schooling &c.

To son Henry 50 acres of land adjoining John Young; to son John Young Bagwell the balance of my land containing 100 acres; wife & friend Isaac Bagwell Ex'rs.; that the said John Bagwell departed his life sometime in the month of Sept. in the year 1796, leaving two children, John & Henry Bagwell and his wife enscient of a child which was born about three months after the death of her said father, John Bagwell the elder, and was called Margaret; that the said Margaret departed this life sometime in the month of May, 1798, an infant & without issue, leaving her mother, Ann Bagwell, and her brothers the aforesaid John &Henry living, and no other brother or sister nor the descendant of any bother or sister; that after the death of the said Anne, his widow, entered upon the said land and held the same until the said Henry Bagwell attained the age of 14 years; that when the said John Bagwell the younger and Henry Bagwell respectively attained their age of 21 years they took possession of the land respectively devised them as aforesaid; that the land in the declaration mentioned is the same land devised as aforesaid to the said John Bagwell the younger, and since his arrival to the age of 21 years has been sold and conveyed by him to the defendant; that the lessor of the plaintiff is the same Henry Bagwell in said will mentioned, and that he attained the age of 21 years on the 28 March 1813; that the said John Bagwell at the time of his death was seized of no other real estate except the land devised in said will to his sons John & Henry; that Anne Bagwell, formerly the wife of the said John Bagwell the elder, departed this life before the institution of this suit; that the said Margaret was neither provided for nor disinherited by the said will &c. 8 May, 1822 - p. 417

Stephen's Lessee
vs. - Ejectment Proceedings.
Jonathan Noright
    That Elisha Stephens, late of the County of Accomack, departed this life on the -- day of Dec. 1800, seized in fee simple of the lands in the declaration mentioned; that on the -- day of --- 1799, he duly made and published his last will & testament which was proved on the 29 Dec. 1800; that the unborn child referred to in said will was born after the date of the said will and was called Sally; the said Damey Stephens referred to in said will departed this life an infant without issue in the year 1802, leaving her mother Sally and her sister the said Sally Stephens living; that the said Elisha at his death left no children except the said Damey & Sally, and the said Damey at her death left no brother or sister except the said Sally; that Sally Stephens departed this life about three months after the death of the said Damey, being at the time of her death an infant & without issue, leaving her mother, the said Sally Stephens, and having no brother nor sister nor the descendant of any brother or sister; that she left no grandfather or grandmother living, either paternal or maternal; the said Sally left the following paternal relations, viz: the lessor of the plaintiff, Polly Stephens, who is the only child of William Stephens, a brother of the whole blood to the said Elisha Stephens, and Hepsey Stephens the only child of Southy Stephens; a brother of the whole blood to the said Elisha; that there were no brother or sisters of the said Elisha Stephens

living at the time of the death of the said Sally Stephens, nor descendants of a deceased brother or sister, except the lessor of the plaintiff and the said Hepsey Stephens; that the said Hepsey Stephens left this commonwealth unmarried and without issue in the year 1816, since which time she has not been heard from; that when she so left, and at the expiration of seven years thereafter, had no father, mother, brother or sister nor their descendants living, nor any grandfather, Grandmother, uncles or aunts, maternal or paternal living, nor any descendant of any such uncle, aunt, except the lessor of the plaintiff, who is the only child of William Stephens, a brother of the whole blood to Southy Stephens, the father of the said Hepsey Stephens; that the lessor of the plaintiff attained the age of 21 years on the 10 Feb. 1820; that after the death of the said Elisha Stephens his widow, Sally Stephens, entered into the lands in the declaration mentioned, and continues seized thereof; that the said Hepsey Stephens departed this life intestate and without issue on the 25 Dec. 1823; That Sally Parks, the widow of Elisha Stephens, was married to Elijah Parks on the -- day of --- 1802 or thereabouts, and that the said Elijah departed this life since the institution of this suit; that Damey Stephens in the said cause mentioned departed this life about the 1 day of Jan. 1801 instead of the time in said cause first mentioned; that at the death of the said Elisha Stephens he had other lands besides 4 ½ acres devised to Damey Stephens - &c. 19 Oct. 1821

LAND CAUSES - 1812 TO 1821

Nathaniel Burwell, John Wedderburn, Thomas G. Smith, Adm'r. with will annexed of William Taliaferro, Richard Taliaferro and Elizabeth Holden, his wife, & William Robinson & Martha Haines, his wife,
vs, - In Debt - Suit for said of land.
Carvey Dunton

That a certain Carvey Dunton of this County is indentured to the complainants in the sum of £1394.40.:3^d, and in order to secure same on the 20 March 1802, executed a deed of mortgage by which he conveyed to your orators Nathaniel Burwell, John Weddeburn & William Taliaferro, since deceased, & whom your orator Thomas G. Smith as administrator now represents, & to your oratrixes Elizabeth Holden Stubs, who hath since intermarried with your orator Richard Taliaferro, & Martha Hains Stubs, who hath since intermarried with your orator William Robinson, a certain plantation & tract of land situate in the County aforesaid on Matchatank Creek, containing 612 acres, being the land formerly sold and conveyed to the said Carvey Dunton by the said parties, to be held by your orators & oratrixes in trust as security for the payment of the aforesaid sum of money, and interest thereon. Nathaniel Burwell of the County of Gloucester & John Waddeburn, William Taliaferro, Elizabeth Holden Stubs & Martha Hains Stubs of King & Queen. - Sept. Court, 1810 - p. 1

Perry Hinman, David Hinman, Elizabeth Hinman, children of Major Hinman, dec., by William Hinman their next friend, & Peggy Hinman, widow of said Major Hinman, dec.

vs. - Suit for dower & partition.

Tabitha Hinman.

That Major Hinman, dec. late husband to Peggy Hinman, one of the complainants, and father to the other complainants & the defendant, departed this life on the -- day of Feb. 1811, intestate, leaving 30 acres of land, more or less, adjoining the land of William Hinman, &c. 27 Nov. 1811 - p. 5

William Seymour, surviving partner of Ker & Seymour

vs. - In debt - Suit for sale of land.

Thomas Tunnell.

That a certain John Tunnell of the County being indebted to the said Ker & Seymour in the sum of 34£18s.6^d in order to secure the payment of same executed a deed of mortgage dated 11 Feb. 1805, on certain lots of land in the Town of Onancock; that after the institution of this suit the said John Tunnell died leaving Littleton Tunnell & Sally Tunnell his children, infants, Mary W. Tunnell his widow, who is appointed guardian of the said infants to defend this suit &c. April Court - 1808 - p. 6

Zorobabel West & Hetty, his wife,

vs. - Partition suit.

John Savage, Richard Savage & Griffith Savage, Inf'ts., William Justice appointed their guardian to defend this suit.

That Richard R. Savage, late of this country, was in his lifetime seized in fee of 100 acres in land in the Parish of Accomack, and being so seized died on the -- day of --- 1807, intestate, leaving Hetty, one of the plaintiffs, John, Richard & Griffin is only children and heirs. &c. 2 Aug. 1811 - p. 11

David Davis & Mary his wife & Skinner Wallop,

vs. - Partition Suit.

Rachel Wallop.

That a certain George Wallop, late of this County, dec. died seized in fee of a plantation in Wallop's Neck, containing --- acres, & of the undivided ½ of a mill called Wallop's Mill; that George Wallop died intestate on the -- day of ---, leaving your orator Skinner Wallop, your oratrix Mary Davis (formerly Mary Wallop) and a certain Rachel Wallop his only children and heirs at law; that a certain Comfort Wallop dec. of this county, was in her lifetime seized in fee of two tracts of land in Accomack Parish, one at Pocomoke Church containing --- acres, and the other containing --- acres adjoining the land of David Watts, the Mifflin land&c. Comfort Wallop died intestate on the -- day of --- leaving your orator Skinner Wallop, your oratrix Mary Davis and the aforesaid Rachel Wallop her only children, &c. 27 Aug. 1811 - p. 14

Stringer
vs. - Partition Suit.
Stringer.

Came Ann Stringer, widow of Thomas Stringer, Sarah Stringer, Revel Custis & Margaret, his wife, by Thomas M. Bayly, their attorney , and James Stringer by Ann Stringer his next friend, and brought their bill in chancery against William F. Stringer: That Thomas Stringer, husband to your complainant, Ann, & father of William Stringer, Margaret Custis, James Stringer & Sarah Stringer, departed this life on the -- day of --- intestate; that before the death of the said Thomas Stringer Sr., by his deed recorded in Accomack County, dated 1 Aug. 1792, he conveyed unto John Floyd Stringer a tract of land containing 105 acres of land (deed state that John F. Stringer is son of Ann; other children Sarah, Thomas, Peggy Smart, William Floyd & James Stringer); that on the 5 May 1804, Ann Stringer, John F. Stringer, Sarah Stringer, William F. Stringer & James Stringer by their deed conveyed 21 acres, part of the said 105 acres, unto John Stringer, son of Hillary Stringer; that on the 24 May, 1804, John F. Stringer conveyed the balance of the said land supposed to contain 75 acres unto William F. Stringer; that on the 4 Feb. 1806, William F. Stringer conveyed to his sister Peggy Smart Custis, the complainant, ¼ of the said land, but the said land has never been legally laid off & assigned to the said Margaret Custis; that it was always understood by the parties and the intention of the parties to the deed of John F. Stringer to William F. Stringer, that the complainant Ann Stringer, widow of Thomas Stringer, should enjoy the land during their natural lives, and that it should then be divided equally between the parties to this suit, viz: William F. Stringer, Margaret Custis, James Stringer and Sarah Stringer, and in consequence of which the said William F. Stringer has given bonds unto the said Sarah Stinger & unto James, that he will convey ¼ part of the said lands unto each of the parties according as he was bound in equity to do, &c. 27 Nov. 1811 - p. 17

Williams
vs. - Partition Suit.
Williams

Came John Williams & Nancy Williams by Samuel Lippincott, their next friend, and brought their bill in chancery against Agnes Williams: That John Williams, dec. late of the county aforesaid, was in his lifetime and at the time of his death seized of a tract of land as of fee, in the County aforesaid, containing ½ acre, and being so seized on the -- day of --- departed this life intestate leaving your complainants John & Nancy Williams & Agnes Williams, the defendant, his only children & heirs at law & leaving no widow, to all of which said children upon the death of the said John Williams the said land and appurtenances descended &c. 26 March 1811 - p. 23

Watts

vs. - Suit for dower & division.

Waterfield.

Come William Watts, Mary Walter & William Brewington & Polly his wife, and brought their bill in chancery against Jacob Waterfield, Nancy Waterfield, George Waterfield & Luther Waterfield; that William Waterfield, Sr., dec., was in his lifetime seized and possessed in fee of a certain tract of land in the County of Accomack supposed to contain 160 acres, adjoining the land of Thomas Waters, John Marshall &c., & being so seized upon the -- day of --- departed this life intestate, leaving William Waterfield the younger, and Elizabeth, the wife of John Evans, Jacob, Nancy, George & Luther Waterfield his only children & heirs, & also leaving a widow, Polly Waterfield; now Polly Brewington, the wife of William Brewington, by reason whereof the said lands descended to the aforesaid children of William Waterfield, Sr., subject to the dower of the widow Polly Waterfield, now Polly Brewington, wife of the said William Brewington and wife pray may be assigned to them by the same commission as may be appointed to make division between the parties in this suit; That the said William Waterfield & --- his wife by deed dated 29 Aug. 1810, conveyed all their interest in the said land unto your complainant William Watts; that the said John Evans & Elizabeth his wife on the 8 July 1811 conveyed their interest in said land to your complainant Mary Walters, by virtue of which your complainants William Watts & Mary Walters & the defendants Jacob, Nancy George & Luther Waterfield are each entitled to one undivided 1/6 part in said plantation, subject to the dower of the complainants William Brittingham & Polly, his wife, &c. 1 Oct. 1811 - p. 25

Powell

vs. - Partition Suit.

Powell

Came William Powell & brought is suit in chancery against Henry Powell, Betsy Powell & Edmund Powell, infant children of Edmund Powell, dec.; that Edmund Powell, father to your complainant and the defendants, departed this life on the -- day --- intestate, leaving the complainant & the defendants his only children' that at the time of his death he was seized of an absolute estate in fee simple of and to 18 acres of land in the Parish of Accomack & adjoining the lands of John Wharton on every side &c. John Snead appointed guardian of the infant defendants to be defend this suit. - 4 April 1812 - p. 34

Custis

vs. - In debt - Suit for sale & division of residue.

Came John Custis & William Robinson Custis, by Major S. Pitts, their attorney and brought their bill in chancery against William Nock & Agnes Nock & Lucretia Nock, children & heirs of Eliz^a Nock, dec.; that a certain William Nock of this County being indebted to the complainants in the sum of 66£ -- in order to secure the same the said William Nock & Elizabeth his wife on the 22 Oct. 1811, executed a deed of mortgage conveying a certain tract of land held by them in right of the said Elizabeth, situate in said county and containing 120 acres; that on the 22 Nov. 1811, the said William Nock became further indebted in the sum of 150£; that sometime after this, to-wit: on the 26 Jan. 1812, the said Eliz^a departed this life leaving the following children, to-wit: Agnes Nock, & Lucretia Nock, to whom the said land descended subject to the aforesaid lien; that after the death of the said Elizabeth the said William Nock continued to hold the aforesaid tract of land as tenant by the curtesy &c. 2 April 1812 - p. 35

Hancock & others
vs. - Partition Suit.
Savage & others.

Came George Hancock, Adah Hancock, Rachel Hancock, Jacob Outten & Mary, his wife in right of said Mary, Richard Walter, Solomon Walter, Abel Walter, Thomas Walter & Richard Cutler & Rachel his wife, in right of said Rachel, and brought their bill in chancery against Ridigal Savage, Hetty Milby, orphan of Gilbert, & John Milby, Elizabeth Milby & William Milby, orphans of John Milby, dec.; that your orators & oratrixes George Hancock, Rachel Hancock, Adah Hancock, Jacob Outten & Mary his wife, in right of said Mary, who was formerly Mary Hancock (all of whom are the only children of Tabitha Hancock, formerly Tabitha Fletcher, dec.) Thomas Walter, Solomon Walter, Richard Walter, Abel Walter, Richard Cutler & Rachel his wife, in right of said Rachel, who was formerly Rachel Walter, (all of whom are the only children of Richard Walter, dec.); That a certain John Fletcher late of this County was in his lifetime seized in fee simple of a certain tract of land situate near the head of Andue Creek, in the County of Accomack, containing 125 acres and being so seized departed this life intestate on the -- day of --- 1811; the said Fletcher at his death leaving neither children nor father living; your orators & oratrixes are advised that his real estate descended to them and to Hetty Milby, orphan of Gilbert Milby, dec., who was a son of Rachel Walter, and to John Milby, William Milby & Elizabeth Milby, orphans of John Milby, dec., who was also a son of the said Rachel Walter, and to Ridigel Savage, formerly Ridigel Fletcher, all of whom are his nearest relatives in the following proportions; To your orator George Hancock & your oratrixes Rachel Hancock, Adah Hancock & Mary Outten, formerly Mary Hancock. all of whom are the only children & heirs of Tabitha Hancock, formerly Tabitha Fletcher, who was a sister of the whole blood to the said John Fletcher, ⅓; to your orators Thomas, Solomon, Richard & Abel Walters and your oratrix Rachel Cutler, formerly Rachel Walter, all of whom are the only children & heirs of Richard Walter, dec., who was a brother of the half blood to the said John Fletcher, dec., 1/6; to Hetty Milby, orphan of Gilbert Milby, dec., who was a son of Rachel Walter, who was a sister of the half blood to the said Fletcher, 1/12; to John, William & Elizabeth Milby, orphans of John Milby, dec., who was another son of said Rachel Walter, 1/12; and to Ridigal Savage who was a sister of the whole blood to the said John Fletcher, the remaining ⅓ &c. 26 May 1812 - p. 39

Leatherbury & wife
vs. - Petition for dower.
Mears.

Came Gilbert M. Leatherbury and Molly, his wife, by Thomas M. Bayly, their attorney, and brought their bill in chancery against Thomas Mears, infant & heir of Jonathan Mears, dec: That said Jonathan Mears of this county died on the 10 Jan. 1811, having first made his last will & testament, which was duly proved 28 Jan. 1811; that the said Jonathan left the complainant, Molly, his widow and Thomas Mears, the defendant, an infant; his only child; that at the time of his death the said Jonathan was seized in fee of a plantation whereon he lived, containing 301 acres, slaves, &c., said slaves now in the possession of Bartholomew Mears, executor of the said Jonathan and guardian of the said Thomas Mears &c. - 3 Sept. 1812 - p. 46

Harvy & wife
vs. - Partition suit.
Jacob.

Came William Harvy & Sally, his wife, by Thomas R. Joynes, their attorney, and brought their bill in chancery against John Jacob & James Jacob, orphans of Richard Jacob, dec.; that a certain Richard Jacob, dec., formerly of this county, was in his lifetime seized in his demesne as of fee in a certain tract of land containing by estimation 100 acres, situate on the waters of Folly Creek, adjoining the lands of Thomas Cropper, John Burton, Sebastian Cropper & the heirs of Scarburgh West, and being so seized departed this life intestate on the __ day of January, 1803, leaving your oratrix Sally Harvy, a certain John Jacob & James Jacob his only children & heirs at law; that since the death of the aforesaid Richard Jacob, your oratrix Sally has intermarried with your orator, William Harvey &c. - 1 Sept. 1812 - p. 49

Nock & wife
vs. - Suit for sale & division.
Guy's Ex'rs.

Came George Nock & Peggy, his wife, by Thomas Evans, their attorney, and brought their bill in chancery against Solomon Nock, Ex'r. of John Guy, dec; That a certain John Guy of the county aforesaid sometime since deceased, was in his lifetime seized in his demesne as of fee of & in a certain tract of land containing by survey 71 ¾ acres, situate near the White Marsh, in the Parish of St. George, adjoining the lands of John Nock &c., and being so seized on the 1 May, 1792, made his last will & testament and among other things devised the said land as follows: I leave my land whereon my mother now lives, after her decease, to be sold to the highest bidder, and the money to be equally divided between my two sisters, Peggy Nock & Amy Nock if my sister Amey [sic] Nock ever has heirs of her body, but if no heirs of her body I give the same to my sister Peggy Nock & her heirs forever, and of the will the said John Guy appointed his mother Exec. & Solomon Nock & John Spiers ex'rs.; that your oratrix is the sister therein mentioned by the name of Peggy Nock & Amey Nock the wife of the said Solomon Nock, the other sister therein mentioned; that the mother of the said John Guy has long since departed this life as has also the said John Spiers; that the said Solomon Nock after the death of the mother of the said John Guy entered upon the lands aforesaid and has ever since retained possession thereof, and taken to himself the profits of the same &c. 30 Nov. 1808 - p. 52

Joynes
vs. - Petition for assignment of dower.
East.
    Came Levin & Thomas Joynes and brought their bill in chancery against Tabitha East, widow of Severn East; that a certain Severn East, deceased, was in his lifetime seized in his demesne as of fee in several tracts of land situate in this County, and being so seized departed this life on the -- day of --- 1811, having first made his last will & testament, devising to his son James East all the remainder of the tract on which the devisor lived, after having first devised to his son Parker East 30 acres of said tract; that since the death of the said Severn East, viz: on the 25 May 1812, the said James East & Rachel his wife, conveyed to your orators all the right of the said James to the land devised to him by his said father; since the conveyance aforesaid your orators have proposed to a certain Tabitha East of this county, widow of the said Severn East, that they should lay off & mark out to the said Tabitha as her dower such portion of the land conveyed to them as she was entitled to by law -- that the said Tabitha refuses under various frivolous & vexatious pretences to agree to the said proposition &c. 1 Sept. 1812 - p. 55

Wilkins
vs. - Partition Suit.
Northam, &c.
    Came George D. Wilkins, John Wilkins & Peggy Wilkins, by Major S. Pitts, their attorney, and brought their bill in chancery against William Northam, John H. Mason & Ann Mason. That a certain Ann D. Wilkins, mother of the complainants was in her lifetime and at the time of her death seized in fee simple of & in a certain tract of land (swamp), situate in the said county on Mesongo, containing about 75 acres, adjoining the land of Col. Cropper &c., that the said Ann departed this life in the year 1797 a feme covert, leaving the following children, to-wit: the present complaintans & Sukey & Rachel Wilkins, to all of whom the said land descended, subject to the right of their father, Henry Wilkins as tenant by the Curtesy therein; that the said Henry Wilkins, the father, departed this life in the year 1802, and the said lands became vested in the aforesaid children of the said Ann; that Sukey, one of the children of the said Ann, sometime afterwards intermarried with a certain George Mason & on the -- day of --- the said George & Sukey his wife conveyed the said Sukey's interest in said land to a certain William Northam of this County; that sometime after this, to-wit: about the month of August, 1810, the said Sukey, the wife of George Mason, departed this life intestate leaving issue to-wit: John H. Mason & Ann Mason,

both of whom are infants; that sometime after this, to-wit: upon the -- day of Oct. 1810, Nathaniel Wilkins, one of the aforesaid children of Ann, departed this life an infant, intestate & without issue, so that his undivided part of the said land descended to the complainants & to John & Ann Mason, the children of Sukey, and so the complainants & William Northam & John & Ann Mason together & undivided hold the said lands &c. 31 Dec. 1811 - p. 58

Wharton
vs. - Partition Suit.
Wharton.

Came Peggy Wharton by Thomas R. Joynes, her attorney, and brought her bill in chancery against Bagwell Wharton, Susanna Wharton & James Wharton; That a certain James Wharton & Sally his wife, who was formerly Sally Shield, dec., were in their lifetime seized and possessed in right of the said Sally, in fee simple of a tract of land in this county situate near the head of Watchaprig & adjoining the lands of William Long, James Shield &c., containing 18 acres, and being so seized the said James Wharton & Sally Wharton have both departed this life, viz: the said James on the -- day of Aug. 1812, and the said Sally on the -- day of Aug. 1806 without having disposed of the said land, leaving your oratrix, Peggy Wharton & Bagwell Wharton, Susanna Wharton & James Wharton, infants, who are the only children of the said Sally Wharton the elder, dec., &c. 1 Dec. 1812 - p. 61

Ames & wife
vs. - Partition Suit.
Hornsby.

Came Shadrack Ames & Elizabeth, his wife, by William A. Parker, their attorney, and brought their bill in chancery against Samuel H. Hornsby & Priscilla Hornsby, heirs of Eli Hornsby, dec. That Eli Hornsby, late of the County aforesaid, dec., was in his lifetime and at the time of his death, seized & possessed in his own right of a tract of woodsland in the county aforesaid, containing 200 acres, and being so seized on the 29 Aug. 1808, departed this life intestate, leaving his widow the aforesaid Elizabeth, your oratrix, and the following his only children & heirs, to-wit: Samuel H. Hornsby & Ann P. Hornsby, to which said children upon the death of the said Eli Hornsby the said land descended, subject to the dower of his widow, the aforesaid Elizabeth &c. 3 Sept. 1812 - p. 63

Booth
vs. - Suit for sale & division.
Booth.

Came Leah, Mehala, Peggy & Convention Booth, infant children of John Booth, dec., by David Watts, their next friend, and brought their bill in chancery against Hetty Booth, widow & Sally Booth Infant of John Booth, dec.; That John Booth, dec., father to your complainants & the defendant Sally, & husband to the defendant Hetty, departed this life on the __ day of Dec. 1811, intestate, being possessed of a small personal estate and about 75 acres of land & marsh on Chincoteague Island &c. 1 Dec. 1812 - p. 65

Kelly
vs. - Suit for partition.
Bayne & others.

Dennis Kelly, by Thomas M. Bayly, his attorney, sued out of the Clerk's Office of the Court of this County his summons in partition against Sally Bayne & Betsy Bayne & William R. Taylor and Bridget his wife, in right of said wife, Southy Bull & Susanna his wife, in right of said wife, Nancy Garrett, Elisha Garrett, Charles Garrett, Samuel Garrett & Sally Garrett, heirs of Elisha Garrett, dec., who together and undivided hold a tract of land in the County of Accomack containing 175 acres, to make partition thereof &c. One moiety or one half thereof and ¼ of one moiety doth belong to the said plaintiff, and ¾ of the other moiety doth belong to the said defendants; that the said defendants do not permit division, although the said Dennis Kelly is entitled to one moiety & ¼ of one moiety of the said lands by virtue of a decree of Accomack County Court 2 April 1812 wherein John Custis & William Robinson Custis were plaintiffs & William Nock & Agnes Nock & Lucretia Nock, children and heirs of Elizabeth Nock, were defendants, the said land being sold according to the said decree, & the said Dennis Kelly being the purcherser of the said land being recovered by the said William Nock & Elizabeth his wife against Joseph Powell in the District Court of Accomack & Northhampton on the 17 Oct., 1808; Sally Bayne appointed guardian to the infant defendant Betsy Bayne, & John Bull guardian to the other infant defendants for the purpose of defending this suit - 16 July 1812 - p. 67

Surveyors report: 14 Jan. 1813 - certain tract of land containing 173 ¾ acres situate near Pocomoke in the county aforesaid, heretofore belonging to Joseph Powell & by him sold to Walter Bayne, Esq., & Elisha Garrett, both now dec., and from whom, or their heirs, William Nock & Elizabeth his wife afterwards recovered ½ & ¼ of ½ in an undivided state, which interest of the said William Nock & Elizabeth his wife in the said lands they afterwards mortgaged to John Custis & William R. Custis, who afterwards obtained a decree of foreclosure & sale thereon, at the sale of which Dennis Kelly became the purchaser, &c.

Bloxom & wife
vs. - Petition for dower & division.
T. & S. Hinman

Came James Bloxom & Polly his wife, by Thomas R. Joynes, their attorney, and brought their bill in chancery against Thomas Hinman & Sarah Hinman, infant children of George Hinman, dec.; that a certain George Hinman late of this County was in his lifetime and at the time of his death seized in fee simple of a tract of land situate on the head of Guilford in this county, containing 200 acres, and being so seized departed this life intestate on the -- day of --- leaving your oratrix Polly, his widow and Thomas, Custis & Samuel Hinman his children and heirs at law; that at the death of the said George Hinman your oratrix was pregnant and was shortly afterwards delivered of a daughter who is named Sally; that after the death of the said George Hinman, viz: on the -- day of Aug. 1805, Samuel Hinman, one of the children of the said George Hinman, departed this life aged about 4 years, and on the -- day of Sept. 1812, Custis Hinman, another of the said children departed this life aged about 11 years, whereby the said land descended to the said Thomas & Sarah Hinman, subject to the dower of your oratrix who since the death of the said George Hinman has intermarried with your orator &c. 31 Aug. 1813 - p. 73

Chandler & wife
vs. - Petition for dower.
Hugh H. Smith, &c.

Came Thomas Chandler & Anne M., his wife, by Thomas B. Joynes, their attorney, and brought their bill in chancery against Hugh H. Smith, Robert Smith, William Smith, Samuel Smith & Walter Smith, children of Robert Smith, dec.; That a certain Robert Smith, dec., was in his lifetime seized in his demesne as of fee of a certain tract of land situate on Andua Creek in said county, continuing __ acres, and being so seized departed this life intestate on the -- day of ---, leaving your oratrix his widow and five infant children, viz: Hugh H., Robert, William, Samuel & Walter Smith; that since the death of the said Robert Smith your oratrix has intermarried with your orator &c. 31 March 1813 - p. 75

Savage
vs. - Partition Suit.
Custis.

Came Margaret Savage, by William H. Smith, her next friend, and brought her bill in chancery against William S. Custis; That a certain John Savage late of this county was in his lifetime and at the time of his death seized in his demesne as of fee among other lands of a valuable plantation and tract of land situate on Metompkin in this County, containing about 500 acres, which said tract of land the said John Savage had purchased of a certain James Henry, and being so seized thereof on the -- day of --- 1792, the said John Savage departed this life, having first made his last will & testament, in which said will the said John Savage among other things directed that his plantation on Metompkin should be rented until his son Joseph arrived to the age of 18 years, and that then the same should be equally divided between all his children who were then living; when the said Joseph Savage arrived to the age of 18 years, there were living of the children of the said John Savage[,] William, Thomas, Charles, Joseph, Severn, the father of your oratrix, and Ann, the wife of a certain William Stone, George, another of the sons of the said John Savage having departed this life previous to that time; on the 8 June, 1803, the aforesaid William Savage conveyed to William S. Custis of this county, who had intermarried with the widow of the said John Savage, all his right to the aforesaid plantation; shortly after the said Joseph arrived to the age of 18 years, viz: on the -- day of --- 1808, a suit in chancery was instituted in this court by the said William S. Custis & Margaret, his wife, S. E. Savage, Ann Savage &

Joseph Savage vs. Thomas W. & Charles Savage for the purpose of assigning to Margaret, the wife of William S. Custis, her dower in the said land, and also for the purpose of dividing the balance of said land among those entitled thereto; division made & dower assigned under said decree; on the 13 July, 1803, Thomas W. Savage conveyed to Severn E. Savage, your oratrix father, all the part of said land which had been allotted to him, also all his right in the reversion in that part of land which had been assigned to Mrs. Custis as her dower; on the 4 April 1812, Joseph Savage conveyed to the said William S. Custis the part of said land which had been allotted to him, and also his part in the reversion in Mrs. Custis' dower; on the 21 Sept., 1811, William Stone & Anne his wife conveyed to William S. Custis all the said Anne's original share of the said land which had been allotted to her, and also her share of Mrs. Custis' dower, and on the 26 Feb. 1810, Charles Savage conveyed to the said William S. Custis all his right in the said land which had been assigned to Mrs. Custis for dower; on the 26 Aug. 1813, the said Margaret Custis departed this life; on the 6 day of Sept. 1808 Severn E. Savage, the father of your oratrix departed t his life intestate, leaving your oratrix his only child & heir at law. Your oratrix is further advised that she is entitled as heir of said Severn E. Savage to ⅓ of the land which had been allotted to Mrs. Custis for her dower, and that the aforesaid William S. Custis, by virtue of the said several conveyances aforesaid is entitled to the two remaining thirds thereof &c. 29 March 1814 p. 78

Custis
vs. - Partition Suit.
Custis
    Came Peter Custis, Frances Custis, Sr. & Frances Custis, infant, child of Thomas Custis by Peter Custis her next friend, and brought their bill in chancery against Edmund R. Custis; That a certain Robinson Custis late of the County of Accomack in his lifetime and at the time of his death was seized in his demesne as of fee in a valuable plantation & tract of land situate on Deep Creek, and was also seized of ½ of the grist & saw mills contiguous thereto on the head of Deep Creek, and being so seized departed this life on the -- day of --- 1798, having first duly made his last will & testament, in which said will among other things he devised to your oratrix Frances Y. Custis, Sr., his widow, his mansion house & outhouses and garden and sufficient ground contiguous thereto for potato patches and other necessary vine patches during her natural life or widowhood, and the remaining part of his real estate to be rented until his son Edmund arrived at lawful age, & the proceeds equally divided among his said widow & his four children, Thomas, Peter, Edmund & Frances, and upon the arrival of the said Edmund at lawful age the whole of his real estate, except what he devised to his wife, to be equally divided between all his aforesaid children; on the 13 May, 1804, your orator Peter Custis conveyed to the said Thomas Custis his undivided ¼ part of said tract supposed to contain 600 acres, and on the 30 May 1804, the said Thomas & Peter Custis conveyed to John Custis (Bay Side) that ¼ part of the aforesaid Mills; on the -- day of --- 1807, the aforesaid Frances Custis, the

daughter of the said Robinson Custis, departed this life under age & without issue, leaving her mother & her three brothers, Thomas, Peter & Edmund Custis living, and her ¼ part of the said plantation descended to her three brothers; the said Thomas Custis departed this life in the month of January 1814, having first made his last will & testament in which he devised his whole estate to your oratrix, Frances Custis, Jr., his daughter, during her natural life with remainder to said Peter & Edmund Custis &c. 1 June, 1814 - p. 83

Wyatt
vs. - Petition for recovery of land.
Robins' Exr's.

Came Isma Wyatt by Thomas Evans, his attorney, and filed his bill in Chancery against Thomas Robins & Carvy Dunton, executors of Arthur Robins, Jr., dec., who was executor of Arthur Robins, Sr., dec., & Arthur Robins (of Thomas), Isaac Robins, John Robins & Bowdoin Robins, devisees of Arthur Robins, Jr., & Richard Cutler. That your orator had heretofore, to-wit: on the 10 April 1790, contracted with Arthur Robins, Sr., of the County of Northampton, now dec., for the purchase of 200 acres of land situate near Bell Haven in the Parish of St. George, County of Accomack, and for the due conveyance of the same the said Arthur Robins, Sr., on his part bound himself, his heirs, Ex'rs. &c. by his bond dated 10 April 1790; that he afterwards duly paid the sum agreed upon for the said land and the said Arthur Robins, Sr., on the 2 Aug. 1790, executed a deed to your orator for the said land, & that your orator entered into the said lands; that on the 28 Sept 1790, the said Arthur Robins, Sr., conveyed a further portion of his said land next adjoining to the said lands of your orator on the South-west, to Mr. Richard Cutler, of the County of Accomack; that the said Arthur Robins, Sr., afterwards, to-wit: on the 25 Nov. 1790, made his last will & testament and devised the use of 400 acres of land on the North side of his tract, contiguous to the said land of your orator on the South-east, to his son Thomas Robins during his life, with a right of dower therein to Lettice Robins, the wife of the said Thomas in case she should survive him, and provided she remain his widow, with remainder in fee to all the children of the said Thomas Robins, and further gave to his son Arthur all the remaining part of his land not before given and appointed his said son Arthur his executor. That upon a survey of the said land there was excluded a considerable quantity of land which by the form of the plat was represented to have been included; that a considerable error has crept into the survey, and that the said Arthur Robins promised to adjust the matter in an equitable manner, but before this was done fell into a pulmonary consumption and died, having first made his will dated 13 Nov. 1802, and devised the lands which he had derived from his father to be rented until the end of the year 1809, and after that period devised the same in several parts by certain metes and bounds to his four nephews, Arthur, Isaac, John & Bowdoin Robins, infant sons of his brother Thomas Robins, in fee, and appointed the said Thomas & Carvey Dunton executors of his said will, who also decline to enter into any arrangement whatsoever relative to the said premises &c. Dec. Court, 1808 - p. 90

Depositions in the above suit - John Sturgis, age 63 or thereabouts - p. 104

Anne Sturgis, age 58 or thereabouts - p. 105

Molly Groten
vs. - Suit for recovery of land.
Peggy Edwards, infant.

That Richard Wells of this county, was in his lifetime and at the time of his death seized in his demesne as of fee in a tract of land situate in this parish of St. George and county aforesaid, near the cross roads, containing 25 acres; the said Richard Wells departed this life intestate in the year 1790 leaving issue Elizabeth Wells his only child and heir at law, who entered upon the said land. The said Elizabeth departed this life on the 23 Dec. 1802, under age, intestate & without issue, and at the time of her death leaving no kindred on the part of her father, the nearest relatives on the part of her mother were your oratrix, Molly Groten, who was a sister of the whole blood to the mother of the said Elizabeth, and a cousin, viz: Peggy Edwards, a bastard child of a certain Esther Edwards, who was also a bastard born in the year 1773, who was a sister of the half blood to the said Elizabeth; on the death of the said Elizabeth to your oratrix was advised that she was entitled to the whole of the said tract of land as heir at law to the said Elizabeth Wells, and according entered and became seized thereof; afterwards, viz: in the year ---- an action of ejectment was commenced in the District Court of Accomack & Northampton in the name of the aforesaid Peggy Edwards vs. your oratrix for a recovery of a part of the said plantation, &c. 29 March 1814 - p. 117

George Layfield & Molly, his wife,
vs. - Suit for dower.
George P. Ewell, infant.

That a certain Daniel Melson of this county departed this life on the -- day of --- 1811 seized & possessed of 100 acres of land, and leaving your oratrix his widow, who has since intermarried with your orator, and one child, to-wit: Daniel Melson who is since dead, and one grandchild, George P. Ewell, the son of one Betty Ewell, who was the daughter of the first named Daniel Melson &c. 2 April 1813 - p. 120

Ann Custis, widow of Thomas,
vs. - Suit for dower.
Frances Y. Custis, Infant.

That a certain Thomas Custis, late of this County who was the husband of your oratrix, being seized in his demesne as of fee of and in a plantation and tract of land situate in this county upon the head of Deep Creek, containing 282 acres 3 rods & 28 perches, and also another tract adjoining the land of William P. Custis & others, and being so seized on the __ day of Jan. 1814, departed this life having first duly made his last will & testament in which he made no provision by way

103

of jointure or otherwise as to the right of Dower of your oratrix; that the said Thomas Custis left issue as only child, viz: Frances Y. Custis, the present defendant, to whom he left the said lands for life with remainder to Peter & Edmund Custis, in fee simple &c. 30 Nov. 1814 - p. 142

John Finney & Margaret, his wife, Catherine Finney, inf't., by John Finney, her
    father, & Euphemia Addison
vs. - Partition Suit.
George K. Bowman & David Bowman, infants.

That a certain David Bowman the elder was in his lifetime and at the time of his death seized in fee among other things of a certain lot of land in the Town of Onancock in this county, containing about 1/5 acre and being so seized departed this life intestate on the -- day of --- leaving six children, viz: David, James Oswald, William, Catharine, Margaret & Euphamia; that on the -- day of 1797 your orator was married to the said Catherine Bowman, who afterwards departed this life on the -- day of --- leaving your oratrix Catherine her only child; that on the --- day of -- your orator was married to his present wife, the said Margaret Bowman; that your oratrix Euphamia was on the-- day of --- married to William B. Addison, since deceased; that the said William Bowman departed this life in 1792 under age & without issue; that the said James Oswald Bowman departed this life intestate & without issue on the -- day of Oct. 1805, leaving your oratrixes & the said David Bowman living; that the said David Bowman the younger departed this life on the -- day of October, 1805, leaving two children, George Ker Bowman and David Bowman, and leaving a widow Isabella, now the wife of William Seymour; that previous to the death of the said David Bowman the younger, he made his last will & testament which is prayed to be taken as a part of this bill of complaint; your orator & oratrixes are advised that by the laws of the commonwealth directing the course of descents, upon the death of the aforesaid David Bowman the elder intestate, the aforesaid land descended to his six children aforesaid, David, James Oswald, William, Catherine, Margaret & Euphemia Bowman, 1/6 part to each; that upon the death of William his part descended to his brothers & sisters; that upon the death of Catherine Finney her 1/5 part descended to your oratrix Catherine, subject to a tenancy by the curtesy in your orator John Finney, her father; that upon the death of James Oswald Bowman intestate & without issue, his 1/5 part descended to his brother David Bowman & his sisters, your oratrixes Margaret & Euphemia, and his niece, your oratrix Catherine. In his will the said David Bowman the younger devised to his wife Isabella, now Isabella Seymour, certain property in lieu of dower, and made no disposition of his interest in the aforesaid lot, and which, therefore your orator and oratrixes are advised descended to his two infant children, George Ker Bowman & David Bowman &c. 30 May 1815 - p. 146

John M. Poulson
vs. - Ejectment Proceedings.
West.

That a certain James Dix, late of this county, was in his lifetime and at the time of his death, seized in his demesne as of fee in a certain plantation and tract of land near the head of Metompkin Creek, and being so seized departed this life on the -- day of --- 1800, under the age of 21 years, intestate & without issue, leaving your orator and a certain Erastus Poulson his nephews & heirs at law, they being the sons of Polly Poulson, formerly Polly Dix, who was a sister to the said James Dix; since the death of the said James Dix, on the -- day of --- 1806 the said Erastus Poulson conveyed to the said John West, late of this county, the whole of the said tract of land containing by estimation 150 acres, although he was only entitled to ½ of said tract, the other ½ of which belonged to your orator; on the 20 Sept. 1810, the said John West, having formerly entered upon and become possessed of the premises, departed this life intestate, leaving John & Harriet West, infants, who are prayed to be made defendants to this suit, his children and heirs at law (Patience West appointed their guardian to defend this suit); at the death of the said James Dix, Anne Duncan, formerly Ann Dix, who was the widow of John Dix, was entitled to ⅓ of the said plantation as her dower during her life, and on the -- day of June, 1812, the said Anne Duncan departed this life &c. 1 Dec. 1813 - p. 153

Edmunds & Wife &c.
vs. - Partition Suit.
Wyatt

That a certain William Wyatt, late of this County, was in his lifetime seized of a tract of land situate near the head of Machapungo Creek, containing 100 acres, and being so seized departed this life intestate about the year 1804; at the time of his death the said William Wyatt left the following children, viz: your oratrix Margaret, who was on the -- day of --- married to your orator, William Edmunds, your oratrix Sally, who on the -- day of Oct. 1813, was married to your orator John Wyatt, your orators Andrew Wyatt & Isma Wyatt and the said Polly Wyatt, &c. 30 Aug. 1814 - p. 158

John Tankard
vs. - In debt - Suit for sale of land.
Allen Kellam, &c.

That a certain Custis Kellam by deed dated 4 Dec. 1807 mortgaged to your orator a certain lot of ground at Bell Haven in this County, containing 1/5 acre; that some time after this, to-wit: on the -- day of March, 1811, the said Custis Kellam departed this life intestate leaving the following children, Allen, Eliza, George & Sarah, Katharine & Ann Kellam and Leah B. Kellam his widow, &c. 30 Nov. 1814 - p. 163

Savage

vs. - Partition Suit.

Savage.

That Richard Savage the younger, a son of Richard Savage the elder, dec., departed this life under age, intestate, possessed of certain land & slaves which were assigned & allotted to him on a division and partition of the land & slaves of the said Richard R. Savage; at the death of the said Richard Savage the younger, he left two brothers and a sister, viz: your orator John Savage, your oratrix Hetty West, formerly Hetty Savage, now the wife of Zorobabel West, and a certain Griffin Savage, all of whom are of the whole blood &c. 26 March 1816 - p. 173

Kellam & wife &c.

vs. - Suit for Dower & Partition.

Milby.

That a certain John Milby, late of this County, father of your oratrix Elizabeth & your orator John Milby, was in his lifetime and at the time of his death seized in fee of a certain tract of land situate near Pungoteague, containing 122 acres; that the said John Milby upon the -- day of --- 1804, departed this life intestate, leaving as his heirs your oratrix, who has since intermarried with your orator Hutchinson Kellam, your orator John Milby & the infant defendant William Milby, the only children of the said John Milby, dec., to whom the said land descended subject to the dower of William Addison & Nancy, his wife, in right of said wife, &c. 25 Sept. 1815 - p. 176

Conquest

vs. - Partition Suit.

Fields &c.

That a certain Jenifer Marshall, formerly of this county, was in his lifetime seized in fee simple of a tract of land near Horntown, & other lands, and being so seized departed this life intestate on the -- day of --- leaving your oratrix Euphemia and a certain Thomas Marshall his only children, to whom the said lands descended; that on the 20 Feb. 1808, the said Thomas Marshall by deed conveyed to a certain John Fields of this county, the undivided ½ of said tract of swamp land, and your oratrix and the said Thomas Marshall by deed dated 9 Oct. 1807, conveyed to the said Fields --- acres of arable land and 4 acres of swamp land; that on the -- day of -- 1811 your oratrix intermarried with your orator, William Conquest; that on the -- day of -- the said John Fields departed this life intestate leaving a widow Esther, and two children, John D. Fields & William B. Fields, to whom all the interest the said John Fields had acquired by said deeds descended, subject to a right of dower in the aforesaid Esther, his widow &c. 31 Aug. 1813 - p. 181

Wilkins & wife &c.

vs. - Partition Suit.

Andrews.

That a certain Robert Andrews late of this county was in his lifetime seized in fee simple of a certain tract of land situate on Pungoteague Creek in this County, and was also entitled to the reversion in two other tracts of land adjoining the same after the death of his mother, Anna Maria Andrews, who held three tracts for life, and being so seized the said Robert Andrews duly made & published his last will & testament on the 22 Oct. 1800, and died on the -- day of Feb. 1803, in the said will there is among other things the following clause: I give & bequeath to my three daughters Anna Maria Hall Andrews, Lucy Stratton Andrews and Elizabeth Stewart Andrews, all my lands, both those in my possession and those in my mother's possession, after the decease, to be equally divided with all my other land between them, Anna Maria Hall's part to be laid off where my mother now lives, Lucy Stratton's part to include the place where Levi Rayfield now lives, and Elizabeth Stewart's part to include my late dwelling plantation" That after the date of the said will, viz: on the 3 June, 1802, the said Robert Andrews mortgaged to Anna Maria Galt of this county 175 acres of said land, being part of the land held by the said Anna Maria Andrews during her life, and which said 175 acres was included in the tract where Levi Rayfield lived as mentioned in said will; that after the death of the said Robert Andrews a suit in chancery was instituted by the said Anna M. Galt against the heirs of the said Robert Andrews to foreclose the equity of redemption in said premises, and at the Nov. term of this Court in the year 1803 it was ordered that the sheriff sell the mortgaged premises, and accordingly the sheriff sold the said 175 acres at public sale and Henry Parker became the purchaser thereof; that the said Anna Maria Andrews departed this life on the -- day of --- 1815; that on the -- day of --- 1815 your orator John Wilkins, Jr., was married to your oratrix Anna Maria Hall, then Anna Maria Hall Andrews; your orator & oratrix are advised that notwithstanding the mortgage above mentioned and the subsequent sale of the premises, that the whole of the aforesaid lands of Robert Andrews, as well thereof which he was possessed in his lifetime as thereof which his mother was possessed, and which were not included in the mortgage & sale, are now subject to partition equally between the three daughters of Robert Andrews, taking care to give your oratrix Anna Maria Hall the late residence of her grandmother, Anna Maria Andrews; to the said Elizabeth Stewart Andrews the former residence of Robert Andrews, and to your oratrix Lucy Stratton Andrews an equal ⅓ in value in some other part of said land, excepting from said division 1 acre of land to be laid off adjoining the family burying ground where Anna Maria Andrews lived, which acre by a codicil to the will of the said Robert Andrews is reserved for a family burying ground &c. 31 Aug. 1815 - p. 204

Fletcher

vs. - In Debt. - Suit for sale of land

Milburn

That William Milburn dec., on the 29 Jan. 1816, executed a deed of mortgage to secure payment of $2,048. due your complainant, Thomas Fletcher; that the said William Milburn died on the -- day of Feb. 1816, without having paid the said sum, leaving Nancy Milburn his widow and Deborah Milburn an infant daughter his only child &c. -- July 1816, p. 214

Parks, &c.

vs. - Partition Suit.

Hickman

That a certain Charles Parks formerly of this county being in his lifetime and at the time of his death seized in his own right of a tract of land containing 22 acres, and being so seized on the 3 April 1792 made and published his last will and testament, and devised the said 22 acres to be sold and the proceeds divided between his two daughters, your oratrix, Peggy Parks & Betty Parks, when they should arrive to lawful age; that the said Betty Parks sometime after married with a certain Arthur Hickman, and sometime after, to-wit: on the -- day of Sept. 1803, departed this life an infant, intestate and leaving issue James Hickman, to whom the said Betty's moiety of the said 22 acres descended; that sometime after this, to-wit: on the -- day of --- 1811, your oratrix sold her undivided part of said land to the said James Fiddeman, so that the said James Fiddeman and the said James Hickman are now tenants in common &c. 31 March 1812.

William Justice, Jr., Samuel Justice, William White & Nancy, his wife, Rachel Miles, Obed Adams & Anna, his wife, Robert P. Broadwater & Sally, his wife, Amey Rowley and Richard Nock

vs. - Partition Suit.

Polly, Anna & Tabitha Justice, infants.

That a certain Richard Justice late of the County of Accomack was at the time of his death seized & possessed of a very considerable real and personal estate; that previous to the death of the said Richard Justice, which happened in the year -- he duly made and published his last will and testament, and among other things devised to his son Ralph Justice his lands in the woods called the Quarters, containing 150 acres; that the said Richard Justice departed this life shortly after the date of the said will leaving the same in his desk and without having altered or revoked the same; that a few days after the death of the said Richard Justice, Thomas Justice, one of his sons to whom no part of the estate of the said Richard Justice was devised, obtained possession of the said will and destroyed it; that shortly after the said Thomas Justice and Benjamin Nock, who had married Rachel Justice, one of the children of the said Richard, to whom also no part of the estate of the said Richard was devised, employed counsel and obtained a writ of partition against your orators, William & Samuel Justice, who are sons of the said Richard Justice, your orator Nancy White who is a daughter of the said Richard Justice, and the said Ralph Justice, all of whom were infants and undefended by counsel; that in the execution of the said writ a part of said Quarter plantation which had been devised to the said Ralph Justice, was allotted to the said Benjamin Nock in right of his wife, another part thereof allotted to your orator, Samuel Justice, and another part to your oratrix Nancy White, then Nancy Justice; that in the year ---- a suit was instituted by your orator William Justice in the Superior Court of Chancery for the Williamsburg District against all the heirs and representatives of the said Richard Justice, setting forth the circumstances above mentioned, and praying the Court to establish the said will in full force; that after various proceedings in said suit, a decree was rendered by said Court in the year 1813, fully establishing the said will as set forth in the bill of complaint; that Ralph Justice departed this life in the year 180- aged upwards of 21 years, intestate and without issue; that at the death of the said Ralph Justice he left living your orators William & Samuel, his brothers, and your oratrix Nancy White his sister, all of the whole blood, your oratrix Rachel Miles, his mother (she having married a certain Roger Miles who is since dead), your orator and oratrixes Richard Nock, Anna Adams, Amey Rowley and Sally Broadwater, all of whom are the children of Rachel Nock, now dec., who was a sister of the half blood to the said Ralph Justice, and Polly, Anna and Tabitha Justice who are children of Thomas Justice dec., his brother of the whole blood; your orators & oratrixes are advised that on the death of the said Ralph Justice the aforesaid Quarter plantation which was devised to him by his father, Richard Justice, descended to his aforesaid heirs in the same manner as if the said will had not been destroyed, and that the same is now subject to partition in the following manner, viz: To your orators Samuel & William Justice & your oratrixes Nancy White & Rachel Miles each a whole share thereof, being 2/11; to your orator Richard Nock and your oratrixes Anna Adams, Sally Broadwater & Amey Rowley, equally to be divided between them, a half share thereof, being 1/11, and to the said Polly, Anna & Tabitha Justice equally to be divided between them a whole share thereof, being the remaining 2/11 &c. 27 Nov. 1816 - p. 230

Copes & wife &c.
vs. - Partition Suit.
Coleburn
    That a certain James Coleburn late of this County was in his lifetime and at the time of his death seized in fee of a tract of land situate on the South side of Folly Creek in said county, containing 398 acres, and being so seized about the year 1795 departed this life intestate, leaving a widow & three children, viz: your oratrix Nancy (who hath since intermarried with your orator Henry S. Copes), your orator James M. Coleburn and the defendant Robert Coleburn, to which said children the said lands descended subject to the dower of the widow therein; that the said widow departed this life in the year 181- so that the lands now belong to be divided between the said three children &c. 26 Nov. 1816 - p. 233

Mason &c.

vs. - Suit for dower & division.

Sterling & wife.

That Jacob Mason, father to your complainants except Mary, to whom he was husband, being seized in his demesne as of fee in and to a tract of land situate near Guilford, in the Parish & county of Accomack, containing 73 acres, departed this life intestate on the -- day of March 1810, leaving the complainants Zadock Mason, Sally, who intermarried with Griffin Bishop, Susannah who intermarried with Elijah Bayly, his children, and of full age, also Nancy Mason, Betty Mason & Benney Mason infants & his children, and Mary Mason, his widow, and Lovey Sterling who intermarried with John Sterling also his daughter &c. 30 Aug. 1810, p. 235

Davis

vs. - Suit for dower.

Watts & wife &c.

That a certain David Davis, late of this county, was the husband of your oratrix, Mary Davis; that the said David Davis was in his lifetime and at the time of his death seized in fee of and in two tracts of land in the County of Accomack, one containing 201 acres, and the other 25 acres, and being so seized on the -- day of December 1815, departed this life intestate and without issue, leaving your oratrix his widow, who is entitled to dower; that the said David Davis left as his next of kin & heir Sarah Watts, his mother (the present wife of David Watts) and Elizabeth Abbott, his sister, to whom the aforesaid lands descended subject to the dower of your oratrix - Feb. 1817 - p. 245

Pitts, et ux. &c.

vs. - Suit for dower.

Hutchinson

That a certain Babel Hutchinson was in his lifetime seized & possessed of a plantation situate on Pungoteague Creek, containing 250 acres, & also certain negro slaves & personal estate, and being so seized on the 13 March 1816, duly made and published his last will and testament and died shortly thereafter; that in the said will the said Babel Hutchinson devised to his son Babel Hutchinson 125 acres of his lands adjoining the lands of Levi Hutchinson, he paying ½ the testator's debts; to his son Perry Hutchinson he devised the remainder of his lands, supposed to contain 123 acres, he paying ½ the testator's debts, and left all the remainder of his estate to be divided between the rest of his children, viz: Rachel, now the wife of your orator Southy Satchell, Elizabeth, now the wife of your orator William Pitts, and Bell Hutchinson, and if any child be born after the date of said will such child to share equally with the rest; that after that time the said Babel Hutchinson had another son born, viz: your orator Hanson Hutchinson; that in said will the said Babel Hutchinson made no provision of any kind for your oratrix, Ann, his wife &c. 2 April 1817 - p. 249

West & wife
vs. - Partition suit.
Tunnell &c.

That William Tunnell of the county of Accomack duly made & published his last will & testament on the 9 July, 1809, and departed this life, which said will was probated 26 Feb. 1810, and which contained the following clause: "Item I lend all my estate real and personal to my loving wife Elizabeth Tunnell during her natural life, and at her death I give and bequeath the same to be equally divided between my children Sarah Taylor, Elizabeth Drummond and Johnson Drummond Tunnell, and their heirs forever;" that the said Elizabeth Tunnell, widow of the said William Tunnell, is now dead; that the said William Tunnell left at his death 100 acres more or less, also a water grist mill and 30 acres of land adjoining said mill, slaves &c., which said land and slaves are now subject to be divided according to the will of the said William Tunnell; that the said Sally Tunnell has intermarried with the plaintiff Isaac West (both under age) &c. 27 Aug. 1817 - p. 260

Catharine Bayly
vs. - Partition Suit.
Zebedee Colony, &c.

That Isma Bayly late of this county being on the 6 Dec. 1805, seized in his demesne as of fee of and in a plantation situate on Occahannock Creek in this County, containing 237 acres, and on that day executed a deed conveying to his eldest daughter, viz: oratrix Catharine, and Margaret and Rosey Bayly, both of whom are since dead, in fee simple 125 acres of said land to include the buildings where the said Isma Bayly then lived; that on the -- day of --- 18-- the said Rosey was married to a certain Watson Colonna, and on the -- day of --- 18-- she died leaving an only child, namely Zebedee Colonna, who is still living; that on the -- day of Dec. 1816, the said Isma Bayly departed this life leaving 5 children and one grandchild, viz: your oratrix Catharine, the said Margaret Bayly and Egbert Rodney and Elizabeth Bayly and the said Zebedee Colonna; the said Egbert Rodney and Elizabeth Bayly being the children of the said Isma Bayly by his last wife; that on the -- day of Feb. 1817, the said Margaret Bayly departed this life unmarried and without issue, leaving no father or mother, but leaving your oratrix Catharine her sister of the whole blood; the said Zebedee Colonna the only child of her dec. sister Rosey Bayly of the whole blood, and the said Egbert Rodney & Elizabeth Bayly her brother & sister of the half blood &c. 1 April 1817 - p. 266

Dolby & wife &c.
vs. - Partition Suit.
Dolby.

That a certain Rachel Dolby late of this county departed this life intestate on the -- day of --- 1817, seized in fee in her own right of a certain plantation containing about 35 acres in Slutikill neck; that at the time of her death she left three children, viz: your orator Anna, the wife of your orator Samuel Dolby, your oratrix Susanna Dolby and your orator William Dolby - &c. 1 April 1818 - p. 270

Haley &c.
vs. - Partition Suit.
Haley

That William Haley late of this county who was the father of your orators, departed this life on the -- day of Nov. 1813, leaving at the time of his death 6 children, viz: William Haley, Leah Haley, Benjamin Haley, George Haley and your orators Jesse Haley & John Haley; that on the -- day of --- 1799 William Haley the elder duly made and published his last will and testament in which he devised to his son James Haley all his lands, but in case of his death without issue, then he gave the same to his son William, and died without having altered or revoked the said will; that at the date of the said will your orator's father had -- children living, and your orators were both born subsequent thereto; that your orators were not provided for by settlement, nor neither provided for nor disinherited in said will, in consequence whereof they are advised that they are entitled to the same portion of their father's estate as if he had died intestate &c. 26 May 1818 - p. 272

Thompson & wife &c.
vs. - Partition Suit.
Selby

That a certain James Broadwater the elder late of this county, was in his lifetime and at the time of his death seized in fee simple of a tract of land situate near Pocomoke in said County, containing 279 acres, and being so seized departed this life on the -- day of --- 1796, leaving five children, viz: James, George, Henry, Rachel & Nancy, and leaving James, George, Gilbert & --- his grandchildren, being the children of his deceased daughter Parker, the wife of Robert Parker; that after various disputes relative to wills said to have been left by the said James Broadwater, it was finally decided upon competent authority that the said James Broadwater died intestate; that previous to the death of the said James Broadwater his daughter Rachel was married to a certain Cutler, and after the death of the said James Broadwater, viz: in the year ----, the said Rachel departed this life intestate leaving your oratrixes Elizabeth Thompson, Margaret Hill and Sarah Benson her only children; that on the -- day of ---- your orator John Thompson was married to your oratrix Elizabeth Thompson, then Elizabeth Cutler, and on the -- day of ---- your orator Shadrack Hill was married to your oratrix Margaret, then Margaret Cutler, and on the -- day of --- your orator Azariah Benson was married to your oratrix Sarah, then Sarah Cutler; that the aforesaid Nancy Broadwater afterwards was married on the -- day of -- to a certain John Finney, since deceased; that the said Nancy Finney at her death on the -- day of --- left two children, viz: your oratrix Elizabeth U. Lewis and William Finney, and the said William Finney died on the -- day of --- under age and intestate and without issue, leaving your oratrix Elizabeth U. Lewis his sister living; that on the -- day of --- 1813, your orator

Stephen I. Lewis was married to your oratrix Elizabeth U. Lewis, then Elizabeth U. Finney; that the aforesaid Gilbert Parker died intestate and without issue, leaving his brothers James & George and his sisters Truit & Milburn living; that the said George Parker departed this life intestate on the -- day of--- leaving your infant orator and oratrix, George & Elizabeth, his only children; that the said George Broadwater departed this life on the -- day of -- having first made and published his last will & testament and devised all his interest in the said land to his brother Henry; that on the -- day of --- the said Henry Broadwater conveyed his interest in said lands to John Finney and others as trustees for certain purposes, and shortly thereafter the said Henry Broadwater and all the trustees in said deed departed this life; that it was decreed by this Court that the executors of the said John Finney, surviving trustee, sell the interest of the said Henry Broadwater in the said land, at which sale your orator Rowland E. Beavans became the purchaser thereof; that on the -- day of -- the aforesaid ---- Parker was married to a certain ---- Truet, and on the -- day of ---- the --- Parker was married to a certain Gilbert Milburn; that on the -- day of --- the aforesaid James Broadwater the younger conveyed his interest in said land to a certain William Selby of this county, and on the -- day of the said James Parker conveyed all his interest in said land to a certain William Selby, and on the -- day of --- the said William Truit and his wife conveyed their interest in said land to the said William Selby, and on the -- day of --- the said Gilbert Milburn and his wife conveyed their interest in said land to the said William Selby; that after the death of the said John Finney his widow, Nancy, married the aforesaid Rowland E. Beavans and died without leaving any issue by him &c. -- May 1816 - p. 275

Burton.
vs. - Partition Suit.
Burton.
That John Burton of the County of Accomack departed this life on the 1 day of Oct. 1817, intestate leaving the plaintiffs Margaret, Polly, Tabitha and John B. Burton his daughters and son, and also the plaintiff John William Burton his grandson, being the son of George W. Burton, dec., who was the son of the said John Burton dec., and also the defendant William W. Burton the heir at law of the said John Burton, dec.; that the said John Burton left a considerable estate, real and personal, the real estate consisting of the plantation whereon he lived near Metompkin, containing 400 acres, and the plantation at the head of Metompkin Bay containing 150 acres, another tract of land near where Gargaphia Church stood containing 82 acres, a tract in Musongoes containing 100 acres and a great water mill at the head of Assawoman Creek and a piece of land containing 25 acres near the said mill &c. 20 Dec. 1818 - p. 280

Garrison &c.

vs. - Partition Suit.

Garrison &c.

That a certain John Garrison late of this county being in his life seized in fee of and in two tracts of land situate in the county aforesaid, containing 370 acres, and being so seized on the -- day of --- 1809 made and published his last will and testament & devised to your orator John W. Garrison 130 acres of land, and 240 acres of land being in two tracts to be divided between his four daughters, Peggy, Elizabeth, Charlotte & Maria Garrison; that the said 130 acres have been laid off and assigned to your orator John; That Maria, one of the aforesaid devisees, departed this life on the -- day of --- 1810 intestate and without issue, leaving her next of heirs the following brothers & sisters on the part of her father, viz: your orators John & Samuel Garrison and Caty, then wife of your orator William Garrison, of the half blood, and Peggy, Elizabeth & Charlotte, sisters of the whole blood, to all of whom the said ¼ of the said Maria in the said 240 acres of land descended; that Caty, the wife of your orator William, departed this life in October 1817, leaving five children, to-wit: William, Sally, Margaret, Smith & Elizabeth Garrison, to whom her said 1/9 of said 240 acres descended equally, subject to the right of your orator William as tenant by curtesy; that your orator John bought of your orator Samuel his 1/9 of ¼ of said lands, so that the said 240 acres of land remains now to be divided as follows: To Peggy, Elizabeth & Charlotte each by virtue of the will ¼, and by descent from Maria 2/9 of ¼; to John W. Garrison 1/9 of ¼ by purchase from Samuel Garrison, and to William, Sally, Margaret, Smith & Elizabeth, children of Caty, 1/9 of ¼ subject to the right of your orator William as tenant by curtesy &c. 1 April 1818 - p. 285

Watson.

vs. - Partition Suit.

Hickman, &c.

That a certain John Hickman the elder late of this county, in his lifetime being seized in fee of a certain tract of land situate on Metompkin, containing 80 acres, made and published his last will & testament, and afterwards departed this life, viz: on the -- day of --- 1813, having devised the said plantation to his widow Peggy during her natural life and after her death to his son John Hickman in fee simple upon his paying his brothers & sisters certain sums; that the said John Hickman the younger departed this life at the same time with his father, John Hickman the elder, both of them being knocked overboard at the same time and drowned in a Gale of wind in the Delaware Bay, the said John Hickman the younger being at that time an infant under the age of 21 years, and leaving neither a widow nor children; that your orators are advised that by the laws of the Commonwealth the aforesaid plantation descended to all the children of the said John Hickman the elder, who were also brother & sisters of the whole blood to said John Hickman the younger, viz: Jesse, George, Nancy, Peggy, Ayres & Maria Hickman, subject to the life estate of the said Peggy Hickman, the widow; that on the -- day of --- the said Jesse Hickman, conveyed to your orator James Watson all his interest in said land; that the said Peggy Hickman, widow of the said John Hickman the elder, departed this life on the -- day of April 1815 &c. 31 May 1815 - p. 292

Kelly
vs. - Partition Suit.
Kelly.

That a certain Charles Kelly late of the County of Accomack departed this life intestate about the year 1798, leaving four children, viz: James, Esther, Anne & Susanna, and leaving his wife enscient of a child who was afterwards born and named Charles; that the said Charles Kelly the elder at the time of his death was seized in fee simple of a tract of land containing 25 acres situate near the head of Watchapreague Creek; that on the 26 Nov. 1816, James Kelly conveyed to your orator Weskit Kelly his interest in said tract of land, and the said Anne Kelly on the -- day of --- 1813, conveyed her right to the said land to your orator, and William Barrcroft and Susanna, his wife, who is the said Susanna Kelly, conveyed their interest in said land to your orator by deed dated -- 1817 &c. 22 Feb. 1819 - p. 296

Wharton &c.
vs. - Partition Suit.
Wharton.

That James Wharton the elder, late of this county, departed this life intestate on or about the -- day of -- 1792, leaving six children, viz: your orator William, your oratrix Nancy, now the wife of James Edmunds, and John, Elizabeth, Charles & James Wharton; that at the time of his death the said James Wharton was seized in his demesne as of fee in a tract of land containing 65 acres; that on the -- day of --- the aforesaid Charles conveyed his interest in said land to your orator William Wharton and to the aforesaid John Wharton; that on the -- day of -- the aforesaid Elizabeth Wharton conveyed her interest in said land to a certain Susanna Wharton; and on the -- day of -- James Wharton the younger conveyed his interest in said land to the said Susanna Wharton; that the said Susanna Wharton departed this life on the -- day of Oct. 1813, being seized of said land and published her last will & testament in which she devised to your orator William Wharton all the lands purchased of the said Betsy & James Wharton - 1 Dec. 1818 - p. 305

Marshall & wife &c.
vs. - Partition Suit.
Evans &c.

That Levin Evans the elder, late of this County, was in his lifetime and at the time of his death seized in fee simple of a tract of land situate near the head of Jenkins Creek, containing 150 acres; that the said Levin Evans on the 24 June 1814, duly made and published his last will and testament in which he devised his whole estate to his wife Sarah Evans during her natural life or widowhood, and after her decease or marrige while estate to be divided between his four children, that the said Levin Evans departed this life on the -- day of Feb. 1815, and left four children, viz: your oratrix Mahala, now the wife of Shadrack D. Marshall, & your orators Levin, John & James Evans &c. 1 Dec. 1818 - p. 309

Ewell
vs. - Partition Suit.
Taylor
    That a certain Teackle Taylor of this County departed this life intestate on the -- day of --- 18-- leaving four children, viz: Henry, James, Hetty & Samuel Taylor; that the said Teackle Taylor at the time of his death was seized in fee simple of a plantation situate near the need of Chincoteague containing 59 acres; that Henry & James Taylor conveyed their interest in said land to William L. Lucas and the said William L. Lucas conveyed his said interest to your orator, William Ewell &c. 1 Dec. 1818 - p. 312

Crippin
vs. - Partition Suit.
Dillastatius
    That a certain Samuel Crippin late of this county, was in his lifetime and at the time of his death seized as of fee in a lot of 2 acres of land, and being so seized departed this life intestate on the -- day of Jan. 1818, without issue, leaving as his next of kin and heirs at law your oratrix Sally Crippen, the only issue of Thomas Crippin, dec., brother of the half blood & Nancy Dillastatius, formerly Nancy Russell, Sarah, John, Robert & Samuel Russell, children of Esther Russell, dec., sister of the whole blood, and Narcissa & John Crippin, the only issue of Savage Crippin, dec., brother of the whole blood, to all of whom the said land descended &c. 1 April 1818 - p. 319

Outten
vs. - Partition Suit.
Wharton
    That a certain Jacob Outten of this County, died intestate about the year 1806, leaving your orator Nathaniel Outten, your oratrix Nancy Taylor, formerly Nancy Outten, wife of George Taylor, and Polly Outten, who is now dead; that the said Jacob Outten at the time of his death was seized of a tract of land containing 200 acres, which descended to his said three children: that the said Polly Outten since the death of her father sold all her interest in said land to a certain John Wharton of this County, and after the death of the said Wharton the said land descended to his widow Elizabeth Wharton during her life, remainder to Thomas T. Taylor, who are prayed to be made defendants to this suit &c. 1 Dec. 1818 - p. 322

White & wife &c.

vs. - Suit for dower & division.

Snead &c.

That a certain Tully Snead late of this county, departed this life on the __ day of April, 1811, having first duly made and published his last will & testament, in which there is the following clause; "Item. I desire that the whole of my estate not hereinbefore disposed of after payment of my debts, should be equally divided between my son Lewis Snead and my daughters Tabitha and Margaret Snead" the said residuary clause being a lot in the town of Onancock containing ½ acre, negroes &c. That your oratrix Rosey, formerly the wife of Tully Snead, and now the wife of Elijah A. White, and the said Tully having made for your oratrix no provision in lieu of her dower in said lot; that your oratrix Tabitha, now the wife of James Stewart, is the same Tabitha Snead mentioned in the will of said Tully Snead &c. 31 March 1819 - p. 341

Rodgers &c.

vs. - Suit for division.

Rodgers.

That a certain Levi Rodgers was on the 12 day of March, 1818, seized and possessed in the fee simple of a large real and personal estate, and being so seized on that day duly made and published his last will and testament in which he bequeathed & devised his said estate among his widow and children; that the said Levi Rodgers departed this life on the -- day of --- 1819; that subsequent to the date of the said will, viz: 28 Dec. 1818, the said Levi Rodgers purchased of a certain George Turner & Esther, his wife, a certain tract of land containing 24 acres, situate in Slutkill Neck; that the said Levi Rodgers made no disposition of the said land either in his will or otherwise, and in consideration of which your orator and oratrixes are advised that the said Levi Rodgers shall be considered as having died intestate as to the said 24 acres, and that the same shall descend and pass to all his children subject to the dower of Euphemia Rodgers as his widow; that at the time of the death of the said Levi Rodgers he left six children, viz: your oratrix Elizabeth P., who has been married to your orator James Boggs since the death of the said Levi Rodgers; Raymond Rodgers; Harriet T.; Lucy; Ann and Jane M. Rodgers - 30 Nov. 1819 - p. 347. (Euphemia Rodgers, widow of Levi Rodgers, married James Eichelberger before 17 Jan. 1820 - p. 349)

Parker

vs. - Partition Suit.

Parker.

That your orator William O. Parker and a certain Henry Parker, late of this County, on the 17 Aug. 1810, purchased of Zorobabel Kellam and Bridget, his wife, a certain tract of land situate near Pungoteague, containing 137 ½ acres; that on the 13 day of August, 1813, the aforesaid Henry Parker conveyed to Henry and William Parker 11 acres and 25 perches of land, being part of the land purchased by the said Henry Parker from Samuel Ross and wife, and adjoining Bull Branch;

that immediately after the execution of the said deed your orator and the said Henry Parker entered upon the said lands; that on the 19 March 1818, the said Henry Parker conveyed to your orator all his right to a certain part of the land purchased as aforesaid by your orator and himself from Kellam and wife, supposed to contain 5 acres; that previous to the death of the said Henry Parker, viz: on the 17 Oct. 1818, the said Henry Parker duly made and published his last will and testament in which he bequeathed to his daughter Sarah Parker ½ of the water grist mill purchased of William Seymour and half the land purchased by my brother William and myself from Xorobabel Kellam and wife, and in a subsequent clause devised to his daughter Sally one half of the land sold to Henry & William Parker, containing about 11 ½ acres, being part of the land purchased of Ross & wife; that the said Henry Parker departed this life on the -- day of Dec. 1818 &c. 1 Sept. 1819 - p. 354

Wilkins
vs. - Partition Suit.
Wilkins &c.

That John Wilkins, father to your complainant, John C. Wilkins, departed this life on the -- day of --- 1818 intestate, leaving your complainant and Harriet Wilkins, Susan Wilkins, Eliza Wilkins, George Wilkins and James Wilkins, infants and Thomas Wilkins & Shepherd Wilkins his only children and heirs at law; that at the death of the said John Wilkins he was seized of the tracts of land nearly adjoining each other at the head of Cradock Creek in the county of Accomack & parish of St. George, to which said land your complainant and the infant children of the said John Wilkins and the said Thomas & Sheppard [sic] Wilkins are entitled to equal shares; your complainant further shows that he purchased by deeds duly recorded the shares of the said Thomas and Sheppard [sic] Wilkins to the said tract of land &c. 30 Nov. 1819 - p. 363

Floyd & wife
vs. - Partition Suit.
Stewart.

That a certain Levin C. Stewart late of this County on the 24 Dec. 1816, duly made and published his last will and testament in which among other things was the following clause; After payment of all my just debts I give and bequeath my whole estate real and personal, of every kind, nature and description to my dearly beloved wife Maria and my daughter Alice Ann Stewart, equally to be divided between them in fee simple; and the said Levin Stewart departed this life shortly thereafter leaving the said will in full force, which was duly proved 27 Jan. 1817; That among the estate which passed under the said devise of his will there is a tract of land situate on the head of Watchaprigue in said county, containing 180 acres; that your oratorix is the same Maria Stewart mentioned in the aforesaid will, she having been married to your orator George Floyd, &c. 30 Nov. 1819 - p. 366

Kellam

vs. - Suit for dower & division.

Kellam &c.

That a certain George Kellam late of this county, departed this life intestate on the -- day of --- 1816, seized in fee simple of a plantation containing 350 acres, situate in Ocahannock Creek, leaving a widow, your oratrix Adah Kellam, and seven children, to-wit: your orator Shepherd and your oratrix Elizabeth, and Stockley, Hutton, Nancy, George & John Kellam; that the said tract of land descended to all his aforesaid children subject to the dower of your oratrix Adah therein, &c. 31 March 1819 - p. 370

Justice &c.

vs. - Suit for sale & division.

Justice &c.

That Thomas Justice departed this life on the -- day of --- intestate, leaving Lovey Justice, Peggy Justice, infant children, & Elizabeth Justice and Sally Justice his only children & heirs; that the said Thomas Justice died seized of 150 acres of land, principally marsh, lying on little Back Creek in the Parish of Accomack, which descended to the aforesaid children &c. 30 Nov. 1819 - p. 374

Edwards, et ux, &c.

vs. - Partition Suit.

Willitt &c.

That a certain George Willett [sic] late of this county departed this life on the 4 day of March, 1813, leaving a will dated 21 Jan. 1813, & leaving a widow Nancy Willett, now the wife of the said John B. Edwards, and the following children, to-wit: Elizabeth, Isaac, James, Edward, Sarah & George and no other children; that since the death of the said George Willett, to-wit: on the 10 May 1817, Edward, one of the children of the said George Willett, departed this life an infant & intestate; since the death of the said George Willett, to-wit: on the 15 day of June in the year 1817, your oratrix Nancy Willett intermarried with the said John B. Edwards; that the said George Willett directed his land on Metompkin to be divided equally between his said children; that on the 6 Sept. 1819, the said Isaac Willett, child of the said George Willett, dec., conveyed all his interest in said land to the said John S. Bundick; that on the 16 May, 1819, your oratrix Elizabeth intermarried with your orator William Lumboard; that at the time of his death the said George Willett was seized of a tract of land on Metompkin containing 50 acres which was directed by the said George Willett to be divided as follows; ⅓ to the said Nancy to be held by her and her husband John B. Edwards as dower during her life, the balance to be divided between the said John S. Bundick who purchased of said Isaac Willett, and William Lumbord [sic] and Elizabeth, his wife, and said James[,] Sally and George Willett &c. 2 June 1820 - p. 376

Baker &c.

vs. - Suit for sale and division.

Baker

That a certain Daniel Baker late of this county departed this life intestate sometime in the year 1819, leaving your oratrix Margaret his widow and two infant children, viz: your orator Charles Baker and Savage Baker, who were his only children; that the said Daniel Baker at the time of his death was seized in fee of a tract of land situate near Gargathy containing 13 acres which descended to the said Charles and Savage Baker, subject to the dower of the said Margaret, &c. - 30 May 1820 - p. 386

Scarburgh

vs. - Partition Suit &c.

Scarburgh

That a certain Americus Scarburgh late of this county, father of your orator Americus Scarburgh, an infant, being in his lifetime seized in fee of a tract of land situate in this county, and being so seized on the 24 March 1818, duly made and published his last will and testament, which was probated on the 27 April 1818, to which said will the testator in the first clause manifested his intention to devise to your orator 215 acres of land, part of the aforesaid tract, subject to the dower of his wife therein, viz: in said 215 acres; that by another clause in said will he devised to his two grandsons, Samuel and John Scarburgh, infants, (Sabra P. Scarburgh their guardian) 300 acres on the west side of his plantation, and in the succeeding clause of said will devised the remainder of his land containing 215 acres to your orator; that by a survey made of said tract of land since the death of the said testator, it is found to contain only 459 acres instead of 515 acres as supposed by the testator; your orator is informed that it was the intention of the said testator that the dividing line between your orator and his said grandsons should start at the head of a gut marked on the said plat &c., and that his grandsons should have the part lying to the westermost of said line, and that your orator should have the part lying to the westward thereof &c. 31 Aug. 1820 - p. 389

Kellam &c.

vs. - Suit for sale & division.

Kellam

That a certain Sacker Kellam late of this county was on the 24 Feb. 1795 seized of a tract of land situate in the White Marsh in the county aforesaid, containing 40 acres, and being so seized to that day duly made and published his last will and testament in which he devised to his wife Charity Kellam the said tract of land during her life or widowhood, with remainder to his sons Smith & Revell Kellam, to be divided equally between them, which said will was proved 29 June 1795; that the said Revell Kellam mentioned in said will departed this life intestate in the year 1817 leaving three children, viz: your oratrixes Sarah and

Nancy Kellam, infants, and a certain Revell Kellam; that the said Charity Kellam departed this life in the year 1819 &c. 29 Nov. 1820 - p. 395

Wright &c.
vs. - Partition Suit.
Wright
That a certain George Wright late of this county departed this life intestate on the __ day of __ 1820, leaving five children, viz: Your orator James Wright , your oratrixes Loves & Henrietta & Elizabeth Northam, now wife of James Northam, and a certain Sally Wright; That the said George at the time of his death was seized in fee of four tracts of land viz: one tract where he resided containing 160 acres, part of which he purchased of George Middleton, and part was devised to him by his father; another tract containing 38 acres; another tract containing 140 acres, and another tract containing 15 acres; that the said lands descended to the said children as aforesaid &c. 25 Sept. 1820 - p. 399

Showard & wife
vs. - Suit for recovery of land.
Singleton.
Came Thomas Showard & Elizabeth, his wife, formerly Elizabeth Boniwell, & represented that previous to the late marriage of your orator & oratrix, in the month of April, 1815, viz: in the month of --- 1814, your oratrix was seized in her own right of a parcel of land situate in the Parish of St. George in Accomack County containing 7 acres, and being so seized a certain Samuel Singleton of this County applied to your oratrix to purchase a certain part of said land supposed to contain one or 1 ½ acres; that your oratrix finally consented to sell the said land; that the said 1 ½ acres has not been paid for, and that it has since been found that the deed called for the whole of the 7 acres &c. - --- June 1817 - p. 403

Tunnell
vs. - Partition Suit.
Watson.
That Elizabeth Tunnell, John W. Watson & Betsy Selby, his wife, together & undivided hold 8 acres of land in the parish of Accomack on Matompkin Creek whereof Selby Simpson late of the said county devised to the said Elizabeth, his widow, now Elizabeth Tunnell, and Elizabeth Simpson, now Elizabeth Watson, and afterwards the said Selby had a child born of the said Elizabeth, his widow, which said child has departed this life an infant, unmarried and without issue, by reason whereof the said Elizabeth is entitled to ⅓ of the said land and the said John W. Watson and Elizabeth are entitled to ⅔ &c. 12 March 1812 - p. 413

Evans &c.

vs. - Partition Suit.

Evans

That a certain John K. Evans, late of the County of Accomack, was in his lifetime and at the time of his death seized of a piece of land in the County of Accomack, containing 80 acres, and being so seized departed this life on the -- day of --- 1815 intestate, leaving your oratrix Margaret Evans his widow and four children, viz: Elizabeth, Thomas, Ann & Margaret, to all of which said children the said land descended subject to the dower of your oratrix, Margaret &c. 30 Aug. 1820 - p. 418

Beach & wife &c.

vs. - Suit for sale & division.

Nock &c.

That a certain Solomon Nock, late of this county, departed this life intestate on the -- day of Feb. 1818, leaving the following children, viz: your oratrix Rosey, wife of your orator George Beach, formerly Rosey Nock; Thomas, Coleburn, Ann, John, Henry & Benjamin; that since the death of the said Solomon Nock, no-wit: on the 10 April 1820, the said John, one of the children of the said Solomon, departed this life intestate & without issue; at the death of the said Solomon he was seized in fee of a tract of land on Watchaprigue containing about 65 acres, slaves &c., which said land and slaves descended to the said children of the said Solomon Nock &c. 29 Nov. 1820 - p. 424

Small

vs. - Partition Suit.

Addison & wife.

That a certain Levi Small, late of this county, departed this life intestate on the 9 day of Feb. 1813, seized in fee of a tract of land situate in said county near Wallops road, containing 223 acres, with a grist mill attached; that the said Levi at the time of his death left two children, your orator Gillett Small and Anne Small who since the death of the said Levi Small has married a certain John Addison of this county; that the said land descended to your orator and his sister Anne &c. 1 May 1821 - p. 428

LAND CAUSES - 1821 to 1826

Custis

vs. - In Debt - Suit for sale of land.

Custis.

That on the __ day of Sept. 1818, your orator, John Custis, became security for a certain Thomas V. Custis, late of this County, to a certain William Seymour for the sum of $2500. payable in fie annual installments to commence on the 1 Jan. 1819, with interest from 1 Jan. 1818; that in order to indemnify your orator the said Thomas V. Custis & Margaret his wife by deed of mortgage dated Sept.

1818, conveyed to your orator a certain lot, together with the houses thereon, situate in the town of Onancock; that your orator has been compelled to pay the sum of $1663.95 as such security; that the said Thomas V. Custis departed this life on the -- day of --- 1821, intestate, leaving six infant children, to-wit: John Custis, Theodore W. Custis, Margaret A. Custis, Edwin Custis and Adeline Custis and Julius Custis; that the wife of the said Thomas V. Custis departed this life sometime previous; that one of the said children, to-wit: Julius, departed this life on the -- day of --- 1821; that since the death of the said Thomas and Margaret, his wife; your orator has frequently applied to the said children, heirs of the said Thomas V. Custis, for payment of the sum as aforesaid paid&c. 29 March 1821 - p. 23

Garrison &c.
vs. - Partition Suit.
Garrison &c.

That a certain Peggy Garrison late of this county, departed this life under the age of 21 years and without issue in the year 1821; that the said Peggy Garrison at the time of her death was possessed in her own right in fee simple of the undivided ⅓ of two tracts of land situate on the waters of the Matshapungo Creek in this county, containing by estimation together 220 acres; that the said lands belonged to the said Peggy Garrison and Elizabeth and Charlotte Garrison as tenants in common, the principal part of the land having been devised to them by their deceased father, John Garrison, and the residue having descended to them from their deceased sister, Maria Garrison; that the said Peggy Garrison at her death left as her next of kin and heirs at law two sisters of the whole blood, viz: the said Elizabeth & Charlotte Garrison, and two brothers of the half blood, John W. and Samuel Garrison, and also left two nephews and three nieces of the half blood, viz: your orators and oratrixes, William, Sally, Margaret Smith & Elizabeth Garrison who are the children of Caty Garrison, dec., who was a sister of the half blood to the said Peggy Garrison &c. 28 Nov. 1820 - p.31

Parker, Assignee,
vs. - In Debt - Suit for sale of land.
Custis &c.

That a certain George Custis & Susanna his wife, late of this county, being indebted to William Gillett & Co. in the sum of £59:19:3, in order to secure the payment of the same, and also other sums of money which they might thereafter become indebted, together with interest, costs &c., upon the 12 July, 1806, executed a deed of mortgage by which they conveyed to the said William Gillett & Co., a certain tract of land situate in the county aforesaid, containing 50 acres, to be held as security &c.; that the said William Gillett & Co., on the 15 Nov. 1804, assigned the same to your orator, Thomas Parker; that upon the -- day of --- the said Susanna Custis in whom the fee simple title of said land was, departed this life leaving the following children, William, John & Sally R. Custis to whom the said land descended subject to the aforesaid claim of your orator, and also subject to the life estate of the said George Custis &c. 27 March 1822 - p. 53

Clayton & wife &c.
vs. - Partition Suit.
Bagwell
    That a certain Charles Bagwell the elder formerly of this county was in his lifetime and at the time of his death seized in fee simple of a tract of land containing 700 acres with a grist & saw mill thereon, situate on Back Creek, and being so seized on the 25 Aug. 1792, duly made and published his last will and testament wherein among other things is the following clause: I give unto my son Charles Bagwell the use of the plantation I bought of James Arbuckle with my two mills during his natural life, and at his death to be equally divided amongst all his children. Which said will was proved 24 June 1793; that immediately after the death of the said Charles Bagwell the elder, his son Charles Bagwell entered upon and became possessed of this said tract of land and mills, and held possession thereof until his death, which happened on the -- day of May, 1819; that at the time of the death of the said last mentioned Charles Bagwell he left six children, viz: your orator & oratrixes Ann Kitson Clayton, wife of George Clayton, Laura Thornton, wife of James Thornton, Charles Bagwell and Sally Bagwell, and also Augustus Bagwell and Elvira Bagwell &c. 31 Aug. 1819 - p. 60

Floyd & wife &c.
vs. - Partition Suit.
Garrison &c.
    That a certain James Garrison late of this county, departed this life in the year 1820 seized of a large estate real and personal; that the said James Garrison at his death left four children, viz: Rachel, the wife of Elijah Floyd, Sally, the wife of John Smith & Ann J. Garrison and James Garrison, infants; that previous to the death of the said James Garrison, viz: on the 20 Aug. 1812, he duly made and published his last will & testament and bequeathed his estate to his four children aforesaid; that after the date of the said will the said James Garrison and Abel Garrison purchased of a certain Arthur Savage two tracts of land situate in this county, by deed dated 24 Nov. 1816; that at the partition of the said land between the said James & Abel, one tract containing 124 acres & the other containing 76 acres were assigned and allotted to the said James Garrison for his part thereof; that in his aforesaid will the said James Garrison made no disposition of the said lands &c. 29 March 1822 - p. 66

Allen &c.
vs. - Partition Suit.
Cropper's devisees
    That your oratrix, Tabitha Allen and your orator James McCollom, by Alexander McCollom, his next friend, that in the year 18-- your oratrix and a certain John Carlton and Peggy, his wife, brought an action of ejectment in the

Superior Court of Law for this County against a certain ---- to recover the one half of one undivided tract or parcel of land containing by estimation 300 acres, more or less, and upon the serving of the declaration in the said suit in ejectment upon the said --- a certain John Cropper entered himself as defendant in the said suit in the room of ----, and that thereupon the said John Cropper confessed the lease entry and ouster and agreed to insist upon the title only; that pending the said ejectment the said John Carlton absented himself beyond seas or elsewhere, and remained absent and unheard of for the space of several years, and being presumed to be dead the said Peggy Carlton intermarried with a certain Alexander McCollom and departed this life on the -- day of ---in the year 181-, during the pendancy of the said suit, leaving her husband the said Alexander McCollom and your orator James McCollom her only child, both of whom are now alive; that on the -- day of 18-- the said John Cropper departed this life, the said suit being pending and undetermined, and that the same was revived by scire facias on his devisees & representatives, and that at a Superior Court of Law held for the county of Accomack on the -- day of Oct. 1821 ---- - the said action of ejectment came on to be heard and a special verdict being found by a jury impanelled to try the same, the Judge of the said Superior Court on consideration of the law arising from facts found in the said special verdict found for the plaintiff ----- and that the plaintiffs recover of the said devisees & representatives of the said John Cropper one half of one messuage & plantation containing 300 acres; that the said John Cropper on the 10 Jan. 1821, duly made and published his last will and testament which was proved 29 Jan. 1821, and that Richard D. Bayly, John G. Joynes & Thomas R. Joynes were appointed executors to the said will; that among other things the said John Cropper devised in his said will that his executors should sell his whole estate not before disposed of, including his military lands in the States of Kentucky and Ohio, and after the payment of debts the proceeds to be divided between all his children living at his death, and the descendants of such as may be dead, (except my daughter Margaret Pettitt Bayly and her descendants) "in case my wife Catherine should refuse to accept the provision made for her and should claim her legal share of my estate, then whole estate to be sold and proceeds to be divided in the same manner as directed in the second clause of my will"; that the said John Cropper left at the time of his death the following children, to-wit: Ann Cropper, Eliz^a Cropper, Catherine Cropper, John Washington Cropper, Thomas B. Cropper, Covington H. Cropper and the following grandchildren: Margaret P. Wise, Henry A. Wise, and John C. Wise, children of Sally Wise, formerly Sally Cropper; Margaret Cropper, and daughter of the said John Cropper; and Catherine Cropper, the widow of the said John Cropper, all of whom are now alive; that the said Catherine, the widow, being unwilling to accept the provision made for in her husband's will renounced the same and has accepted a certain share of her husband's estate in lieu of dower therein; that the tract of land of which your orator and oratrix are entitled to one half by judgment of the Superior Court of Law for Accomack County was devised by a certain John Allen to his three sons, Stephen, Edmund & John Allen to be equally divided between them, and that your oratrix and Peggy, the mother of your orator, derived their title from the said Edmund Allen &c. 30 April 1822 - p. 72

Edwards &c.
vs. - Suit for Dower & division.
Badger &c.

That a certain John Edwards late of this county on the 4 Dec. 1799, was seized in fee simple of a tract of land near the White Marsh containing 60 acres, and being so seized duly made and published his last will and testament in which among other things he devised the land where he then lived to be equally divided between his two sons, David & John; that the said John Edwards departed this life on the -- day of Dec. 1800 seized and possessed as aforesaid leaving the said will in full force; that your orator John A. Edwards is the same John A. mentioned in the said will, and your oratrix Rosey Badger was formerly the wife of the said John Edwards, dec., she being now the widow of a certain William Badger, dec.; that after the death of the said John Edwards your orator & David Edwards entered upon and became seized of the said land and held possession of the same until the said David Edwards departed this life intestate on the -- day of January, 1819, being at the time of his death and for a number of years previous thereto non compos mentis, and being at his death aged about 24 years, that he left no widow nor children, but left his mother, your oratrix, your orator, his brother of the whole blood, and three sisters and one brother of the half blood, viz: Margaret, Robert, Susanna & Elizabeth Badger, who are children of your oratrix by her second husband, the aforesaid William Badger &c. 29 Jan. 1821 - p. 89

Lewis &c.
vs. - Suit for sale and division.
Lewis.

That a certain William Lewis departed this life intestate in the year 1819 leaving six children: your orators & oratrixes Nathaniel, Jane, Samuel & Meshack Lewis, infants, and Charles Lewis and William Lewis, who were his children by his deceased wife Esther Parker; that the said William Lewis at the time of his death was seized & possessed as tenant by the Curtesy of a tract of land containing 12 acres which land at the death of the said Esther Lewis descended to his aforesaid children subject to the right of the said William Lewis as tenant by the Curtesy &c. 29 May 1822 - p. 95

Ames & wife &c.
vs. - Suit for dower & division.
Hornsby

That a certain Edmund Hornsby late of this county departed this life intestate in the year 1805 seized in fee of a tract of land situate near Andua Creek, containing 100 acres; that at the time of his death the said Edmund left two children, viz: your oratrix Sally, now the wife of Thomas H. Ames, and a certain Elizabeth B. Hornsby, and also left a widow, your oratrix Elizabeth, now the wife of your orator Shadrack Ames; that the said land descended to the said Sally Ames and Elizabeth B. Hornsby subject to the dower of your oratrix Elizabeth Ames; That a certain William Hornsby departed this life intestate in the year 1806 and without issue, leaving as his next of kin your oratrix Sally and the said Elizabeth B. Hornsby; that the said William Hornsby at the time of his death was seized in fee of a tract of land containing 75 acres adjoining the aforesaid tract belonging to the said Edmund Hornsby &c. 30 July 1821 - p. 98

Ardis
vs. Suit for sale & division.
Ardis
That a certain James Ardis late of this county, departed this life on the -- day of Sept. 1818, intestate seized in fee of a tract of land containing 80 acres, and leaving the following children, to-wit: your orator & oratrixes, James Ardis, Sally Ardis & Betsy Ardis and Azariah, George, John, Margaret and Nancy Ardis, infants; that the said land descended to his said children equally &c. - 29 May 1822 - p. 110

Laws
vs. - Partition Suit.
Russell.
That a certain Robert Russell late of this county departed this life on the -- day of Oct. 1821; that previous to his death, viz: on the 12 Sept. 1821, the said Robert duly made and published his last will and testament and directed that there be an equal division of his property among his children except his son Henry; that among other property of which the said Robert was seized at the time of is death was two tracts of land, one situate near Chincoteague containing 220 acres, the other situate near Kegotank containing 250 acres, and a lot of 2 acres near Kegotank; that the said Robert Russell at the time of his death left the following children exclusive of his son Henry, viz: John C. Russell, Robert Russell, Sally Russell, Samuel Russell and Nancy Laws, then the wife of the said William Laws; that since the death of the said Robert Russell the said Nancy Laws has departed this life leaving your orator Robert Russell Laws her only child &c. 1 Oct. 1822 - p. 118

Powell & wife
vs. - Suit for dower & division.
Roberts &c.
That a certain William S. Roberts late of this county departed this life intestate on the __ day of Jan. 1816, leaving his widow Elizabeth, now the wife of the said Arthur R. Powell, and the following children, to-wit: Louis, Edwin, Elizabeth and Ann Roberts; that since the death of the said William S. Roberts, to-wit: on the 12 June, 1817, your oratrix, Elizabeth, intermarried with your orator Arthur R. Powell; that at the death of the said William S. Roberts he was seized in fee of a tract of land on Matchapungo containing 405 acres, also 100 acres

purchased of Arthur Savage, which land descended to the said children of the said William S. Roberts subject to the dower of your oratrix Elizabeth Powell &c. 29 Oct. 1821 - p. 122

Custis & wife
vs. - Partition Suit.
Rodgers &c.

That a certain Jacob Bird late of this county departed this life intestate on the -- day of --- 1813, leaving four children viz: your oratrix Malinda Custis, now the wife of William Custis, Jacob, Elizabeth & Ebern Bird, and also leaving a widow Polly, now the wife of a certain Samuel M. Madox; that the said Jacob Bird at the time of his death was seized in his own right in fee simple of two tracts of land situate near the New Church containing 200 acres and the other situate near the head of Onancock containing 110 acres, which tracts of land descended to his four children aforesaid subject to the dower of his said widow; that since the death of the said Jacob Bird his widow Polly has married a certain Samuel H. Maddox, who by deed dated ____ conveyed to a certain William T. Rodgers all the right of dower of said Polly in the aforesaid land &c. 1 June 1821 - p. 126

Revell& wife
vs. - Partition Suit.
Hopkins &c.

That a certain Susanna Armistead late of the county of Northampton departed this life intestate sometime in the year 181-, seized in her own right in fee simple of a plantation on the waters of Hungars Creek in said county, containing 350 acres and being also seized of one other plantation situate near Occahannock Creek in said County containing 500 acres; that at the time of the death of the said Susanna Armistead she left no children nor descendants of children living except your oratrixes Ann, now the wife of John B. Revell, and Susan Hopkins and your orator Charles and Elison Hopkins, all of whom now reside in this county, and were the children of Elizabeth Hopkins, dec., who was a daughter of the said Susanna Armistead; that the land above mentioned descended to your orators and oratrixes as grandchildren of the aforesaid Susanna; that a certain Maximilian Hopkins, late of the said County of Northampton departed this life intestate in the year 1818, being seized in his own right in fee simple of a tract of land in the said County of Northampton containing 160 acres, and adjoining the first named tract belonging to the said Susanna Armistead; that at the death of the said Maxamilian Hopkins he left four children, viz: your oratrixes Ann and Susan, your orator Charles and the aforesaid Elison Hopkins, the aforesaid Maximilian Hopkins having formerly been the husband of the said Elizabeth Hopkins; that at the death of the said Maximilian Hopkins the said land descended to his aforesaid children &c. 24 Sept. 1821 - p.131

Scarburgh
vs. - Suit for Dower.
Scarburgh &c.

That a certain William Scarburgh late of this county departed this life on the -- day of March 1821, seized in his own right in fee simple of a tract of land situate on Occahannock Creek in the said County, adjoining Americus Scarburth and others; that the said William H. Scarburgh at his death left your oratrix Elizabeth Maria Scarburgh his widow, and two children, viz: Elizabeth P. Scarburgh and Jane M. Scarburgh, infants; that the said William M. Scarburgh previous to his death duly made and published his last will and testament, but not having in said will made and disposition of is said land the same descended to his two aforesaid children; that the said William M. Scarburgh did not in his will or in any other manner made any provision for your oratrix in lieu of her dower in said lands, so that your oratrix, as she is advised, is entitled to one third of the said land during her life as her dower therein &c. 27 Nov. 1821 - p. 135

Boggs &c.
vs. - Suit for sale & division.
Boggs &c.

That a certain John Boggs late of this county departed this life intestate on the -- day of July 1822; seized in fee simple of a tract of land situate in Slutkiln Neck containing 140 acres, slaves &c., and also left the following children and grandchildren to whom the said land descended subject to the dower of Peggy Boggs, the widow of the said John Boggs, viz: your orators Elijah & James Boggs & your oratrixes Rachel, now the wife of William Rodgers & Catharine Moore who are the only surviving children of the said John Boggs, and your oratrix Elizabeth Custis, wife of William Custis, who is the only child of William Boggs, dec., who was a son of the said John Boggs, and your oratrixes Nancy Northam, wife of Custis Northam, Peggy Parker, wife of John Parker & William, Mary, Jane, Elizabeth, Lucy & Henry Boggs, all of whom are children of Arthur Boggs, dec., who was a son of the said John Boggs &c. 1 Oct. 1822 - p. 139

Wilkerson
vs. - Partition Suit.
Wilkerson

That a certain William Wilkerson the elder late of this county departed this life intestate on the -- day of --- 1818, seized in fee of a tract of land situate in this county, containing 5 acres; that the said William Wilkerson at his death left two children, viz: your orator William Wilkerson & a certain Solomon Wilkerson to whom the said land descended; that a certain Elizabeth Wilkerson, who was the widow of the said William Wilkerson, also departed this life intestate on the -- day of 1821, being at that time seized in her own right in fee simple of a tract of land containing 33 acres; that at her death the said Elizabeth left two children, your orator William Wilkerson & the said Solomon Wilkerson to whom the said land descended &c. 20 Oct. 1828 - p. 147

Merrill & wife
vs. - Partition Suit
Coleburn

That a certain Abel Coleman late of this county departed this life intestate in the year 1817, leaving 5 children, viz: your oratrix Elizabeth, now the wife of John Merrill, and Henrietta, John, William, Riley and James Coleburn; that the said Abel Coleburn at the time of his death was seized in fee of a tract of land located in the neighborhood of Jenkins Bridge, containing 165 acres, which land descended to his five children aforesaid; that the said Henrietta Coleburn departed this life an infant & without issue in the year 1819, and all her interest in said tract descended to her aforesaid brothers and sister &c. 27 Nov. 1821 - p. 150

Broadwater &c.
vs. Partition Suit.
Nock.

That a certain Caty Nock late of this county departed this life in the month of October, 1810, seized in her own right in fee simple of a tract of land situate in this county containing 53 acres, and one other tract of land containing 16 acres, also the moiety of a mills stream and mill seat at the head of Assawoman; that the said Caty Nock at the time of her death left seven children, viz: your oratrixes Tabitha, now the wife of Robert Broadwater, Mary, Elizabeth, Thomas, Joseph, Caty and Charles Nock, to whom the said land descended subject to the right of Benjamin Nock, her husband, as tenant by the curtesy; that the said Benjamin Nock departed this life in the year 1811; that the said Caty Nock & Charles Nock both departed this life in the year 1811 under age, intestate and without issue, so that the two tracts of land became subject to partition between the five remaining children of the said Caty Nock; that on the 31 Jan. 1817, the said Thomas Nock, conveyed his interest to said tracts to your orator Robert P. Broadwater, &c. 28 Jan. 1823- p. 153

Mathews &c.
vs. - Partition Suit.
Mathews.

That a certain John Mathews late of this county departed this life intestate sometime in or about the year 1804, seized in fee simple of a tract of land situate near Log Town in the county aforesaid, containing 200 acres & leaving four children, viz: your orators John R. Mathews & Thomas R. Mathews & Samuel & Joseph Mathews, infants, to whom the said land descended; that the said Joseph Mathews departed this life an infant, without issue in the year 1820, and his interest in said land descended to your orators & the said Samuel Mathews who are his next of kin & heirs at law &c. 26 Nov. 1822 - p. 158

Welburne &c.
vs. - Suit for sale and division.
Wallop &c.

That a certain Elizabeth Wallop, late the wife of a certain Skinner Wallop, Sr., departed this life on the -- day of --- 1792, the said Skinner and Elizabeth being seized in fee simple in right of said Elizabeth of and in a tract of land situate on Chincoteague Island containing 42 acres; that the said Elizabeth Wallop at the time of her death left six children, viz: John Wallop, William Wallop, George Wallop, Peggy Watts, then the wife of a certain David Watts, Ibbey Coard, then the wife of a certain John Coard & Polly Welburn, then the wife of a certain Drummond Welburn; that upon the death of the said Elizabeth Wallop the said land descended to all her aforesaid children subject to the right of the aforesaid Skinner Wallop, Sr. during his life as tenant by the curtesy; that the said Skinner Wallop departed this life sometime in the year 1816; that the aforesaid William Wallop departed this life subsequent to the death of the said Elizabeth Wallop intestate leaving four children, to whom his interest in the said land descended, viz: your oratrix Sally Welburn, wife of William Welburn, your oratrix Betsy Wallop and your orators William and Rosella Wallop; that the said Peggy Watts also departed this life subsequent to the death of the said Elizabeth Wallop leaving four children, viz: John Watts, David Watts, Jr., Nancy Drummond, the wife of a certain William R. Drummond, & Betsy Wishart, formerly the wife of a certain James Wichart, and the said Betty Wishart [sic] has since died leaving two children, viz: Joshua and David Wichart; that the said Ibbey, the wife of the said John Coard, has also died since the death of the said Elizabeth Wallop, leaving six children, viz: Arthur Coard, William Coard, your oratrix Elizabeth Fletcher, wife of Thomas Fletcher, Nancy Evans, the wife of a certain John Evans, Parker Coard and Hepsey Brittingham, formerly the wife of a certain John Brittingham, and the said Parker Coard is since dead leaving one child named Ibbey, and the said Hepsey Brittingham is also since dead leaving two children, Maria and William; that since the death of the said Elizabeth Wallop the aforesaid Polly Welburn has departed this life leaving four children, viz: Thomas, Mary, Skinner and John Welburn; that since the death of the said Elizabeth Wallop the aforesaid George Wallop has also departed this life leaving two children, viz: your orator Skinner Wallop and Mary Davis, formerly Mary Wallop; That since the death of the said Skinner Wallop, Sr., the aforesaid tract of land is subject to division into six parts, one of which shall be allotted to the aforesaid John Wallop, and one other share to the descendants of each of the aforesaid deceased children of the aforesaid Elizabeth Wallop, &c. 3 April 1823 - p. 161

Jester &c.
vs. - Suit for sale & division.
Jester.

That a certain John M. Jester of the county of Accomack was in his lifetime and at the time of his death seized in fee of a certain tract of land on Chincoteatgue Island containing 78 acres, and being so seized departed this life intestate on or about the -- day of 1821, leaving your orator James Jester, your oratrix Sarah, who intermarried with your orator William Wimbler, and Rachel Jester and Elijah Jester, Kendall Jester, Leah Jester and Anne Jester, his only children & heirs, all of whom are now alive &c. 30 Dec. 1822 - p. 171

Bundick & wife &c.
vs. - Partition Suit.
Hickman.

That a certain Richard Hickman late of this county departed this life intestate on the -- day of --- 1820, leaving his widow and the following children, to-wit: your oratrix Elizabeth, now the wife of George Bundick, your orator William, George & Zeporah Hickman infants; that since the death of the said Richard Hickman his widow who intermarried with a certain Charles Copes, has departed this life without any other children than the above; that at the death of the said Richard Hickman he was seized in fee of a tract of land on Metompkin containing 130 acres, and of another plantation lying on Wallops road containing about 80 acres; that the said land descended to his aforesaid four children &c. 30 March 1821 - p. 174

Mears & wife &c.
vs. - Suit for sale & division.
Chandler.

That a certain Nancy Bull late of this county departed this life intestate on the -- day of --- 1821 under age and without issue; at the death of the said Nancy Bull she was seized in fee simple of a parcel of land on Folly Creek containing 18 acres, and that the said land descended as follows: to your oratrix Bridget Mears, wife of William Mears, ¼; to your orators William & James Bull ¼ and to Bagwell Chandler & Mary Chandler, infant children of Mary Chandler, formerly Mary Bull, who departed this life on the -- day of --- 1818, and who was sister of said Nancy Bull, the other ¼ - 30 March 1821 - p. 184

Gladding
vs. - Suit for sale & division.
Gladding.

That a certain John Gladding departed this life intestate on the -- day of --- 1821, leaving the following children, your orators & oratrixes Henry, Sally, John and Nancy Gladding, and the infant defendants George & Milcah Gladding; that at the time of his death the said John Gladding was seized of a plantation on Pocomoke containing 118 acres, which said land descended to your orators and oratrixes and the infant defendants, &c. 31 March 1821 - p. 187

Taylor &c.

vs. - Suit for sale & division.

Taylor.

That a certain Staton Taylor late of this county departed this life intestate sometime in the year 1821, leaving six children, viz: your orator and oratrix Edmund and Harriett Taylor and Sarah Ann, Comfort, John & Mary Taylor; that the said Staton at the time of his death was seized in fee of a tract of land containing 100 acres, and one other tract of six acres which land on the death of the said Staton Taylor descended to his aforesaid children &c. 30 Dec. 1822 - p. 190

Kellam &c.

vs. - Suit for sale & division

Kellam

That a certain Robert Kellam late of this county was on the -- day of --- 1811 seized in fee simple of a tract of land situate near Andue containing 150 acres & also considerable personal estate; that the said Robert Kellam on the same day duly made and published his last will and testament and among other things devised the tract of land aforesaid to his son James Kellam with a contingent limitation to his son Argil Lewis Kellam; that the said Robert Kellam departed this life on the 4 day of January 1823, leaving the said will in full force; that since the date of the said will the said Robert Kellam purchased from a certain James Kellam a tract of land situate in the neighborhood of Occahannock containing 30 acres; that the said testator made no disposition of said land in his will, and the same therefore descended as if the said Robert Kellum had died intestate; that the said Robert Kellam at the time of his death left five children, viz: your orator and oratrix, Argil Lewis Kellam and Charlotte Kellam, and James, William & Sally Kellam, &c. 25 Feb. 1823 - p. 193

Matthews &c.

vs. Suit for division.

Matthews.

That a certain George Matthews late of this county departed this life intestate sometime in or about the year 1813 leaving three children, viz: your orator Meshack Matthews, your oratrix Mary W. Waterfield, wife of Jacob Waterfield, and a certain Margaret Matthews; that at the time of his death he was seized in fee simple of two tracts of land, one containing 111 acres, and the other containing 55 acres; that at the death of the said George Matthews the said two tracts of land descended to his then children aforesaid, &c. 28 April 1823 - p. 200

Chance

vs. - Suit for sale & division.

Chance

That a certain Elijah Chance late of this county departed this life on or about the -- day of --- intestate, leaving a widow and the following children, to-wit: your oratrix Nancy and William, Elijah, John, Thomas and Margaret Chance; that since the death of the said Elijah, Margaret Chance, his widow, has departed this life intestate; that at the time of the death of the said Elijah Chance he was seized in fee simple of 50 acres of land, and that the said land descended to his aforesaid children to be equally divided between them &c. 25 Feb. 1823 - p. 203

Custis & wife
vs. - Suit for Dower.
Meshack &c., slaves.

That a certain William Selby late of this county was in his lifetime seized in fee simple of a large real estate situate in this county, and being so seized on the 22 July 1818 duly made and published his last will and testament in which said will he devised to his negroes "the land purchased of Francis Houston by my father; also the land I purchased of Samuel W. Pitt; also the land I purchased of the heirs of James Broadwater; also 40 acres purchased by Drummond & William Welburn, containing 403 ½ acres" That the said William Selby departed this life on the -- day of March 1821 leaving the said will in full force; that the said William Selby at the time of his death left your oratrix Sally Selby his widow, and on the -- day of Feb. 1823, she was married to your orator John Custis; that in said will there is no provision made for your oratrix in lieu of dower, &c. -- April 1823 - p. 207

William Silverthorn & Susanna, his wife, formerly Susanna Dickerson, assignees of Thomas Fletcher
vs. - In Debt - Suit for sale of land.
Poulson.

That a certain Henry Custis late of this county on the 4 July 1802, being indebted to a certain Fletcher of this county as administrator of Leah Dickerson, for the purpose of securing the payment of same conveyed to the said Thomas Fletcher a certain tract of land containing 30 acres, situate on the head of Guilford Creek; that the said Henry Custis departed this life intestate on the -- day of Dec. 1809, leaving a daughter Tabitha his only child & heir at law; that the said Tabitha Custis on the -- day of Oct. 1807, intermarried with a certain Erastus Poulson, and on the-- day of May 1815, the said Tabitha Poulson departed this life leaving her husband Erastus Poulson and two children, viz: John & Edward A. Poulson living; that on the -- day of May 1815, your orator was married to your oratrix, &c. 30 Oct. 1815 - p. 220

Marshall &c.
vs. - Suit for sale & division.
Ewell & wife &c.

That a certain George Marshall late of this county departed this life on the -- day of Sept. 1814, age 21 years, and upwards, intestate and without issue; that the said George Marshall at the time of his death was seized in fee simple of a tract of land situate near Horntown, containing 100 acres; that at the death of the said

George Marshall he left neither children, father, mother, brother nor sister; that your orator and oratrixes are further advised that by the laws of this commonwealth in this case the inheritance must be divided into two moieties, one of which shall go to the paternal and the other to the maternal kindred, preferring first the grandfather, and if there be no grandfather, then the grandmother, uncles and aunts and their descendants; that at the death of the said George Marshall he left neither grandfather nor grandmother, but on the paternal side he left an aunt, the sister of his dec. father George Marshall, and a number of descendants of the deceased brothers and sisters of the said George Marshall the elder; and on the maternal side he left the descendants of a dec. uncle who was a brother to his mother, Leah Dickerson; the kindred of said George Marshall on the paternal side were as follows: First the descendants of William Marshall, dec., the eldest brother of said George Marshall the elder, viz: your orators John Marshall and William Marshall and your oratrixes Polly Nock, wife of Littleton Nock, Peggy Hargis, wife of Thomas Hargis & Frances Duncan, wife of Thomas Duncan, who are children of said William Marshall, also your orators Stringer Marshall, Solomon Marshall and William Marshall of Solomon, and your oratrixes Nerissa Taylor, formerly Nerissa Marshall, Elizabeth Williamson, wife of William Williamson, Euphamia Johnson, wife of Caleb Johnson, and Frances Marshall, who are the children of Solomon Marshall, dec., a son of said William Marshall; also your orator Lemuel Henderson, your oratrixes Polly Welburn, wife of Drummond Welburn and Scarburgh Aydlott, wife of John Adylott, who are the children of Rhoda Marshall, a daughter of said William Marshall;

Secondly the descendants of John Marshall, dec., second brother of said George Marshall the elder, viz: your orators John Knox and Robert Knox and your oratrix Barbara Knox, who are children of Barbara Knox, dec., formerly Barbara Marshall, a daughter of said John Marshall, also your orator George Marshall of Levin and your oratrix Edy Taylor, wife of Revell Taylor, who are the only children of Levin Marshall, dec., who was a son of John Marshall, dec., also your orators John L. Melvin and James W. Melvin, who are children of Betsy Melvin, formerly Betsy Marshall, a daughter of said John Marshall the elder;

Thirdly the descendants of Daniel Marshall dec., third brother of said George Marshall the elder, viz: your orator Isaac Marshall and your oratrixes Comfort Hudson, formerly Comfort Marshall, and Nancy Bowen, formerly Nancy Marshall, who are the only children of the said Daniel Marshall;

Fourthly the descendants of Charles Marshall, dec., fourth brother of said George Marshall the elder, viz: your orators William Wallop and Revell Wallop & your oratrixes Sally, Elizabeth & Nancy Wallop, infant children of William and Bridget Wallop, dec., formerly Bridget Marshall, a daughter of said Charles Marshall;

Fifthly the descendants of Leavin Marshall, dec., viz: your orator Shadrack D. Marshall

Sixthly the descendants of Polly Welburn, dec., formerly Polly Marshall, who was the elder sister of said George Marshall the elder, viz: your orators William Welburn and Drummond Welburn who are the children of said Polly Welburn, also your orators Sebastian Cropper and William D. Cropper and your oratrix Polly Marshall, wife of John Marshall, who are children of Barbara Cropper dec., formerly Barbara Welburn, a daughter of the said Polly Welburn;

Seventhly your oratrix Elizabeth Murrer formerly Elizabeth Marshall, the second sister of said George Marshall the elder, dec.

Eightly the descendants of Leah Marshall, the <u>second</u> sister of said George Marshall the elder, dec., viz: your orator James Marshall her son;

That the kindred of the said George Marshall the younger of the maternal side are as follows: viz: Jesse Dickerson, William Ewell and Sally, his wife, formerly Dickerson, Elizabeth White, wife of James White, formerly Elizabeth Dickerson, Susanna Silverthorn, wife of William Silverthorn, formerly Susanna Dickerson, the said Jesse, Sally, Elizabeth & Susanna being the children of Jesse Dickerson dec., a brother to Leah Marshall, formerly Leah Dickerson, the mother of the said George Marshall the younger, &c.

By leave of the court the complainants in this cause made the following amendments to their bill:

2nd Page after the end of the 6th line add "and the descendants of a deceased aunt who was a sister of his mother, Leah Dickerson" 3rd Page after the end of the 15th line add "and a certain Elizabeth Custis, the daughter & only child of Elizabeth Custis who was a daughter of Martha March (Marsh?) formerly Martha Dickerson, a sister to the mother of said George Marshall" &c. 29 Nov. 1815 - p. 230

Revell & Wife
vs. - Partition Suit.
Seymour

That a certain George Seymour late of the county of Accomack departed this life intestate sometime in or near the year 1803 leaving three children, viz: Elizabeth, Rosey Seymour, the mother of your oratrix Rosey Revell, and a certain William B. Seymour; that the said George Seymour at the time of his death was seized in fee simple of a tract of land situate near Pungoteague containing 400 acres, and that the land descended to his three children aforesaid; that after the death of the said George Seymour your oratrix Elizabeth intermarried with your orator, William A. Christian, and the said Rosey, Seymour intermarried with your orator John B. Revell, and she has since died leaving issue of the said marriage your oratrix Rosey Revell who is her only child, &c. 25 Aug. 1823 - p. 240

Lilliston & wife
vs. - Partition Suit.
Bell &c.

That a certain William Welch late of this county departed this life intestate on the -- day of April 1811, leaving five children, viz: your oratrixes Nancy, now wife of Elijah Lilliston and Elizabeth Welch, and Margaret, now the wife of George Bell, and William Welch and Sally Welch; that the said William Welch at the time of his death was seized in fee simple of a tract of land situate in the

White Marsh containing 200 acres, which land on the death of said William Welch descended to all of his aforesaid children, &c. 27 Oct. 1823 - p. 243

Floyd &c.
vs. - Partition Suit.
Floyd.

That a certain William Floyd the elder, late of this county,. departed this life intestate on the 13 day of March 1823, leaving the following children and grandchildren, viz: William, James, Eliza, Polly, Esther, Sally, Susan and John Floyd, Margaret Burton, wife of Joshua Burton, and a certain Thomas Floyd, all of whom were his children, and also your orators Thomas and Edward Bull who were his grandchildren, being the children of his deceased daughter Rachel; that at the time of his death the said William Floyd, Sr., was seized in fee simple of a tract of land on Watchapreague containing 200 acres, and one other tract situate on Hog Island in the County of Northampton containing 400 acres, which said land at the death of the said William Floyd, Sr., descended to his children and grandchildren &c., 27 Oct. 1823 - p. 246

Boggs
vs. - Suit for Dower.
Boggs.

That Francis Boggs late of this county on the 1 day of March 1820, duly made and published his last will and testament in which among other things he devised to his wife, your oratrix Elizabeth, his whole estate until the first day of Jan. 1834 on consideration that she make no charge against his children for their support, and he then devised the land given him by his father to his son Joseph; your orator, to his son John C. Boggs he devised 40 acres purchased of Nathaniel Burnell and others, and all his other estate to be divided as follows: to your oratrix, his widow, 1/9, to his son Joseph 1/50, to his son John 1/20, and the balance equally between his children Mary Ann, Susanna, Leah, Thomas, Eliza, Margaret and Sally Boggs, and the said Francis Boggs departed this life on the -- day of Sept. 1823, leaving the said will in full force; that your oratrix at the Sept. term of court 1823, renounced all benefit under the said will and claimed the provisions allowed her by law &c. 23 Feb. 1824 - p. 250

Cole
vs. - Partition Suit.
Taylor.

That a certain Comfort Taylor late of this county deceased departed this life intestate and a feme covert in the year 1817 leaving four children viz: Edward, Harriott, Sarah Ann and Comfort Taylor; that the said Comfort Taylor at the time of her death was seized in her own right in fee simple of two tracts of land on the head of Assawoman Creek containing 97 acres and ¾ more or less subject to a life estate in Staton Taylor as tenant by the curtesy; that the said Staton Taylor departed this life in the year 1820, and the said land descended to the aforesaid children equally; that on the 21 March 1823 Crippin Taylor, Joseph Conquest and George Warner, Jr., conveyed to the said Edward, Harriott, Sarah Ann and Comfort Taylor a tract of land containing 7 acres adjoining the above mentioned land; the said Comfort Taylor the younger departed this life on the -- day of --- 1823, an infant without issue, leaving the said Edward, Harriott & Sarah Ann her next of kin and heirs at law; that on the 1 Jan. 1824, the said Edward Taylor conveyed to your orator John Cole his interest in said land &c. 23 Feb. 1824 - p. 255

Gunter &c.
vs. - Suit for Dower & division.
Gunter.

That a certain Laban Gunter the elder late of this county departed this life intestate in the year 1822 leaving your oratrix Sarah his widow and nine children, viz: your orator William L. Gunter, your oratrix Polly Henderson, wife of Robert Henderson, and Margaret, Edward, Anna, Sally, Betsy, Laban & Maria Gunter, and leaving his wife enscient with a child, who was afterwards born and died within two days of its birth; that at the time of his death the said Laban Gunter was seized in fee simple of a tract of land near Drummondtown containing 100 acres, also one other tract containing 50 acres and of one other tract situate near New Church containing 30 acres; that at the death of the said Laban Gunter the said land descended to his aforesaid children subject to the dower of your oratrix Sarah &c. 26 Nov. 1823 - p. 260

Lilliston & wife &c.
vs. - Suit for sale and division.
White.

That Levin White late of this county departed this life on or about the year 1794 seized of 43 acres of land, leaving William White, Elijah, Nancy, John, Henry, Catharine & Betsy his children, so that upon his death the said children are equally entitled as his heirs to the said 43 acres of land; that Betsy White died in or about the year 1798 under the age of 21 years, without issue, leaving her aforesaid brothers and sisters, her mother Bridget White and her half brother William Welch to whom her undivided part of the said land descended; that John White died on or about the year 1811 leaving as his next of kin his mother Bridget White and his aforesaid brothers and sisters and his half brother William Welch to whom his interest in said land descended; that Nancy White died in 1818, leaving an only child Napoleon White to whom her undivided share in said land descended; that Elijah White died in 1810 leaving issue John his only child to whom his share of said land descended; that Catherine White died in 1819 without issue leaving her mother Bridget White, her brother Henry White, Levin, Daniel, William, Betsy, George, Elijah, Hanna & Sally White, children of William White who died in the year 1815, Napoleon White, the child of Nancy White, John the child of Elijah White, Betsy, Nancy, Margaret, William and Sally Welch, children of William Welch who died in the year 18--, the said Nancy Welch being now the wife of your orator Elijah Lilliston, and the said Margaret being now the wife of your orator George Bell; that Henry White died in the year 18-- leaving his only children, to-wit: Adeline & Bridget White; that William White, Jr., son of William, Sr., died in the year 1818 under age and without issue leaving his brothers and sisters, Levin, Daniel, Betsy, George, Elijah, Hanna & Sally White; that Daniel died in the year 1821 of full age, leaving his mother Sarah and his aforesaid brothers and sisters as his next of kin and heirs at law; that by deed dated ---- Nancy and John White conveyed their right in said land to Bridget White; that on the -- day of ---- William White conveyed his interest in said land to Bridget White, and that Henry White by deed dated ---- conveyed all his interest in said land to Elijah A. White, so that your orators and oratrixes and the said Napoleon White, son of Nancy White, dec., John White, son of Elijah White, dec., Adeline White & Bridget White, children of Henry White, dec., Betsy Welch, William Welch and Sally Welch, children of William Welch, dec., original parties to this suit, and Sarah the mother of Daniel White, Levin White, Betsy, George, Elijah, Hanna and Sally White, brothers and sisters of Daniel White, and Anne Kellam, daughter of Zorobabel who are permitted by the court as parties to this suit, are entitled to have division of said land &c. 2 April 1824 - p. 264

Tyler &c.
vs. - Suit for sale & division.
Tyler.

That a certain David Tyler late of Tangier Island departed this life intestate on the -- day of July 1823, seized in fee simple of a tract of land on Tangier Island containing 3 acres of arable land and about 100 acres of Marsh, commonly called Norse Hammock; that at the time of his death the said David left the following children and grandchildren, viz: your orators and oratrixes, Thomas, William and John Tyler of David, and Nelly Evans, wife of George Evans, Zeporah Croswell, wife of William Croswell, and Anne Tyler, all of whom are his children, and John, George, Thomas & Ann Mary Tyler his grandchildren, they being the children of his deceased son Severn Tyler, formerly of this county; that at the death of the said David Tyler intestate the said tract of land & marsh descended to his aforesaid children and grandchildren &c. 25 Aug. 1823 - . 266

Rodgers
vs. - Suit for sale and division.
Rodgers.

That a certain Mary Ann Rodgers late of this county departed this life intestate and without issue on the -- day of --- 1822, seized in her own right of a tract of land containing by estimation --- acres; that the said Mary Ann Rodgers at the time of her death left as her next of kin and heirs at law your orators George & Lewis Rodgers and a certain John H. Rodgers her brothers &c. 29 June, 1824 - p. 280

Nock

vs. - Suit for sale and division.

Nock.

That a certain Samuel Nock late of this county departed this life, intestate on the -- day of --- 1820, leaving six children, viz: your orators & oratrixes, Elijah, William, Levin, John and Mary Nock infants, and a certain Nancy Nock, all infants; that at the time of his death the said Samuel Nock was seized in fee simple of a tract of land in the White Marsh containing 55 acres, which land descended to his aforesaid children - 27 Jan. 1823 - p. 283

Pewsey & wife

vs. - Suit for sale and division.

Hickman

That a certain John Hickman late of this county departed this life intestate on the -- day of --- 1812, leaving his widow Peggy who departed this life on the -- day of 1817, and the following children: your oratrix & orators George, Peggy and Ayres Hickman; that since the death of the said John Hickman, to-wit: on the -- day of Sept. 1820, your oratrix Nancy intermarried with your orator Thomas Pewsey; that at the death of the said John Hickman he was seized in fee simple of a parcel of land about three miles from Drummondtown, containing about 8 acres, which said land descended to his aforesaid four children &c. 30 March 1821 - p. 286

Warner & wife &c.

vs. - Partition Suit.

Savage.

That a certain Hetty Mason, formerly Hetty James, late of this county, departed this life in the year 1817 leaving one child named Delight Mason, and being seized together with her husband Teackle Mason of 35 acres of land on Kegotank Creek, which 35 acres were devised to the said Hetty in fee simple by her deceased brother, ---- James; that at the death of the said Hetty Mason the said tract of land descended to the said Delight Mason subject to the right of her husband Teackle Mason during his life as tenant by the curtesy; that the said Delight Mason departed this life intestate, an infant and without issue in the year 1819, and the said Teackle Mason departed this life in the year 1821; that your oratrix Elizabeth Warner, wife of George Warner, Jr., is a sister of the whole blood to the said Hetty Mason; that your oratrixes Elizabeth, Mary and Sarah Ann James are the only children of David James, dec., who was a brother of the whole blood to the said Hetty Mason; that your orator and oratrixes Rosanna, Sarah and Robert J. Broadwater are the only children and heirs of Robert J. Broadwater, dec., who died in the year 1820, intestate, and who was a brother of the half blood to the said Hetty Mason, and that Mary Anne and Sally C. Savage are the only children of Nancy Savage, dec., who was a sister of the whole blood to the said Hetty Mason, &c., 27 Nov. 1821 - p. 289

Gray

vs. - Suit for sale and division.

Russell.

That a certain Thomas Gray late of this county departed this life intestate in the month of July 1824, leaving your orators and oratrix Dennis Gray, James Gray and Sarah Gray his children, and leaving one grandchild Colmore Russell, who was the only child of his dec. daughter Elizabeth Russell; that at the time of his death the said Thomas Gray was seized in fee simple of a tract of land containing 12 acres, which upon the death of the said Thomas Gray descended to his said children & grandchildren &c. 27 Sept. 1824 - p. 293

East & wife

vs. - Suit for sale & division.

Bonwell.

That a certain Clement Bonwell late of this county departed this life intestate on the -- day of --- 181- leaving four children, viz: your oratrix Elizabeth, now the wife of Richard East, your orator James and Robert & Elijah Bonwell; that the said Clement Bonwell at the time of his death was seized in fee simple of a lot of land containing 1 acre in the town of Onancock, which descended to all his aforesaid children &c. 28 June 1824 - p. 295

Mears & wife &c.

vs. - Suit for division.

Smith.

That on or about the -- day of --- 1803, a certain Charles Smith late of this county intermarried with a certain Hannah Powell; that the said Hannah Powell departed this life sometime about the year 1813; that the said Hannah at the time of her intermarriage with the said Charles Smith was seized in her own right in fee simple of the undivided one half of the following real estate formerly belonging to James Powell of this county, viz: one tenement in Belle Haven containing about 12 acres, and a plantation situate near Belle Haven containing about 12 acres, and a plantation situate near Belle Haven containing about 300 acres, and situate partly in the county of Accomack and partly in Northampton, the other half of said real estate belonged to a certain Mahala Powell, sister of the said Hannah Powell; that the said Mahala Powell sometime in the year 1807 was married to a certain John Smith of this county and departed this life shortly thereafter leaving her said husband and one child not named living; that the said unnamed child departed this life shortly after the death of the said mother, Mahala Smith, an infant, whereby the interest of the said Mahala in said land descended to the said Hannah Smith the maternal aunt of the said unnamed child, subject to the life estate of the said John Smith as tenant by the curtesy; that the said John Smith conveyed his life estate in said land to the said Charles Smith; the said Hannah Smith left at her death two children, viz: your oratrix Ann, now the wife of Thomas W. Mears, and James Smith, an infant, to whom the whole of the said real estate descended, subject to the life estate of the said Charles Smith as tenant by the curtesy in one moiety thereof and the remaining moiety subject to the right of the said Charles Smith during the life of the said John Smith by virtue of the deed aforesaid; the said Charles Smith departed this life intestate in the year 1823 leaving six children, viz: your oratrix, your orator James, and also George, Charles, Elizabeth and John Smith; your orator and oratrix are advised that on the death of the said Charles Smith your orator James and your oratrix Anne became entitled immediately to one moiety of the said land, and that the remaining moiety during the life of the said John Smith descended to all the children of the said Charles Smith equally &c. 27 Sept. 1824 - p. 298

Broadwater
vs. - Partition Suit.
Broadwater.

That a certain Elias Broadwater the elder late of this county departed this life intestate in the year 1823 leaving three children, your orator Caleb, your oratrix Nancy, wife of Savage Broadwater, and Walter Broadwater, and leaving also two grandchildren, viz: Walter Broadwater and Alfred Broadwater, children of Elias Broadwater, Jr., son of the said Elias, Sr.; that the said Elias Broadwater, Sr., at the time of his death was seized in fee simple of a tract of land situate in the neighborhood of Pocomoke and containing 80 acres, which land at the death of the said Elias Broadwater, Sr., intestate, descended to his aforesaid children and grandchildren &c. 30 Nov. 1824 - p. 303

Broadwater & wife &c.
vs. - Suit for sale and Division.
Scarburgh.

That a certain Charles Tunnell the younger being on the 13 Feb. 1810, seized in fee simple of a house and lot in the town of Onancock in this county, containing about 2 acres, duly made and published his last will and testament in which he devised to his wife Maria during her life or widowhood, the aforesaid houses & lot, and at her death or marriage he devised the same in fee simple to his nephew Littleton Tunnell; the said Charles Tunnell also bequeathed to the said Littleton Tunnell his negro woman Sally, which said will was proved 27 Aug. 1810; that Charles Tunnell, Sr., on the 6 June, 1815, duly made and published his last will and testament in which he bequeathed to his grandson the said Littleton Tunnell, in fee, a negro girl named Nina, which said will was recorded 29 July 1816; that the said Maria Tunnell, the widow of the said Charles Tunnell, Jr., departed this life on the -- day of --- 1810; that the said Littleton Tunnell being seized of the house and lot and negro slaves aforesaid, departed this life under age, intestate and without issue on the -- day of April 1819; that at the time of his death the said Littleton Tunnell's father, John Tunnell, was dead; that the said Littleton Tunnell left at his death his mother, viz: your oratrix Mary, one sister of the whole blood, viz: Sally, now the wife of Americus Scarburgh, she being the daughter of your oratrix Mary and the said John Tunnell, and also two sisters of the half blood, viz: your oratrixes Elizabeth and Mary, your oratrix Elizabeth being the daughter of your oratrix Mary by John Massey her second husband, and your oratrix Mary being the daughter of your oratrix Mary by your orator Joseph Broadwater, her third husband, to whom the said houses and lot & negroes descended, giving to your oratrixes Mary Broadwater, Sr. and Sally Scarburgh whole shares, and to your oratrixes Elizabeth Massey and Mary Broadwater, Jr., each half shares, &c. 26 June, 1820 - p. 306

Nock
vs. - Partition Suit.
Nock.
    That a certain John Nock departed this life on the -- day of Sept. 1820, intestate and without issue, being at that time seized in fee simple of a tract of land near the Last Shift in this county containing 200 acres; that the said John Nock left no father nor mother living, nor any issue, but left four brothers, viz: your orators James and Levin and Samuel Nock and Edmund Nock, and leaving a niece your oratrix Anne Joynes, the only child of his deceased sister Anne Joynes; that at the death of the aforesaid John Nock the said land descended to his aforesaid four brothers and niece; that the said Samuel Nock departed this life intestate a few days after the death of the said John Nock, leaving his infant children viz: your orators and oratrixes Elijah, Mary, William, Lewis, John and Nancy Nock, to whom descended the said Samuel Nock's undivided share of said land &c. 30 Oct. 1820 - p. 314

Bloxom
vs. - In Debt - Suit for sale of land.
Bloxom.
    That a certain Abbott Bloxom late of this county was on the 30 July 1821 indebted to sundry persons, and your orator Richard Bloxom was bound as his security, and being so indebted the said Abbott Bloxom in order to secure the said Richard Bloxom conveyed to him a tract of land containing 17 acres; that the said Abbott Bloxom departed this life intestate on the -- day of --- 1822, leaving two children Mahala & Richard Bloxom to whom the said land descended, subject to your orator's lien &c. 3 April 1823 - p. 318

Smith &c.
vs. - Partition Suit.
Hall.
    That a certain Erastus Hall late of this county departed this life intestate sometime in the year 18-- seized in fee simple of a tract of land near Pocomoke containing 60 acres; that the said Erastus Hall at his death left no children nor their descendants, nor father nor mother, but left four brothers and sisters, viz: your orator & oratrixes Abigail Smith, Luther Hall, Mary Hall and a certain Dixon Hall, to whom the said land descended, giving the whole blood whole shares and the half blood half shares &c. 30 Nov. 1824

Custis &c.

vs. - In Debt - Suit for sale of land.

Evans &c.

That a certain Levin Evans, late of this county, departed this life intestate and without issue sometime in the year ----; that previous to his death, viz: on the 25 Jan. 1819, the said Levin Evans was indebted to your orator and a certain Bagwell Wharton jointly & in order to secure the payment of the same executed a deed of mortgage conveying a tract of land containing 100 acres; that at his death the said Levin Evans left as his next of kin & heirs at law his mother, Sarah Evans, one sister, Mahala Marshall, the wife of Shadrack Marshall, and two brothers, John and James Evans; that on the -- day of --- 182- the said Bagwell Wharton departed this life &c. 7 Feb. 1824 - p. 338

Edmunds

vs. - Suit for sale and division.

Edmunds.

That a certain Margaret Edmunds, late the wife of William Edmunds, dec., late of this county, departed this life on the -- day of March 1818, seized in fee simple of a tract of land near Garrison's Chappel, containing 31 acres; that the said Margaret at her death left three children, viz: your orator Thomas Edmunds, your oratrix Nancy, wife of Henry Stewart, and a certain Margaret Edmunds, inf't., to all of whom the said land descended subject to the life estate of the said William Edmunds as tenant by the curtesy; the said William Edmunds departed this life in the year 1824 - 27 Dec. 1824 - p. 348.

Bloxom

vs. - Partition Suit.

Bloxom.

That a certain Major Bloxom late of this county departed this life intestate in the year 1824 leaving 5 children, viz: your orators Edward and Major P. Bloxom, your oratrix Hetty, wife of William Bloxom, and Nancy and Narcissa Bloxom; that the said Major Bloxom at the time of his death was seized in fee simple of two tracts of land, one containing 300 acres and the other containing 60 acres, which said land at the death of said Major Bloxom descended to his aforesaid children &c. 25 April 1828 - p. 355

Marshall

vs. - Suit for sale and division.

Marshall.

That a certain James Marshall, late of this county, departed this life intestate in the year 1816, leaving five children viz: your orators John, James & George Marshall, and Peter and Josiah Marshall, infants; that at his death the said James Marshall was seized in fee simple of three tracts of land near Horn Town, one containing 100 acres, one other containing 4½ acres, and the other containing 23 acres, which said lands descended to the aforesaid children to be equally divided &c. 30 Nov. 1824 - p. 390

Parker
vs. - Suit for Dower.
Finney.
That a certain Henry Parker on the 17 Oct. 1818 duly made and published his last will and testament in which among other things he devised to his daughter Ann Parker a tract of land situate on Andua Creek, containing 175 acres, which formerly belonged to Robert Andrews, and also 20 acres of land near Ames' Ridge; that the said Henry Parker in his lifetime made no provision by deed, will or otherwise for your oratrix Agnes Parker, his widow; that after the death of the said Henry Parker the said Ann Parker married with a certain Henry F. Finney, and she has since died leaving her said husband and one child, Susan Finney, living; that at the death of the said Ann Finney the said land descended to the said child, Susan Finney in fee simple, subject to the right of the said Henry F. Finney during is life as tenant by the curtesy, and also subject to the right of your oratrix aforesaid &c. 20 Sept. 1825 - p. 400

Nock
vs. - Partition Suit.
Parker.
That a certain John Watson formerly of this county departed this life intestate in the year ---- leaving two daughters, Nancy& Margaret Watson, and being seized in fee simple of a tract of land situate in the White Marsh near Walker's Folly containing 100 acres, which land descended to his two daughters aforesaid; The said Nancy G. Watson on the 3 Feb. 1815, conveyed her undivided moiety of the said land to George S. Fisher, who on the same day conveyed the same to a certain William Seymour; that the said William Seymour departed this life in the year 1821 having first duly made and published his last will and testament in which he directed his executors to make sale of all his real estate for the payment of his debts; that the said undivided moiety of the tract above mentioned was purchased at said sale by your orator William Nock; the said Margaret Watson married a certain Samuel Parker and has since died leaving one child named Margaret Ann, and leaving her said husband living, and her moiety of the said land descended to her said husband for life, with remainder to her said child in fee simple &c. 31 Oct. 1825 - p. 403

Lilliston & wife &c.
vs. Suit for sale and division.
Fitzgerald
That a certain Charles Fitzgerrald late of this county departed this life intestate on or about the 1 day of Oct. 1815, leaving his widow Rosey and the following children, to-wit: Julia Ann, Elizabeth, Samuel, Sally and Thomas Fitzgerrald; that the said Charles Fitzgerrald at the time of his death was seized in

fee simple of a tract of land near the head of Folly Creek, containing 37 acres; that since the death of the said Charles Fitzgerrald your oratrix, Julia Ann, has intermarried with your orator Thomas Lilliston on or about the 19 Dec. 1822; your orator James Carmine with your oratrix Elizabeth on or about the -- March 1823, and your orator Thomas Peusey with your oratrix Sally on or about the 10 Aug. 1825; that since thee death of the said Charles Fitzgerrald dower has been assigned to his widow aforesaid &c. 27 Sept. 1825 - p. 406

Savage.
vs. - Suit for sale and division.
Savage.

That a certain Charles S. Savage late of this county departed this life intestate on the -- day of ---- 1811 leaving three children, viz: your oratrix Rosey Ann & Severn E. and Charles S. Savage, and leaving your oratrix Lovea his widow; that the said Charles S. Savage at the time of is death was seized in fee simple of a tract of land situate on Folly Creek containing 65¼ acres, which said land descended to the three children of the said Charles S. Savage subject to the dower of your oratrix Lovea &c. 31 Oct. 1825 - p. 409

Custis
vs. - In Debt - Suit for sale of land.
Outten.

That a certain Matthias Outten late of this county in his lifetime, viz: on the 7 April 1821, was indebted to a certain Thomas R. Fisher, dec., of whose last will and testament your orator, William P. Custis, was the executor; that in order to secure the same the said Matthias Outten on the 7 April 1821 conveyed to your orator a tract of land containing 40 acres and also two lots in the town of Drummond, containing by estimation 1 acre; that on the 17 March 1824, the said Matthias Outten became indebted to your orator and in order to secure the same conveyed to your orator a tract of land near Drummondtown containing 50 acres, also one other tract of land situate near Drummond Town containing 34 acres, and one other tract near Drummond Town containing 22 acres, also one lot of land in Drummond Town containing by estimation 2 acres; that on the 17 July 1824, the said Matthias Outten duly made and published his last will and testament which said will was proved 25 Oct. 1824, in which he devised to his daughter Sally T. Coleburn, wife of James H. Coleburn, for life, with remainder to his grandaughter Betsy F. Coleburn, his plantation called Snead's & Hargis, containing 40 acres, with a contingent limitation to William D. Outten & John M. Copes & Elizabeth Copes; the said Mathias Outten devised to his grandchildren John H. and Elizabeth Copes his two lots in the town of Drummond, and also devised to his son William D. Outten his field called the Joynes field, also the houses and lots on which the testator lived containing 1 acre; he also directed that the lands purchased by him from William R. Bunting, and also the 16 acres purchased by him from Mckeel Bonwell should be sold for the payment of his debts, and also gave his executor the right to sell the field called the Monger field if necessary for the same purpose, and appointed your orator and the said William D. Outten executors. The land devised by the said Matthias to his daughter Sally T . Coleburn, in the same land mentioned by the said Matthias in the second deed above mentioned to your orator, and expressed therein as containing 50 acres, the lots devised to his grandchildren John H. and Elizabeth Copes in the said will are the same lands conveyed by the first deed of mortgage to your orator; the land devised to the said William D. Outten is the same lot conveyed by the second deed to your orator; the land devised to the said William D. Outten called the Joynes field is the same conveyed in the second mortgage to your orator; the land directed to be sold and purchased by the testator from William R. Bunting is the same land conveyed in the first deed of mortgage; the land directed to be sold called the Monger field, is the same land conveyed in the second deed of mortgage containing 20 acres; the land directed to be sold purchased from Mckeel Bonwell was conveyed to neither of the aforesaid deeds; after the death of the said Mathias Outten your orator ascertained that the testator was indebted to a certain John B. Walker, his late ward, in a greater sum than the value of the whole real estate, and that there is still a considerable balance due the said Walker &c. __ March 1825 - p. 413

John Jackson & wife &c.
vs. - Suit for sale and division.
Bayly &c.
That a certain Edmund Core late of this county, departed this life intestate sometime in the year 1823, being at that time seized in fee simple of a tract of land containing 68 acres; the said Edmund Core at his death left no children nor their descendants, nor father, mother, brother or sister or their descendants, nor grandfather nor grandmother; that the said Edmund Core left the following paternal relatives, your orators John, William and Zorobabel Laws and your oratrixes Rebecca, wife of John Jackson, & Mary Laws, who are the only children of Adah Laws, formerly Adah Core, the only sister of the father of the said Edmund Core, and left no other paternal relatives; the said Edmund Core left the following maternal relatives, viz: Anne Bayly, the wife of Thomas S. Bayly, and sister of the whole blood to the mother of the said Edmund Core, William Justice, a brother of the whole blood to the mother of the said Edmund Core, Polly Savage, formerly Polly Hickman, the only daughter of Polly Justice, a sister of the whole blood to the mother of the said Edmund Core, James Justice, a brother of the half blood to the mother of the said Edmund Core, and Catharine Mears, the wife of Thomas Mears, a sister of the half blood to the mother of the said Edmund Core, Elizabeth Savage, wife of John Savage, half sister to the said Core's mother, and no other maternal uncles nor aunts nor their descendants; the said William Justice is since dead leaving three children, viz: Tinney White, the wife of James White, Polly Fletcher, the wife of Henry Fletcher, and Joice Laylor, your orators & oratrixes, to whom the said land descended &c. 11 Dec. 1824 - p. 438

Laylor

vs. - Suit for sale & division.

Chandler.

That on the 3 day of March 1820, James R. Ashmead and Elizabeth his wife, late of this county, duly executed a deed conveying to a certain Patience Laylor with remainder in fee to your oratrix and Mary Chandler, the daughter of Mitchell Chandler, a lot of land in the town of Onancock containing 1 acre, with reservation of a life estate to said Elizabeth Ashmead; that the said Elizabeth departed his life shortly after the date of said deed and the said Patience Laylor departed this life in the month of Jan. 1824, so that the said lot is now subject to division between your oratrix Cynthia Laylor and the said Mary Chandler; that your oratrix is deaf and dumb, and Luther H. Reed has been appointed curator of her estate &c. 31 Oct. 1823 - p. 442

Thomas.

vs. - Partition Suit.

Thomas.

That a certain Hepsy Rodgers late of this county departed this life on or about the 27 Aug. 1825, intestate and without issue, leaving one niece to-wit: your oratrix Margaret L. Thomas, daughter of John B. Thomas, the only heir and representative of Elizabeth Thomas, formerly Elizabeth Rodgers, sister of the said Hepsey Rodgers, dec., one sister Susan Taylor, wife of Thorowgood Taylor, formerly Susan Rodgers, and two brothers, John W. Rodgers and Levin Rodgers; that the said Hepsey in her lifetime and at the time of her death was seized in fee simple of ⅓ part of a certain tract of land situate in White Marsh near Holly Meeting House, containing by estimation one hundred and --- acres, also ⅓ part of one other tract of land, viz. the timber now growing and that may hereafter grow, containing by survey 10 acres, and also possessed of three negroes and considerable personal estate; that on the death of the said Hepsey Rodgers the said land and negroes descended to your orators & oratrixes &c. 26 Dec. 1823 - p. 447

Tunnell &c.

vs. - Suit for recovery of land.

Wharton.

That a certain Joseph Tunnell late of this county being in the year 1797 seized in his own right in fee simple of a certain tract of land containing 75 acres, and being indebted to a certain John Wharton, late of this county, in order to secure the same conveyed by deed of mortgage to the said John Wharton the aforesaid tract of land; that the said John Wharton in the year 1802 took possession of the said mortgaged premises and continued to hold possession thereof until his death in the year 1814, when he devised all his estate, real and personal, to his wife Elizabeth Wharton during her life with remainder to such persons as would have been his heirs at law had he died intestate, and appointed a certain Bagwell Wharton and others executors; that the said John Wharton having left no children nor father nor mother, a certain Bagwell Wharton, Ann

Taylor, the wife of Thomas T. Taylor and Tabitha Watson, the wife of Ephraim Watson, the said Bagwell, Anne and Tabitha being the only brother and sisters of the said John Wharton, would have been his heirs at law if he had died intestate, and were consequently entitled to the remainder after the death of the said Elizabeth Wharton, in the estate of the said John Wharton under his said will; that the said Elizabeth took possession of and continued to hold the said premises; that the said Joseph Tunnell departed this life intestate on the -- day of --- leaving four children, your orator Isaiah Tunnell, your oratrix Elizabeth Corbin, wife of Robert Corbin, your oratrix Polly Marshall, wife of Sampson Marshall, and a certain Rosey Tunnell; that the said Rosey Tunnell departed this life intestate without issue on the -- day of --- 1812; that at the death of the said Joseph Tunnell his whole estate descended to his said four children, and upon the death of Rosey Tunnell her part descended to her surviving brother and sisters &c. 1 Feb. 1817 - p. 463

Wharton, assignee, &c.
vs. - In Debt - Suit for sale of land.
Burton.

That William W. Burton late of the county of Accomack, deceased, being indebted to Bagwell Wharton of the same county, now deceased, for the purchase of two tracts of land & mill, and in order to secure the same the said William W. Burton and Ann D., his wife, executed a deed of mortgage on the said two tracts of land and water grist mill, the one tract called Whittington, the other tract called the woodland; that the said Bagwell Wharton on the 7 Sept. 1820, being indebted to the said Elizabeth Wharton, the complainant, assigned the said mortgage to the said Elizabeth Wharton; that on the -- day of --- the said Bagwell Wharton departed this life having first made his last will and testament; and appointed John Custis his executor; that the said John Custis on the 11 Dec. 1823, under his own hand and seal assigned the said deed of mortgage to the complainant; that William W. Burton departed this life on the -- day of --- having paid no part of said debt, and having made no will Theodore W. Adair qualified as his administrator; that on the 6 Aug. 1822, the said Theodore Adair made payment of $679. toward paying the said bond which is credited on said bond; that the said Ann D. Burton, widow of the said William W. Burton intermarried on the -- day of --- with James Duncan; that the said William W. Burton left Annabella Burton, Mary Adair Burton, Maria Burton, Ann Burton & Louisa Burton his only children and heirs at law, and that the said lands have descended to them &c. 10 April 1824 - . 482

Hadlock
vs. - In Debt - Suit for sale of land.
Coward's Executors &c.

That on the 27 Dec. 1820, Samuel Coward of this county, being seized in fee of a tract of land hereafter mentioned, being indebted to Robert Hadlock, in order to secure said indebtedness, conveyed by deed of mortgage the said tract of land containing 400 acres, situate on the Chesapeake Bay, to the said complainant; that the said Samuel Coward duly made and published his last will and testament bearing date 20 March 1821, and thereby gave to his wife Catherine Coward during her widowhood, and in lieu of dower, his plantation called the Vale of Shirans in Scarburgh's Neck whereon he then resided, and devised the said plantation to his son Samuel William Coward when he should arrive to lawful age, but in case he died before coming to age gave the said plantation to his three daughters, Jane O. Addison, Eliza E. Coward and Louisa W. Coward; that the said Samuel William Coward departed this life in the year 1821 without revoking the said will; that Catherine Coward, the widow, relinquished all benefit under the devise in said will; that Jane O. Addison mentioned in the said will is the wife of Kendall Addison, and that the plantation called the Vale of Shirons [sic] and mentioned in said will is the same tract of land conveyed by the testator to your orator &c. 6 Dec. 1822 - p. 490

Justice.
vs. - Suit for division.
Taylor.
That a certain William Justice late of this county departed this life intestate on the -- day of --- 1817, leaving nine children, viz: your orator & oratrixes John, Richard & Rosey Justice, Sukey Taylor, the wife of Southy Taylor, Polly Justice, Mahala Justice, Parker Justice, William Justice and Elizabeth Justice; that the said William Justice the elder at the time of his death was seized in fee simple of a tract of land on the Bayside Road near the head of Back Creek, containing 130 acres; that on the death of the said William intestate the said land descended to all his children aforesaid &c. 27 July 1819 - p. 510

Boggs.
vs. - Suit for sale & division.
Rodgers.
That your orators & oratrixes, James Boggs & Elizabeth, his wife, John W. Hutchinson and Harriott his wife, together with Jane M. Rodgers, their sister, and the defendant, all of the county of Accomack, are now seized in fee simple in possession as tenants in common, of the following lands and Marsh; one parcel containing 34 acres; one parcel containing 23 acres; another parcel containing 91 acres of which Raymond R. Rodgers died seized, which several parcels were devised to the said Raymond R. Rodgers by Levi Rodgers, dec., the father of your oratrixes this defendant and the said Raymond; that the above parcels of land descended to your oratrixes and this defendant as heirs at law of the said Raymond R. Rodgers, deceased who died before he attained the age of 21 years, and your orators James Boggs and Elizabeth P. his wife are now entitled to one undivided 1/5 part or share thereof, being heirs of the half blood, and then your orators & oratrix John W. Hutchinson and Harriott his wife being of the whole blood to the said Raymond R. Rodgers are entitled to 2/5, and the defendant Jane M. Rodgers to the remaining 3/5 &c. 26 June 1826 - p. 514

Finney

vs. - Partition Suit.

Beach.

That William Finney late of this county departed this life in the year 1813, having first duly made and published his last will and testament in which he devised to his son John W. Finney, your orator, 100 acres of arable land, also all the Marsh adjoining the said 100 acres; to his three daughters, Mary Ann, Sarah & Tabitha slaves & the remaining land; that the said Tabitha has since married a certain William Beach &c. 26 Dec. 1823 - p. 522

Revell & wife &c.

vs. - Partition Suit.

Hopkins.

That Charles Hopkins late of this county departed this life intestate and without issue in the year 1825, leaving as his next of kin & heirs at law two sisters and one brother, viz: your oratrixes Susan, wife of Edmund Poulson, Ann, wife of John B. Revell, and a certain Elison Hopkins. That the said Charles Hopkins at his death was seized in fee simple of a tract of land in Northampton County containing 167½ acres, which said land at the death of the said Charles Hopkins descended to the aforesaid brother and sisters &c. 25 April 1826 - p. 527

Joynes.

vs. - Suit for sale & division.

Hargis.

That a certain John R. Bull late of this county departed this life intestate in the year 1820, and administration of his estate was granted to your orator Levin L. Joynes, who took possession of the said estate and proceeded to administer same according to law; that the said John R. Bull was at the time of his death & seized of a tract of land situate near the New Church, containing --- acres, which at his death descended to his three children, viz: Susan, wife of William Hargis, John R. and Ann Bull &c. 12 March 1825 - p. 530

INDEX

ASHBY, James 59, 60
  John 59
  Robert 83
  Samuel 59
  Sarah 59, 60, 83
  Susanna 60
  Susannah 59
  Tamer 60
  William 59
ASHMEAD, Elizabeth 148
  James R. 148
AYDLOTT, John 135
  Scarburgh (HENDERSON) 135
AYRES, Francis 2
BADGER, Elizabeth 38, 126
  Elizabeth (WHITE) 38
  Margaret 126
  Robert 126
  Rosey 126
  Susanna 126
  William 126
BAGGALY, Jarvis 5
BAGWELL, Alexander 21
  Ann 89, 90
  Ann Kitson 124
  Anne 90
  Augustus 124
  Charles 21, 124
  Elizabeth Jones 83
  Elvira 124
  George 83
  George P. 83
  Henry 21, 89, 90
  Isaac 90
  Isaiah 83
  John 89, 90
  John Young 89, 90
  Laura 124
  Margaret 83, 90
  Margaret (DRUMMOND) 6
  Peggy 82, 83
  Sally 124
  Spencer 21
  Thomas 79, 82, 83
  William 83

BAILEY, Ann 31, 32
  Richard 5
  Thomas 31, 32
BAKER, Betsy 53
  Charles 120
  Daniel 45, 51, 120
  Esther 51
  Finney 51
  Grace 53
  Grace (BAKER) 53
  Henry 51
  Hezekiah 53
  Jemima 53
  John 51, 53
  Margaret 120
  Molly 51
  Nancy (COPES) 45
  Patience (BUNDICK) 52
  Preeson 52
  Rachel 52
  Rachel (BUNDICK) 52
  Richard 52
  Samuel 53
  Savage 120
  Stephen 53
  Susanna 51
  Tabitha 52
  Viola 51
  William 52, 53
BALEY, Charles 5
  Henry 6
  Richard 6
  Rosanna 6
  Southy 6
BARCLAY, William 33, 70
BARKER, Abigail (SCOTT) 66
  William 66
BARNES, Parker 77
BARRCROFT, Susanna (KELLY)
  115
  William 115
BARRY, Alice 35
  Allah 35
  James 35
  Rebecca 35

154

BARRY, Thomas 35
BAYLEY, Anne 30
 Elizabeth 6
 Tabitha 12
 Thomas 30
BAYLY, Alice (KER) 48
 Alice (SCARBURGH) 48
 Ann 32
 Anne 27, 33, 36
 Anne (DRUMMOND) 34
 Anne (JUSTICE) 36, 147
 Betsy 41
 Catharine 111
 Charles 27
 Charlotte 41
 Edmund 19, 41, 47, 54
 Edward 19, 41
 Egbert Rodney 111
 Elijah 110
 Elizabeth 111
 Elizabeth Wise 27
 Isma 111
 John 19, 22
 Margaret 27, 111
 Margaret Pettit (CROPPER) 87,
  125
 Nancy 41
 Peggy (BULL) 89
 Richard 17, 41
 Richard D. 87, 125
 Robert 19
 Rosey 111
 Sarah 27
 Susannah 27
 Susannah (MASON) 110
 Thomas 32, 33, 34, 35, 46, 47, 48,
  63
 Thomas M. 68, 93, 96, 99
 Thomas S. 147
 Thomas Simpson 36
BAYNE, Betsy 99
 Sally 99
 Walter 99
BEACH, Ezekiel 59, 60
 Mary 60

BEACH, Rosey (NOCK) 122
 Sarah 60
BEAVANS, Nancy 113
 Nathaniel 24
 Rowland E. 113
 William 4
BELL, Anne 67
 Edward 80
 George 136, 139
 Jeodiah 7
 Margaret (WELCH) 136, 139
 Mary 67, 80
 Peggy 67
 Robert 67
 Sally 67
 Sarah 67
 Sarah (BRADFORD) 7
 Susanna 67
 Thomas 67
 William 36, 67
BELOTE, Hancock 16
 James 89
BENSON, Azariah 112
 Sarah (CUTLER) 112
BENSTON, James 44
 John Savage 44
 Joyce 44
 Peggy 44
 Polly 44
 Posey 44
BENTHALL, Elizabeth 32
BERKELY, William 25
BERRY, Alice 35
 Allah 35
 James 35
 Rebecca 35
 Thomas 35
 William 35
BEVANS, William 14
BIRD, Daniel 22
 Ebern 128
 Elizabeth 128
 Jacob 80, 128
 Malinda 128
 Polly 128

BISHOP, Elizabeth 44
  Griffin 110
  Henry 44
  Nancy 44, 59
  Nancy (WARNER) 77
  Nathaniel 59
  Polly 44
  Sally (MASON) 110
  William 44
BLAKE, David 1
  Dennis 1
  John 1
  Sarah (RATCLIFF) 1
  William 1
BLOXOM, Abbott 143
  Argil 40
  Edward 144
  Hetty 144
  Hetty (BLOXOM) 144
  James 99
  Mahala 143
  Major 144
  Major P. 144
  Nancy 89, 144
  Narcissa 144
  Polly 99
  Richard 143
  Southy 83
  William 144
BLOXUM, Levin 51
  Major 50
  Major Simpson 51
  Margaret S. 51
  Richard 50, 51
BOGGS, Arthur 129
  Catharine 129
  Elijah 75, 129
  Eliza 137
  Elizabeth 129, 137, 150
  Elizabeth P. 150
  Elizabeth P. (RODGERS) 117
  Francis 137
  Henry 129
  James 117, 129, 150
  Jane 129

BOGGS, John 129
  John C. 137
  Joseph 137
  Leah 137
  Lucy 129
  Margaret 137
  Mary 129
  Mary Ann 137
  Nancy 75, 129
  Peggy 129
  Rachel 129
  Sally 137
  Sarah 38
  Sarah (WHITE) 38
  Susanna 137
  Thomas 137
  William 38, 129
BOISNARD, James 82
  John 56, 80, 82
  Leah (COPES) 82
BONIWELL, Elizabeth 121
BONNEWELL, Anne (BRADFORD)
    7
BONWELL, Clement 141
  Dolly (SHRIEVES) 52
  Elijah 141
  Elizabeth 52, 141
  Hetty (BULL) 89
  James 141
  John 52
  Keely 80
  Kitty 89
  Mckeel 146, 147
  Molly (BULL) 89
  Robert 141
  Sally (BULL) 89
BOOTH, Convention 98
  George 15
  Hetty 98
  Jemimah 56
  John 15, 98
  Leah 98
  Mehala 98
  Peggy 98
  Sally 98

BOWDOIN, Ann 4
  Peter 2, 4
  Susanna 2
  Susanna (PREESON) 2
BOWMAN, --- (Maj.) 17
  Catharine 104
  Catherine 104
  David 35, 47, 48, 104
  Edmund 17
  Euphamia 104
  George K. 104
  George Ker 104
  Isabella 104
  Isabella (KER) 48
  James Oswald 104
  Margaret 104
  William 104
BRADFORD, Anne 7
  Bailey 7
  Bayley 8
  Bayly 64
  Bridget 7
  Bridget (ADDISON) 45
  Fisher 7, 64
  John 7, 37
  Nathaniel 7, 8, 64
  Sarah 7, 37
  Thomas 7
  William 7, 8, 45, 64
BREWINGTON, Polly 94
  William 94
BRIMER, John 12, 13
  Mary 12
  Robert 12, 13
  Samuel 12
BRINMER, John 12
  Mary 12
  Robert 12
  Samuel 12
BRITTINGHAM, Hepsy (COARD)
    131
  John 131
  Maria 131
  William 94, 131
BROADWATER, --- 112

BROADWATER, Alfred 142
  Betsy 40
  Caleb 40, 142
  Catherine 45
  Elias 142
  George 112, 113
  Henry 112, 113
  Hetty 40
  James 45, 112, 113, 134
  Joseph 143
  Mary 143
  Nancy 112, 142
  Nancy (BROADWATER) 142
  Rachel 40, 112
  Robert 40, 130
  Robert J. 140
  Robert P. 108, 130
  Rosanna 140
  Sally 45, 108
  Sally (NOCK) 109
  Sarah 140
  Savage 142
  Tabitha (NOCK) 130
  Walter 142
  William 45
BROOKS, Francis 28
  Henry 28
BROTHERTON, Mary 8
BROUGHTON, Anne 27
  Anne (BAYLY) 27
  James 27
BROWN, Nancy (MARSHALL) 135
BULL, Abel 89
  Ann 151
  Betsy 89
  Bridget 88, 89
  Dianna (TURNER) 46, 63
  Dina (TURNER) 63
  Edward 137
  Elizabeth 69
  Elizabeth (NOTTINGHAM) 69
  Hetty 89
  James 132
  Jesse 89
  John 70, 99

BULL, John R. 151
  Mary 132
  Molly 89
  Nancy 132
  Nichols 69
  Peggy 89
  Rachel (FLOYD) 137
  Richard 88, 89
  Sally 89
  Scarburgh 89
  Southy 99
  Susan 151
  Susanna 99
  Teackle 89
  Thomas 137
  Tobias 89
  William 46, 132
BUNCLE, Ann 31
  Anne 30
BUNDICK, Betsey 53
  Betsy 53
  Elias 52
  Elizabeth (HICKMAN) 132
  George 53, 132
  John S. 119
  Keziah 52
  Leah 52
  Levin 52
  Nancy 53
  Patience 52
  Rachel 52
  Richard 52, 53
  Sally 52, 53
  Tabitha 52, 53
  William 53
BUNTING, Anne (WEST) 29
  Betty 71
  Elijah 72
  Elizabeth 71, 72, 73
  Esme 71, 72
  George 71, 72
  Hollowell 71
  Jonathan 71, 72, 73
  Phamy 72
  Severn 71, 72

BUNTING, Smith 29
  William R. 146, 147
BURDETT, Elizabeth 33
  Elizabeth D. 60
  Elizabeth Jenny 61
  Tabitha 61
  Thomas 33
  Thomas William 60, 61
  William 33, 60, 61
BURNELL, Nathaniel 137
BURTON, Agnes 29
  Ann 149
  Ann D. 149
  Annabella 149
  George W. 113
  John 75, 96, 113
  John B. 113
  John William 113
  Joshua 137
  Louisa 149
  Margaret 113
  Margaret (FLOYD) 137
  Maria 149
  Mary Adair 149
  Polly 113
  Tabitha 113
  William 20, 28
  William W. 113, 149
BURWELL, Nathaniel 36, 91
BYRD, Daniel 22
CARLTON, John 86, 87, 124, 125
  Margaret 86
  Peggy 124, 125
  Peggy (ALLEN) 87
CARMINE, Elizabeth
    (FITZGERALD) 146
  James 146
CARRUTHERS, Robert 11
  Tabitha 11
CARSS, John 39
  Peggy 39
CHAMBERS, Catherine (WEST) 29
  Edmund 28, 29
  Katharine (WEST) 28
  Katherine (WEST) 29

159

160

161

DIX, James 105
  James Henry 77
  John 76, 77, 78, 105
  John Savage 77
  Julius Petit 77
  Leah 76
  Levi D. 77
  Polly 105
  Rachel 38
  Rachel (EVANS) 38
DOLBY, Anna 112
  Rachel 66, 111
  Samuel 112
  Susanna 112
  Thomas 66
  William 112
DOUGLAS, George 72
DOWNING, Arthur 35
  John Robins 30
  Phamy (BUNTING) 72
  Sally 35
  Sally (LATCHUM) 35
DRUMMOND, Ann 4, 30, 31
  Anne 34
  Betty 31
  Bradhurst 12
  Charles 31
  Daniel 43
  Drake 7
  Elitia 31
  Elizabeth 30, 31, 32
  George 4, 5, 30, 31, 32
  Hill 6
  James 6
  John 6, 7, 32, 36
  Leah 43
  Margaret 6
  Mary 6
  Nancy 43
  Nancy (WATTS) 131
  Patience 43
  Peggy 36
  Richard 5, 6, 8, 30, 31, 34
  Robert 6, 7, 28, 43
  Sarah 8, 31, 32

DRUMMOND, Scarburgh 2
  Sophia 36
  Spencer 30, 31
  Stephen 47
  Susanna 43
  William 12, 30, 43
  William R. 131
DUBBERLY, Annabella 14
  John 14
DUN, Moses 35
  Nicholas 20
  Rebecca 35
  Rebecca (BERRY) 35
DUNCAN, Ann D. 149
  Anne 105
  Frances (MARSHALL) 135
  James 149
  Thomas 135
DUNTON, Alice 21
  Benjamin 83, 84
  Bridget 84
  Carvey 91, 102
  Carvy 102
  Catherine (BROADWATER) 45
  Elizabeth 83
  Esther 83, 84
  Isaac 21
  Jacob 83, 84
  Mary (COLEBURN) 46
  Michael 67
  Rachel 84
  Sarah 67, 84
  Selby 45
  Susey 84
  William 46
DYE, Elizabeth 4
  Margaret 4
  Sarah 4
EAST, Elizabeth (BONWELL) 141
  James 38, 97
  Parker 97
  Rachel 38, 97
  Richard 141
  Severn 97
  Tabitha 97

EDMUNDS, James 115
  Margaret 144
  Margaret (WYATT) 105
  Nancy 144
  Nancy (WHARTON) 115
  Thomas 79, 89, 144
  William 144
EDWARDS, David 126
  Esther 73, 103
  John 126
  John A. 126
  John B. 119
  Nancy 119
  Peggy 73, 103
  Rosey 126
EICHELBERGER, Euphemia 117
  James 117
EMMERSON, Arthur 8, 62
EVANS, Ann 122
  Edward 38, 40
  Elizabeth 122
  Elizabeth (WATERFIELD) 94
  George 139
  Hepse 38
  James 116, 144
  Johannes 38, 40
  John 38, 40, 94, 116, 131, 144
  John K. 122
  Levin 115, 116, 144
  Mahala 116, 144
  Margaret 122
  Nancy 38, 40
  Nancy (COARD) 131
  Nelly (TYLER) 139
  Rachel 38
  Sarah 115, 144
  Thomas 96, 102, 122
  William 38, 40
EVINS, James 69
EWELL, Betty (MELSON) 103
  Comfort (HOPE) 4
  George P. 103
  Mark 4
  Sally (DICKERSON) 136
  Sally (DICKINSON) 50

EWELL, Sarah (DICKINSON) 50
  William 50, 75, 116, 136
EYRE, Ann (UPSHUR) 47
  John 47
  Littleton 10
FALDO, Richard 6
FENN, Richard 13
FIDDEMAN, James 108
FIELDS, Esther 106
  John 106
  John D. 106
  William B. 106
FINNEY, Ann (PARKER) 145
  Catherine 104
  Elizabeth U. 112, 113
  Euphemia 75
  Henry 88
  Henry F. 145
  John 49, 104, 112, 113
  John W. 151
  Margaret 104
  Mary Ann 151
  Nancy (BROADWATER) 112
  Sarah 151
  Susan 145
  Tabitha 151
  Walter 88
  William 112, 151
FISHER, George 65, 66
  George S. 145
  Thomas R. 146
FITCHETT, Salathiel 80
FITZGERALD, Charles 145, 146
  Elizabeth 145, 146
  Frances 70
  Julia Ann 145, 146
  Peter 70
  Rosey 145
  Sally 145, 146
  Samuel 145
  Thomas 145
FLETCHER, Elizabeth (COARD)
    131
  Henry 88, 147
  John 95

FLETCHER, Matthew 75, 88
 Polly (JUSTICE) 147
 Ridigel 95
 Tabitha 95
 Thomas 50, 108, 131, 134
FLOYD, Benjamin 65
 Elijah 124
 Eliza 137
 Elizabeth 65
 Esther 137
 George 118
 James 137
 John 137
 Margaret 137
 Maria 118
 Molly 65
 Polly 65, 137
 Rachel 137
 Rachel (GARRISON) 124
 Sally 137
 Susan 137
 Thomas 137
 William 28, 137
FOSTER, Absalom 55, 56
 Betty 55, 56
 Bridget 20
 Charity 56
 Delilah 20
 George 56
 John 20
 Joshua 55, 56
 Leah 56
 Peggy 55, 56
 Sally 56
 Samuel 56
 Sinah 20, 55, 56
 William 36, 56
FOXCROFT, Bridget 17
FREEMAN, Elizabeth 4, 69
 Joshua 69
 William 4, 5
FRESHWATER, Christopher 59
 Elizabeth (MEERS) 20
 George 20
 Nathaniel 59

FRESHWATER, Polly 59
 Susanna 59
 William 59
GALT, Anna Maria 107
GARGANUS, Elias 13
GARRETT, Bridget 70
 Charles 70, 99
 Elisha 70, 99
 Elishe 70
 Nancy 70, 99
 Sally 70, 99
 Samuel 70, 99
 Susan 70
GARRISON, Abel 124
 Ann J. 124
 Caty 114, 123
 Charlotte 114, 123
 Elizabeth 114, 123
 James 124
 John 114, 123
 John W. 114, 123
 Jonathan 32
 Margaret 114
 Margaret Smith 123
 Maria 114, 123
 Peggy 114, 123
 Rachel 124
 Sally 114, 123, 124
 Samuel 114, 123
 Smith 114
 William 114, 123
GARTNER, Elizabeth (BISHOP) 44
 John 44
GASCOIGNE, William B. 7
GIBB, Esther (WHEELTON) 47
 Joseph 47
 William 36, 37
GIBSON, James 2
 Sarah 2
 Sarah (PREESON) 2
GILCHRIST, George 24
GILLETT, William 123
GLADDING, George 132
 Henry 132
 John 132

HEATH, Robert 75
HENDERSON, Lemuel 135
　Polly 135
　Polly (GUNTER) 138
　Rhoda (MARSHALL) 135
　Robert 138
　Scarburgh 135
HENRY, Elizabeth 58
　Hugh 58
　Isaac 58
　James 58, 100
　Nancy 58
　Sarah 58
　Susannah 58
　William B. 58
HEZLET, Alice 35
　Alice (BERRY) 35
　Robert 35
HICKMAN, Arthur 108
　Ayres 114, 140
　Betty (PARKS) 108
　Custis 56
　Elizabeth 132
　George 114, 132, 140
　Hepsey (WARNER) 77
　Isaiah 36
　James 108
　Jesse 114
　John 51, 52, 114, 115, 140
　Joshua 55
　Maria 114
　Nancy 114, 140
　Parker 51, 52
　Peggy 114, 115, 140
　Peggy (FOSTER) 56
　Polly 52, 147
　Polly (JUSTICE) 147
　Revel 77
　Richard 132
　Sally 36
　Sarah 52
　Sarah (JUSTICE) 36
　William 51, 52, 132
　Zeporah 132
HILL, Margaret (CUTLER) 112

HILL, Richard 2, 3
　Shadrack 112
　Tabitha 10
HINMAN, Bayly 70
　Custis 99, 100
　David 92
　Elizabeth 92
　Frances (FITZGERALD) 70
　George 99, 100
　Major 92
　Peggy 92
　Perry 92
　Sally 100
　Samuel 99, 100
　Sarah 99, 100
　Tabitha 92
　Tabitha (BUNDICK) 52
　Thomas 99, 100
　William 52, 92
HITCHENS, Gerard 22
　Mary 22
HOPE, Ann 39
　Charles 39
　Comfort 4
　George 2, 3, 4, 39
　Thomas 3, 39
　William 2
HOPKINS, Ann 128, 151
　Charles 128, 151
　Elison 128, 151
　Elizabeth (ARMISTEAD) 128
　Maximilian 128
　Susan 128, 151
HORNSBY, Ann P. 98
　Betty 80
　Edmund 126, 127
　Eli 98
　Elizabeth 126
　Elizabeth B. 126, 127
　Leah 80
　Major 80
　Molly Rose 80
　Priscilla 98
　Rosey 80
　Sally 80, 126

JOYNES, Thomas R. 87, 96, 98, 99, 125
  Thomas Robinson 37
JUSTICE, Anna 108, 109
  Anne 36, 147
  Betsey 36
  Bridget 36
  Comfort 4
  Comfort (HOPE) 4
  Elizabeth 119, 150
  James 147
  John 150
  Lovey 119
  Mahala 150
  Nancy 43, 108, 109
  Parker 150
  Peggy 119
  Polly 108, 109, 147, 150
  Rachel 43, 108, 109
  Ralph 3, 36, 43, 108, 109
  Richard 3, 43, 108, 109, 150
  Robert 4
  Rosey 150
  Sally 119
  Samuel 43, 108, 109
  Sarah 36
  Sinah 36
  Sukey 150
  Tabitha 108, 109
  Thomas 43, 108, 109, 119
  Tinney 147
  William 43, 92, 108, 109, 147, 150
KELLAM, Adah 119
  Allen 105
  Ann 105
  Anne 139
  Argil Lewis 133
  Bridget 117
  Bridget (ADDISON) 44, 45
  Charity 120, 121
  Charles 43
  Charlotte 133
  Custis 105
  Eliza 105
  Elizabeth 119

KELLAM, Elizabeth (MILBY) 106
  George 105, 119
  Hutchinson 106
  Hutton 119
  James 133
  Jesse 81
  John 25, 119
  Joseph 33
  Katharine 105
  Leah (HORNSBY) 80
  Leah B. 105
  Nancy 43, 119, 121
  Nancy (JAMES) 43
  Parker 38
  Parker (WHITE) 38
  Revel 80
  Revell 120, 121
  Richard 20
  Robert 133
  Sacker 120
  Sally 133
  Sarah 105, 120
  Shepherd 119
  Sidney 80
  Smith 120
  Spencer 38
  Stockley 119
  William 133
  Xorobabel 118
  Zorobabel 44, 45, 117, 139
KELLEM, Jesse 79
KELLY, Anne 115
  Charles 115
  Dennis 99
  Esther 115
  James 115
  Susanna 115
  Weskit 115
KENDALL, John 3
  Littleton 67
  William 17
KER, Alice 48
  Ann 48
  Catherine 48
  Edward 47, 48

168

MIFFLIN, Daniel 28
  Warner 55
MILBURN, --- (PARKER) 113
  Deborah 108
  Gilbert 113
  Nancy 108
  William 108
MILBY, Elizabeth 95, 106
  Gilbert 95
  Hetty 95
  John 30, 95, 106
  William 95, 106
MILES, Rachel 108, 109
  Roger 109
MOORE, Catharine (BOGGS) 129
  Catherine 22
  James 39
  Joseph 39
  Robert 39
MORRYSON, Francis 25
MURRER, Elizabeth (MARSHALL)
    136
  George 136
NIBLET, Caleb 22
  Sarah (TAYLOR) 22
NICKLESS, Hancock 1
NICLESS, Hancock 30, 31
NOCK, Agnes 94, 95, 99
  Amey 43, 96, 97, 109
  Amy 96
  Ann 122
  Anna 109
  Anne 43, 143
  Benjamin 43, 108, 109, 122, 130
  Caty 130
  Charles 130
  Coleburn 122
  Comfort 49
  Edmund 143
  Elijah 49, 140, 143
  Eliza 94, 95
  Elizabeth 95, 99, 130
  Elizabeth (POWELL) 67, 68
  Elizabeth (WARNER) 77
  George 77, 96

NOCK, Henry 122
  James 49, 143
  John 52, 96, 122, 140, 143
  Joseph 130
  Levin 140, 143
  Lewis 77, 143
  Littleton 135
  Lucretia 94, 95, 99
  Mary 49, 130, 140, 143
  Nancy 77, 140, 143
  Peggy 96, 97
  Polly (MARSHALL) 135
  Rachel 109
  Rachel (JUSTICE) 43, 108
  Richard 43, 108, 109
  Rosey 122
  Sally 43, 109
  Samuel 140, 143
  Solomon 96, 97, 122
  Tabitha 130
  Thomas 122, 130
  William 20, 67, 77, 94, 95, 99, 140,
    143, 145
NORTHAM, Custis 129
  Elizabeth (WRIGHT) 121
  James 121
  John 24
  Nancy (BOGGS) 129
  Southy 24
  William 97, 98
  Zerobabel 24
NOTTINGHAM, Abel 69
  Anne 61
  Benjamin 61, 62
  David 69
  Elizabeth 69
  Isaac 61, 62
  Mary (JACOB) 67
  Michael 62
  Molly 61
  Peggy 61
  Robert 61, 62
  Sally 62
  Sarah 69
  Severn 67

175

176

179

WALKER, John 9, 28
  John B. 147
  Joseph 9
  Sarah 9
WALLOP, Betsy 131
  Bridget (MARSHALL) 135
  Comfort 92
  Elizabeth 131, 135
  George 92, 131
  Ibbey 131
  John 131
  Mary 92, 131
  Nancy 135
  Peggy 131
  Polly 131
  Rachel 92
  Revell 135
  Rosella 131
  Sally 131, 135
  Skinner 92, 131
  William 60, 131, 135
WALTER, Abel 95
  Mary 94
  Rachel 95
  Richard 95
  Solomon 95
  Thomas 95
WARD, Mary 61, 62
  William 25, 61
WARNER, Elizabeth 77
  Elizabeth (JAMES) 140
  George 77, 78, 138, 140
  Hepsey 77
  Isaac 77
  Jacob 77, 78
  Lucretia 77
  Nancy 77
  Polly 77
  Solomon 77
  William 77, 78
WARRINGTON, William 36
WATERFIELD, Elizabeth 94
  George 94
  Jacob 94, 133
  Luther 94

WATERFIELD, Mary W.
    (MATTHEWS) 133
  Nancy 94
  Polly 94
  William 94
WATERS, Elizabeth 18
  Elizabeth (LITTLETON) 16, 17
  Richard 16, 18
  Spencer 37
  Thomas 94
WATSON, Benjamin 58
  Betsy (SELBY) 75
  Betsy Selby 121
  Bezelel 75
  Bezelell 88
  Daniel 75, 88
  Director (LINGO) 74
  Elizabeth 121
  Ephraim 149
  James 114
  John 75, 145
  John W. 121
  Levi 58
  Margaret 145
  Nancy 145
  Nancy G. 145
  Rosey 58
  Tabitha (WHARTON) 149
  William 58, 88
WATT, Adam 14
  James 14
  Scarburgh 14
WATTS, Betsy 131
  David 92, 98, 110, 131
  John 131
  Nancy 131
  Peggy (WALLOP) 131
  Sarah 110
  William 51, 52, 94
WEDDERBURN, John 91
WEELBURN, William 79
WELBURN, Barbara 136
  Drummond 131, 134, 135
  John 131
  Mary 131

WELBURN, Polly (HENDERSON)
   135
 Polly (MARSHALL) 135, 136
 Polly (WALLOP) 131
 Sally (WALLOP) 131
 Skinner 131
 Thomas 131
 William 131, 134, 135
WELBURNE, Ann 1
 Daniel 1
 Elizabeth 1
 Samuel 1
WELCH, Ann 75
 Betsy 138, 139
 Elizabeth 75, 136
 Margaret 136, 138, 139
 Margaret R. 75
 Nancy 136, 138, 139
 Sally 136, 138, 139
 Sarah 75
 William 75, 136, 137, 138, 139
WELLS, Elizabeth 73, 103
 Richard 73, 103
WEST, Abel 21, 85
 Agnes 28, 29
 Agnes (BURTON) 29
 Alexander 9
 Ann 16
 Anne 15, 29
 Anthony 29, 84, 85
 Catherine 15, 29
 Charles 14
 Comfort 29
 Comfort (COPES) 57, 82
 Elizabeth 29
 Harriet 105
 Hepsy 68
 Hetty 92, 106
 Isaac 111
 Jane 30
 Jean 29, 30, 84
 John 5, 11, 15, 28, 29, 30, 36, 52,
   77, 84, 85, 105
 Katharine 28
 Katherine 29

WEST, Leah (BUNDICK) 52
 Major 29
 Mary 9, 15, 29, 30
 Mary (SHRIEVES) 52
 Mary Scarburgh 84
 Matilda 29, 30, 84
 Matilda (SCARBURGH) 11
 Mitchel S. 68
 Mitchell 68
 Patience 105
 Richard 16
 Salathiel 68
 Sally (TUNNELL) 111
 Sarah Taylor (TUNNELL) 111
 Scarburgh 15, 29, 57, 82, 96
 Susanna 29
 Susey 68
 Thomas 52
 Zorobabel 92, 106
WHARTON, Ann 148
 Anne 149
 Bagwell 98, 144, 148, 149
 Betsy 115
 Charles 115
 Elizabeth 115, 116, 148, 149
 James 46, 98, 115
 John 94, 115, 116, 148, 149
 Nancy 115
 Peggy 98
 Sally 98
 Sally (SHIELD) 46
 Susanna 98, 115
 Tabitha 149
 William 115
WHEALTON, Scarburgh 14
 William 14
WHEELTON, Betsey 49
 Betsy 47
 Charles 47
 Daniel 49
 Elisha 47
 Esther 47, 49
 George 47
 James 47
 Joshua 49

WHEELTON, Nancy 47, 49
  Polly 49
  Sally 47
  William 47
WHITE, Adeline 139
  Ambrose 8, 9, 13
  Betsy 138, 139
  Bridget 138, 139
  Catharine 138
  Comfort 8
  Daniel 138, 139
  Elijah 138, 139
  Elijah A. 117, 139
  Elizabeth 38
  Elizabeth (DICKERSON) 136
  George 138, 139
  Hanna 138, 139
  Henry 17, 38, 138, 139
  James 75, 136, 147
  John 138, 139
  Levin 138, 139
  Nancy 108, 138, 139
  Nancy (JUSTICE) 108, 109
  Napoleon 138, 139
  Nathan 38
  Parker 38
  Rosey 117
  Sally 138, 139
  Sarah 38, 139
  Tinney (JUSTICE) 147
  William 17, 108, 138, 139
WHITTINGTON, Arthur 51
  Esther (LITTLETON) 16
  Smart 11
  William 11, 16
WICHART, Betsy (WATTS) 131
  David 131
  James 131
  Joshua 131
WILKERSON, Elizabeth 129
  Solomon 129
  William 129
WILKINS, Ann 32, 98
  Ann D. 97
  Anna Maria Hall (ANDREWS) 107

WILKINS, Catherine 10
  Eliza 118
  George 118
  George D. 97
  Harriet 118
  Henry 32, 97
  James 118
  John 10, 11, 97, 107, 118
  John C. 118
  Nathaniel 98
  Peggy 97
  Rachel 97
  Shepherd 118
  Sheppard 118
  Sukey 97, 98
  Susan 118
  Thomas 118
WILLET, Garthery 33, 35
  William 33, 35
WILLETT, Agnes 29
  Agnes (WEST) 29
  Ambrose 39
  Ann (STRINGER) 24
  Edward 119
  Elizabeth 119
  George 77, 119
  Isaac 119
  James 119
  Jonathan 28, 29
  Nancy 119
  Sarah 119
  Susanna 39
  William 2, 3
WILLIAMS, Agnes 93
  Francis 17
  John 93
  Nancy 93
  Richard 4
  Samuel 20
  Sarah 4
  William 20
WILLIAMSON, Elizabeth
   (MARSHALL) 135
  William 135
WILSON, Rebecca 1

WILSON, Samuel 71
WIMBLER, Sarah (JESTER) 132
  William 132
WISE, Elizabeth Jones (BAGWELL)
    83
  George E. 83
  Henry A. 87, 125
  James 80
  John 13, 59, 80
  John C. 87, 125
  Margaret D. P. 87
  Margaret P. 125
  Sally (CROPPER) 125
  Sarah 87
  Thomas 5
WISHART, Betsy (WATTS) 131
  James 51, 131
  Joshua 51
  Maria 51
WITCHARD, Phillip 15
WRIGHT, Abel 76
  Elijah 76
  Elizabeth 76, 121
  George 76, 78, 121
  Henrietta 121

WRIGHT, Henry 76
  Jacob 76, 78
  James 121
  Leah 76
  Loves 121
  McWilliams 76, 78
  Ned 68
  Rachel 76
  Sally 121
  Sinah 76
WYATT, Andrew 105
  Elizabeth 74
  Isma 102, 105
  John 105
  Littleton 74
  Lusy (LINGO) 74
  Margaret 105
  Peggy (MELSON) 65
  Polly 105
  Sally 105
  Sarah 27
  Sarah (BAYLY) 27
  William 105
YOUNG, Elizabeth 75
  Thomas 75, 88

www.ingramcontent.com/pod-product-compliance
Lightning Source LLC
Chambersburg PA
CBHW070428270326
41926CB00014B/2995